LUTON TOWN
Staring into the Abyss

LUTON TOWN
Staring into the Abyss
MINUS 30:
THE COLDEST PLACE IN FOOTBALL

Rob Hadgraft

DESERT ISLAND BOOKS

First published in 2008
by
DESERT ISLAND BOOKS LIMITED
7 Clarence Road, Southend on Sea, Essex SS1 1AN
United Kingdom
www.desertislandbooks.com

© 2008 Rob Hadgraft

The right of Rob Hadgraft to be identified as author of this work has
been asserted under The Copyright Designs and Patents Act 1988

British Library Cataloguing-in-Publication Data
A catalogue record for this book is available from the British Library

ISBN 978-1-905328-46-8

Printed in the UK
by the
MPG Books Group

All photographs in this book were taken by the author or gratefully
received from private collections

CONTENTS

No Luton sand, no Luton sea,
    Just lots of chalk and River Lea,
But there's something still I can't pin down
    That draws me to the town.
It's certainly a place I'd choose
    To court the muse,
I'm glad I had the chance to stay there as a guest,
    It's where my first poems came.
There's little corners I could name
    That I believe are deeply blessed:
The Scandinavia Cafe in High Town;
    The Great Northern Public House;
The woodland above Pope's Meadow;
    The tea area below the stand at Kenilworth Road.

By performance poet and Luton fan John Hegley
(gratefully reproduced with permission)

Foreword

This book chronicles a remarkable series of catastrophic events at our club over the last 50 years, and shows how Luton Town became trapped in a cycle of financial meltdowns. My colleagues and I from LTFC2020 are striving to end this and ensure there are no more chapters of misery to be written.

Since we took control of the club we've been heartened by the faith and goodwill shown by the people who matter – the fans. The wave of support from football supporters in general has been wonderful: we've had around 5,000 messages, many saying Luton are now their 'second club' due to the severity of the sanctions we suffered earlier this summer. The Luton 'soap opera' will continue well into the 2008-09 season and there will undoubtedly be both heartache and joy. There will be a gladiatorial struggle between fellow sufferers Rotherham and Bournemouth and ourselves. We believe we can survive and that next May there will be the biggest celebration party Bedfordshire has ever seen.

As I understand it, there are currently more than 40 League clubs on a financial knife edge, possibly within weeks of going into Administration, so the law of averages suggests more will take that step soon. After all the stress, heartache and nightmares we suffered here, I wouldn't wish such turmoil on anyone else, but it does seem inevitable.

You might call us old-fashioned, but we at LTFC2020 think the small-town football club is one of this country's great institutions. It is worth fighting to preserve. When Luton went into Administration for a third time in late 2007, the LTFC2020 bid to take over focused firmly on key principles, such as transparency, the engagement of supporters, sensible, achievable plans within a prudent financial structure, an independent feasibility study to select the future location of a new stadium, the inclusion of the Trust and other supporters' groups in shaping the future, and the inclusion of the community to build a stronger fan base.

We are totally committed to rebuilding the youth structure for which this club is famous and will work within the community. We will bring the soul back to our club. Whatever happens, all at LTFC2020 are totally committed to our long-term plan. We are all genuine, long-standing Luton fans ourselves, and we know the club is nothing without the support of the fans. We believe the future is very bright. It's taken another crisis, the most serious yet, to truly unite our fan base, but united it is. Our club will never die while we stand together.

STEPHEN BROWNE
Director, LTFC2020 Ltd

Introduction

Over the last 50 years Luton Town FC seems to have lurched from one calamity to another. The sporting press is fond of applying the prefix 'crisis club' whenever anybody hits hard times, but in Luton's case no other Football League outfit is better qualified for such a label.

Not only are Luton the only team to have plummeted from First to Fourth Divisions twice, they have suffered more off-field fiascos than any other professional outfit. After being docked an unprecedented 40 points during a nine-month period, they were facing a third successive relegation in 2009.

Life hasn't always been this way. In the mid to late-1950s the Hatters were a happy little club, sensibly managed and establishing itself steadily as a footballing force. Sixteen successive campaigns in Division Three had been followed by eleven in the Second Division, with promotion to the top flight finally achieved for the first time in 1955. It was solid, steady, upward progress in anybody's book.

It was only when a taste of the big time came along that things began to go wrong. Luton's zenith would be reached in the early autumn of 1958, when the club surged proudly to football's summit – to the top of the league, number one in a field of 92. It was no fluke, for they possessed a much-admired forward line of genuine power and flair. However, reaching the top seemed to have a dizzying effect on all concerned and, paradoxically, this spell of unprecedented success would merely kick-start a remarkable decline.

Manager Dally Duncan had taken nearly ten years to get Luton to the pinnacle, but within days of getting there he was tempted away by big wages at Blackburn Rovers. Luton never recovered once their leader left the bridge. The directors dithered and failed to appoint a replacement for eight months, during which time the team slithered back down the league table. The only bright spot was an FA Cup run in which a team selected by committee survived a series of narrow squeaks to reach Wembley for the first time. Lacking proper leadership, the Cup final performance against Nottingham Forest was abysmal. The decay that had set in after Duncan's shock exit gained significant momentum on that sultry May afternoon beneath the famous twin towers.

One observer likened Luton's subsequent fall to that of a broken elevator plummeting to earth. The facts back this up. In 1960 the club was in Division One (then England's top tier, of course), but by 1965 they had arrived in Division Four. They went from the penthouse to the basement in five miserable years. Such a rapid decline had never been seen before. To further illustrate the extent of the slump, consider this: In early October 1958 the Hatters were top of Division One, but by December 1966 were 90 places worse off and second-bottom in Division Four (a nadir achieved after a 1-8 hammering by the only club below them!).

This crazy, untrammelled tumble through the divisions represented the first of what would be a long series of crises at Luton Town. The settled years were gone forever. In the 50 years since the trouble began in 1958, there have certainly been highs as well as lows, but the good times have always seemed like mere respites from longer periods of torment.

Talk of moving away from the ancient, hemmed-in Kenilworth Road stadium began in the 1950s. Since then there has been a succession of blue-prints, planning applications, pipedreams and other machinations, but half a century later a new ground seems no nearer reality. Various owners have come and gone, attracted no doubt by the property development aspect, but none achieved what they set out to do. Worse, some of them left the club in a worse state than when they arrived.

For 50 years Luton Town has been taking two steps forward and three back. The club has gone close to extinction more frequently than any other currently in the League. Between 1999 and 2007 it was placed in adminis-tration no fewer than *three* times – a record. Some of the off-field events at Kenilworth Road have simply beggared belief. Fans have learned not to expect a quiet life, nor to look much beyond the next match or two.

For many years a Luton Town 'crisis' has been expected every ten years or so. Recently it has seemed more like every ten weeks. This book chron-icles the troubles of the last 50 years and proves that, when it comes to Luton Town, truth is stranger than fiction.

ACKNOWLEDGEMENTS:
As a Kenilworth Road regular for around 35 years, I have observed most of the crises described in this book at close quarters, but nevertheless I would like to thank a number of other devotees for their help, including Gary Sweet, Nick Owen, Kevin Lennon, Scotty, Kevin Barrett, Jane Ledsom, RV Kempson, Caz Meers, Mark Ledsom, Bernard Elwen, Cherry Newbery, Kevin Catlin, Graham Sharpe, Brian Ellis, John Pyper, Andrew Cornelius, Donald Gunn and John Hegley.

BIBLIOGRAPHY:
Luton Town, The Modern Era – Roger Wash (Desert Island Books);
Luton Town at Kenilworth Road: A Century of Memories – Roger Wash (Desert Island Books);
Luton Town , An Illustrated History – Roger Wash (Desert Island Books);
The Luton Town Story 1885-1985 – Timothy Collings (LTFC);

Luton Town, a Pictorial Celebration of Their Cup History – Timothy Collings (LTFC);
The Definitive Luton Town FC – Bailey, Ellis & Shury (AFS);
Kenilworth Sunset – Tim Kingston (Book Castle);
A Hatter Goes Mad – Kristina Howells (Book Castle);
MIG Crew – Tommy Robinson (Pennant);
Supermac – Malcolm Macdonald (Highdown);
Joe Kinnear: Still Crazy – Hunter Davies (Andre Deutsch);
In The Time of Nick – Nick Owen (Brewin);
A Little Thing Called Pride – Alec Stock (Pelham);
Football Club Manager – Alec Stock (Sportsman's BC);
Tales From the Boot Camps – Steve Claridge & Ian Ridley (Gollancz);
My Father and Other Working Class Football Heroes – Gary Imlach (Yellow Jersey);
Big Fry – Barry Fry (CollinsWillow);
Sam Bartram, the Story of a Goalkeeping Legend – Mike Blake (Tempus);
The Story of Luton – Dyer, Stygall & Dony (White Crescent);
Greetings From Bury Park – Sarfraz Manzoor (Bloomsbury);
Irons in the Fire – Russell Brand (Hodder Stoughton).

OTHER RESEARCH:
Luton News, Luton Today, Beds on Sunday, Herald & Post, Evening Post, Saturday Telegraph, The Times, Daily Telegraph, Independent, Guardian, Mirror, People, News of the World, Daily Mail, Evening Standard, Daily Express, Financial Times, BBC Three Counties Radio, Chiltern Radio, Trust in Luton, Loyal Luton Supporters Club, Vital Luton, Lutonfc.com, lutontown-mad, Luton Outlaws, Official Luton Town Supporters Club, *When Saturday Comes, Charles Buchan's Football Monthly, Four Four Two, Mad as a Hatter.*

ROB HADGRAFT
July 2008

CRISIS 1 (1958-66)
A Club in Decay

PART 1: BEFORE THE STORM

The early morning mist at the eastern end of the chalky Chiltern Hills covered large parts of Luton on the morning of Saturday, 27th September 1958. But as kick-off loomed at Kenilworth Road, light southerly winds and sunny intervals created a pleasant autumnal afternoon, just in time for the arrival of famous visitors from Preston North End.

Proud Preston currently topped the league, unbeaten in four away matches so far. Today's encounter pitched established stars from a northern footballing stronghold against young upstarts from Bedfordshire, less familiar with life at soccer's sharp end. The surrounding terraced streets were alive with excitement as the crowds converged on the ground, where the BBC TV's *Sports Special* had already set up their cameras. More than 23,000 squeezed inside, anticipating another attacking display from their favourites, knowing victory might see the Hatters go top.

Promoted to the top division in 1955 for the first time, Luton had surprised with their potent, fearless football. Managed by Scotsman Dally Duncan, this unfashionable small-town club had chalked up some remarkable scoring feats on the big stage: Three visits from mighty Sunderland, for example, saw the Hatters bang in an astonishing total of 21 goals (8-2, 6-2 and 7-1).

Preston's celebrated England winger Tom Finney received a warm welcome, but the respect ended there as Luton ripped into their visitors. Inside two minutes inside-forward Allan Brown sent new winger Billy Bingham scampering down the right, from where his low, driven cross caused panic in the Preston rearguard. Defender Joe Walton tangled with goalkeeper Fred Else, and Irishman George Cummins roared in to score. Straw boaters were tossed into the air and Luton were on their way.

Preston centre-forward Denis Hatsell equalised, but home favourite Gordon Turner made his first-ever penalty miss before Luton hit their visitors with a three-goal salvo. Two strikes from outside-left Jim Adam and Bingham's debut goal completed a 4-1 romp. The Hatters leapfrogged Preston and Bolton and sat proudly on top of the league.

Luton had briefly hit top spot in previous seasons, but either in August, when league tables were relatively meaningless, or for a couple of days in midweek, when the tables were not published anyway. But the hammering of Preston on a Saturday meant Luton would be top in all the Sunday papers for the whole world to see.

PART 2: MELTDOWN

Surely a top division football club can't be run by any old Tom, Dick and Harry? One would think not. But for much of that 1958-59 season, an unlikely trio called Tom, Fred and Percy found themselves in charge at Luton Town.

For nearly an entire season pub landlord Tom Hodgson, farmer/estate agent Percy Mitchell, and pensioner Fred England were in charge of Luton as the team battled to stay near the top of Division One. Deciding that the club didn't need a manager for the time being, the three of them – average age 62 – signed players, controlled finances and had the final say in picking the team.

Once a week, Percy would park his tractor and meet up with Tom, mine host of The Warden Tavern, and they would be joined by their elderly pal Fred. The threesome would study a scrap of paper on which was written the eleven names recommended to play the next game. Team skipper Syd Owen and head trainer Frank King had input over the list of names, but it was Tom, Fred and Percy who had the final say. Assisted, no doubt, by a stiff drink or two, they would mull over the list and then deliver their verdict. It seems a strange way for a team facing the likes of Manchester United, Spurs and Wolves to be put together.

This sort of thing could only happen at Luton Town. Not for nothing was the club known as the Mad Hatters. Luton may have been the very first southern club to turn professional (in 1890), but some of what went on behind the scenes retained a distinctly amateur air nearly 70 years later. Going top of the league in the autumn of 1958 seemed to induce a sort of altitude sickness, for they would soon be heading back down the mountain again. Mid-table Blackburn approached Luton's popular manager Dally Duncan with a view to him taking charge at Ewood Park. To dismay in Bedfordshire, Duncan – after nearly ten years of unprecedented success – grasped the opportunity and walked out of Kenilworth Road.

Having finished the previous season (1957-58) in a best-ever eighth place, Luton had a settled team, considered one of the most potent attacking forces around. With recent signing Bingham rampaging down the right flank, the Hatters were widely feared. When he made his famous comment 'you've never had it so good' in nearby Bedford at a 1957 Tory rally, Prime Minister Harold Macmillan might easily have been addressing Luton fans. But all good things come to an end, and as the autumn leaves began to fall along the tree-lined A6 out of Luton, so the Hatters' hopes of maintaining their lofty status fluttered away in the breeze. On the October day that Duncan headed north, Town's prospects went west. The *Luton News* pictured him waving farewell from a train window as he set off for Blackburn. It would prove a turning point in Luton's 73-year history.

Duncan left behind an ageing team. A period of transition was looming that would need careful handling. The rebuilding of the Luton Town machine would need to be overseen by someone with foresight, know-how and experience. The last thing needed was for recruitment, planning and team selection to fall into the hands of inexperienced amateurs. But that is exactly what happened. Club chairman Mitchell, committed and amiable but not universally popular, decided Duncan's shock departure need not be a problem. In fact it suited him just fine. The vexed question of a new manager could wait. This was Percy's big chance to grab complete control of his beloved Luton Town.

To most folk associated with The Hatters, both inside and outside the club, the obvious successor to Duncan as manager was veteran centre-half and part-time coach Owen, a defensive rock and natural leader whose playing days were coming to an end. Indeed, the board seemed happy to make the 36-year-old the next manager, but Owen wanted to finish the 1958-59 season as a player before hanging up his boots, and was committed in the short-term to part-time coaching at Oxford University. Owen made it clear he would consider becoming manager the following summer, but for now wanted to play on.

No problem, said the chairman, who then announced his solution: The club would not have a team manager for the time being and would be run indefinitely by a three-man ad-hoc committee. He defended the decision, saying that one of the trio – Tom Hodgson – was a former player and thus had 'inside' experience – and if necessary they would take advice from senior players like Owen and Allan Brown, and trainer Tom Mackey. This arrangement would last until the end of the season, at least, and be reviewed in April 1959. It looked like a 'make-do-and-mend' arrangement and met with a few raised eyebrows. The board's recent record regarding transfers had made them less than popular and many felt they already meddled too much with on-field affairs. It looked like the void left by Duncan's departure was being filled in a ham-fisted manner.

With Duncan gone, Luton's league form dipped, although the team still produced the goods in the FA Cup. Spectacular victories mixed with narrow scrapes carried managerless Luton to Wembley for the first time, for their first Cup final. Paradoxically, this cup success only accelerated the club's general decline, for it disguised the fact that ploughing on without a proper manager had been a major blunder. The creaking joints of the team meant judicious changes were clearly needed, but with nobody in place to make them, the problem was simply brushed under the carpet.

One of the more inexplicable policies of the committee was to keep the same eleven men for all cup-ties, regardless of current form. Thus, the eleven who beat Leeds in round three in early January were selected for all nine ties through to the final against Nottingham Forest. The main problem with this, as far as the fans were concerned, was that the eleven who faced Leeds did not represent Luton's strongest team. Top scorer Gordon Turner and flying winger Jim Adam had been surprisingly dropped that day. Inevitably, both men soon forced their way back into the league side, but the rigid selection policy saw them step aside for Cup action. Turner, who had rattled up a record 177 goals in eight seasons, missed Wembley purely because he'd been absent for the third round. It seemed an utter nonsense.

The inflexibility angered the fans, who worshipped Turner and felt he must play at Wembley. Turner and Adam's absence allowed John Groves and Tony Gregory – neither of whom were regulars – to play beneath the famous twin towers. Both were decent players, but was this really the strongest side Luton could field in its finest hour? Before the final, a reporter telephoned Blackburn to ask Dally Duncan about Turner being left out, and the former Town boss said Luton would be 'committing suicide' if they played without him. Recriminations would rage in Luton for years afterwards. Investigations by journalist Tim Collings for his centenary history of the club suggested that at least one director – Tom Hodgson – wanted Turner to play, but chairman Mitchell was under pressure to stick with the 'regular cup line-up'. Whatever the truth, the whole affair was an embarrassing mess.

Away from the Cup, Luton's league form stuttered badly and they sank from first place to 17th. They finished comfortably clear of relegation, but it was a disappointing campaign all the same, and all was clearly not well behind the scenes. Chairman Mitchell, for all his good intentions, was known to have 'favourites', and inevitably this contributed to festering discontent that began to rip the heart out of a previously happy little club. Wembley or not, a truly astonishing decline now set in.

The delight in reaching the Cup final camouflaged all the problems. Cup fever was rife in the town after the semi-final victory over Norwich, with black and white favours everywhere and scores of shop windows carrying special displays, the famous locally made straw boaters particularly prominent. Luton had seen nothing like it since the celebrations at the end of the war. The fans did their bit, but sadly the club was found wanting on its biggest day. To compound the daft selection policy, the club shot itself in the foot by failing to make special arrangements in the build-up. The players were not taken to a resort or a hotel, as was traditional, which was hardly the way to boost team spirit.

In the days before the final, skipper Owen played his valedictory league game before heading to London to collect the Football Writers' Player of the Year award. But for the rest of the squad nothing out of the ordinary happened, apart from an incessant demand from fans for tickets. For the most part it was business as usual. The players assembled on the coach at Kenilworth Road on the morning of the final – just as they did for any other match in southern England – right-half John Groves even strolling to the ground after jumping off a corporation bus in Dunstable Road.

On the big day the leaderless Hatters produced a limp and desperately disappointing performance and were beaten 1-2 by a Forest side reduced to ten men after Roy Dwight's broken leg. A magnificent turnout of Hatters fans could hardly believe the anticlimactic nature of Town's display. Interviews with the players in the ensuing years revealed the true nature of the shambles behind the scenes. The lack of general planning even extended to tactics for the game itself. Formations and strategy was barely discussed, the players say.

A few days afterwards Syd Owen was appointed manager as expected, and the ever-optimistic fans looked forward to this trusty old stalwart reviving the good times. Lanky Syd, whose craggy appearance made him look older than his 37 years, was seen as perfect for the job. It was anticipated he would manage the same way he played: sensibly, single-mindedly, and without undue fuss. He had been a rock at the heart of Luton's defence for twelve seasons, and although he lacked speed and agility (teammate Dave Pacey reckoned Owen hobbled around 'like an old man') he was effective and consistent. There was, of course, sentiment involved when the national football writers voted him 1959's Player of the Year to coincide with his retirement, but it was widely agreed he had been unlucky not to win more than three England caps. He was the most consistent English centre-half of the decade, far superior to Billy Wright and Neil Franklin, insisted Pacey.

Having finally appointed a manager, chairman Mitchell busied himself with his project to build a new stadium for Luton Town. At a pinch, Kenilworth Road could hold up to 30,000, but even by 1960 standards the ground was fast becoming antiquated. It offered neither a comfortable nor convenient location for watching football, despite the stirring atmosphere generated inside. Mitchell's dream was to create a new 50,000-capacity stadium at Lewsey Farm, midway between Luton and nearby Dunstable. The chairman was an estate agent and farmer himself, so knew a thing or two about land acquisition and planning matters. Supporters therefore assumed things were moving in the right direction. Fifty years later and we are still waiting!

Predictably, Mitchell's plans provoked opposition from Lewsey area residents – nobody wants a football ground on their doorstep – and the matter ended up in front of a planning inquiry in January 1960. The man from the Ministry came to Luton and pulled on his wellies for a site visit. It was then a matter of waiting for the verdict. This took so long that the great Lewsey scheme soon began to fade from the memory, with the worrying displays on the field holding the attention to a far greater extent.

Popular magazine *Charles Buchan's Football Monthly* examined what was going wrong at Kenilworth Road. It labelled the town a 'disgrace' for not supporting the team in greater numbers (the average gate had fallen to 17,000). Mitchell offered an explanation: 'Transport is [our] main bugbear. Most clubs, particularly in the north, have special football buses laid on by the local transport body but we cannot obtain this advantage. Lack of parking facilities is another headache. People from outlying areas of town are chary of coming by car owing to this difficulty. In some cases the only alternative is to walk.'

Interestingly, the magazine noted that much of Luton's support came from outlying towns such as Hitchin, Hemel Hempstead and Aylesbury. The Hatters were 'of scant interest' to most Luton townsfolk, large numbers of whom were not true locals, having arrived in search of work since the 1930s. Half a century after these observations, it is clear that little has changed regarding the demographic make-up of Luton's support.

The downturn in results and drop in crowds put pressure on Owen to strengthen his team, but he seemed unable to find men of the calibre he wanted. Highly-rated 17-year-old Harvey McCreadie was recruited from Accrington, but would prove a flop. In fact he made headlines for all the wrong reasons, needing hospital treatment after an incident at the California Ballroom in Dunstable left him with nasty facial wounds. Owen also found another so-called 'wonder boy' – wing-half Mark Lownds from County Durham – but again it was a signing which did nothing to help the club's immediate plight.

When Luton took a 1-4 home hammering from Wolves in the FA Cup, and then failed to sign Bradford City centre-forward Derek Stokes, the board took drastic action. Despairing at their manager's failure in the market, they took matters into their own hands and went over his head to recruit unsettled Scottish centre-forward Joe McBride from Wolves. Owen was said to be furious, as he didn't fancy McBride and didn't appreciate his job being done by amateurs. McBride, 21, cost a five-figure fee, so had to be played whether or not Owen rated him. Owen must have had mixed feelings when McBride headed a cracking goal on his debut.

The transfer deadline passed without significant additions by Luton, so when the club then announced record profits of £40,000, the fans wondered what was going on. Why hadn't this money been spent on bolstering the team for the relegation fight? Despite a few goals from the 'unwanted' McBride, by the time of the club's annual meeting in April 1960, Luton were all but relegated. The atmosphere was tense and the meeting turned into a battleground, lasting a record two hours. Shareholders' anger centred on the decision to use half the profits to appease the taxman instead of investing in the team. The chairman hit back, saying sooner or later the tax bill would have to be paid to stabilise the accounts, and they had given the manager a free hand to find new men (a fact disputed by Owen), but he had not found the right material.

Mitchell declared that First Division football had no future in Luton unless they moved to a new ground. Kenilworth Road had a sub-standard pitch which meant it could never stage representative games, and its slope and poor drainage had earned the club an unwanted reputation. Another issue was the lack of parking space. The only answer was a new ground, and the club were still awaiting a reply from the Ministry following the inquiry into the Lewsey Farm proposals.

Shareholders blamed Mitchell for apparently writing off First Division football simply because of the inadequacies of the ground. He also stood accused with his board colleagues of 'meddling' in team affairs, but insisted that manager Owen had 'sole control' and picked the team himself. Owen was the first Luton manager who did not have to submit his selections for approval.

Owen himself did not attend the meeting, but disagreed with the fiction that the board never interfered with team affairs. Huddersfield star Denis Law and Bradford City's John McCole were two who might have signed had the board cooperated. The poisonous fall-out from this meeting proved the final straw for Owen. What with the Joe McBride affair, the board's refusal to re-engage his trusted colleague Wally Shanks as coach, plus the fact that relegation was about to be confirmed, the time was right to walk away. Owen sat down and penned a resignation letter.

Less than 48 hours after the AGM, Town hosted West Ham in their penultimate game of the season. Their only chance of avoiding relegation was to win both remaining games and hope Birmingham and Leeds both lost all three of theirs. It was clearly a lost cause and barely 11,000 turned up at Kenilworth Road. Owen also didn't believe in miracles, for his resignation letter had by now already been submitted. Although a reshuffled Luton scored a surprise 3-1 victory, Birmingham beat Sheffield Wednesday 4-2 to condemn the Hatters to the drop. The board accepted Owen's resignation, informing him during the second half of the match, at which point Luton were 3-0 up. Instead of drowning his sorrows at the end, the dedicated Owen is said to have dashed from the stadium to catch a fourth-team Hellenic League game at Bicester.

Luton's final farewell after five years in the top flight was a 0-2 defeat at Preston on a day overshadowed by the retirement of Preston and England winger Finney. Before kick-off the players and officials linked hands to sing *Auld Lang Syne*, accompanied by a brass band. After the predictable home win, modest Tom disappeared down the tunnel, foiling attempts to hoist him shoulder-high for a hero's farewell. Luton's players disappeared equally quickly, their First Division life over.

Town finished bottom, five points adrift of safety, and were relegated alongside Leeds. Another small-town club, Burnley, pinched the league championship despite only amassing 55 points – just 25 more than wooden spoonists Luton. Luton's main problem in 1959-60 had been a lack of goals, with their final tally of 50 the lowest by anybody in the top division for eight years.

With Owen gone, directors Mitchell, Hodgson and England regained control of team affairs. A a new manager would not be appointed until after a close-season tour of Czechoslovakia. They also released eleven players, a quarter of the squad, and withdrew the fourth team from the Hellenic League. Owen became chief coach at Leeds and was soon joined at Elland Road by Luton's assistant trainer Les Cocker. They would go on to enjoy huge success as the largely unsung backroom team who would help Don Revie build the all-conquering Leeds side of the late 1960s and early 70s.

The summer of 1960 drifted by and Luton Town remained rudderless. Finally, during the week when Fred Trueman and Brian Statham bowled England's cricketers to victory against South Africa in the Edgbaston sunshine, Luton's board made its move. After an approach to one potential candidate (thought to be Manchester United coach Jack Crompton) came to nothing, Mitchell reluctantly decided to advertise for a 'team manager-coach', thus confirming that the new man would not enjoy the control supposedly given to Syd Owen. Accused of 'meddling' recently, the board evidently now wanted an even greater say in team affairs.

From a short-list of applicants, 46-year-old York boss Sam Bartram was sent a telegram while he holidayed in Bournemouth, inviting him for interview. Bartram, a popular figure in the game after 21 years as Charlton goalkeeper, was seen last of all and promptly given the job on the spot. In four seasons under 'Big Sam', York had finished 7th and 13th in Division Three (North), which mean they missed the 'cut' and dropped into the new Fourth Division in 1958. He guided York to promotion a year later, only for instant relegation to follow. It was not a distinguished record, so Bartram was delighted to get the Luton job, particularly as his daughter Moira was already attending a boarding school near the town.

There were soon signs of discontent in the dressing room as the new boss made it clear there would be changes. Several senior men departed at the start of 1960-61, following those earlier released by the board. By the end of October Luton had won only three of seventeen games, so a swift promotion to Division One looked highly improbable. Then followed the national pay crisis which nearly led to a players' strike. Feisty Scot Allan Brown was the Luton players' union representative. He reported from the dressing room that an overwhelming majority of teammates would strike if necessary and backed the PFA all the way in its battle to abolish the maximum wage. Rumours that Luton's under-performing footballers were trying to earn better money wasn't especially welcomed in many areas of the town. After all, hundreds were being laid off at the town's Vauxhall car factory, and a three-day week was introduced at one point at the Commer plant in neighbouring Dunstable.

The car workers' worries lingered, but the footballers celebrated when PFA chairman Jimmy Hill helped negotiate the end of the maximum wage in early January 1961. A few days later the Football League backed down on other aspects of so-called 'football slavery', and the rules that tied a player to one club were scrapped. Later the club chairmen would renege on some of the agreements, but football was still being dragged into the modern era.

Luton's chairman ignored the gloom among the fans to announce that the club was ready to 'break into the upper crust', thanks to its ambitions. He was referring to the plan, currently mired in red tape, to move lock, stock and barrel to a new site at Lewsey Farm. Mitchell was reportedly confident the new ground would be built by 1965, and had been assured by friends in high places that Luton would then stand a good chance of staging group games in the 1966 World Cup. Mitchell's optimism would prove misplaced. Like many chairmen of his era, he was typical of the old guard, his grip on the game loosened by the increasing demands of the players and by the closer relationship being fostered with television.

Now that Luton's glory days of the late 1950s were over, there was a procession of departing players. They left behind a patchwork of fading veterans and inexperienced youngsters. Morale was low and sinking lower. Some 33 players were used in 1960-61 – a huge number in pre-substitute days – including five different goalkeepers. As Alf Ramsey's Ipswich stormed to the Second Division title, The Hatters stuttered to a finishing position of 13th, and average gates slipped below 13,000.

This unhappy season would be mainly remembered for a curious FA Cup episode against Manchester City. In appalling conditions at rain-soaked Kenilworth Road, Town went 2-0 up in twenty minutes, only to collapse dramatically as quicksilver Denis Law netted no fewer than six times. Salvation came after the drenched referee called the players off after 69 minutes with the score 6-2 to City. According to club historian Roger Wash, he intended to restart the game when the rain eased, but Luton's players wisely made themselves scarce and the game had to be abandoned.

Three days later the restaged contest ended with Town winning 3-1 in the mud. Law scored again and his tally of seven while finishing on the losing side remains unsurpassed.

The malaise that set in after Dally Duncan walked out in 1958 was never more apparent than on the final day of the campaign. Just 8,373 turned up for a meaningless 0-0 draw with Scunthorpe, the ground echoing to slow handclapping. The gloom was a long way from the excitement of Wembley less than two years earlier. Not surprisingly, the manager engineered a clearout in the summer of 1961 and fourteen players were released. Trying to build a side capable of mounting a promotion challenge, Bartram must have cast envious eyes to his native North East, when fellow Second Division Sunderland paid Middlesbrough £45,000 for the prolific Brian Clough (197 goals in 213 games). Bartram's main buy was Manchester United centre-half Ron Cope for less than a quarter of the Clough fee. Cope was made captain, but would not prove the defensive rock Bartram needed and was eventually dropped. Although Gordon Turner chipped in with his usual twenty goals, the 1961-62 season was another disappointment, Town again finishing 13th in Division Two.

A combination of paying higher wages to players while enduring lower attendances meant the club was losing money fast, and Bartram could not plunge into the market to put things right. As 1961-62 petered out and gates dropped below 7,000 (less than half the break-even figure), Bartram made a team selection that had everyone questioning his sanity. For an Easter Monday match with Leyton Orient he dropped leading scorer Turner and played veteran goalkeeper Ron Baynham at centre-forward. The experiment was a flop and Town lost 1-3. Bartram had evidently taken the step as a gesture of protest against the lack of money available, and to shake up established players like Turner.

After the game a furious Turner said he was insulted by the ridiculous team selection and slapped in a transfer request. The chairman, who chose not to consult his manager on such matters, told no one and ripped up Turner's request. Press coverage and football gossip was not as intense as in later decades and most Luton fans were unaware of these shenanigans behind the scenes. Had such events been public, it would not have come as a shock when Sam Bartram and Luton duly parted company shortly after the end of the 1961-62 season.

Rather like Prime Minister Harold Macmillan, who in the same week boldly told the East German government to 'pipe down' over the Berlin Wall crisis, Sam Bartram was an angry man and was not content to button his lip. He met with reporters from the *Sunday People* in order to 'lift the lid on Luton', as they put it. In a frank catalogue of revelations that was serialised over five weeks, Bartram pulled no punches, and Luton's internal squabbles involving interfering directors and lazy players were aired under big headlines over Britain's breakfast tables.

'Sam Bartram Uncensored,' screamed the billboards on 17th June 1962 and the *Sunday People* rocketed off the sales stands in Bedfordshire. Luton fans were fascinated by the sort of juicy gossip they'd never enjoyed before. Bartram wrote: 'My departure from Luton was not by mutual consent [as stated]. They just fired me – and refused to state any reason beyond saying that my integrity was beyond question. The Football League is trying to emphasise the need for loyalty these days, but where has it got me?' He said the decline in Luton's fortunes was due to a host of problems, including meddling directors, broken promises, and players whose only interest was earning as much money as possible. Directors' wives even insisted certain players must not be dropped as they were 'good looking'.

'Football has turned sour on me. I was worried when I went into management six years ago that the small-time local businessmen who become directors seldom want experts to advise them, or managers or team builders. All they appear to need are stooges, can carriers and yes-men. The public is being conned by self-glorifying directors and couldn't-care-less players. If I left out the likes of Baynham, Morton, Groves, Kelly and Turner, who were all getting on and losing form, I was criticised by a section of the board to whom they were old favourites.' He criticised petty squabbling and bickering involving the directors, who were only interested in humouring their chairman.

It was sensational stuff for the time, and Bartram added: 'Try as I would at Luton, and I tried pretty nearly everything, I could never get most of the [players] to face up to the debts they owed as public performers ... most of them struggled to get [into training] by 10am and many would just jog-trot through the exercises at their own speed and in their own set ways. Training was for them a nuisance, a bore.'

There was talk that the Luton chairman wanted Dally Duncan back to replace Bartram, but Duncan did not fancy a move south again. Other names in the frame were said to be former Chelsea pair Ted Drake and Roy Bentley, neither of whom apparently fancied the Luton role. After Bartram's newspaper revelations, the job looked something of a poisoned chalice. Candidates approached by the club started ruling themselves out of the running for 'travel' or 'health' reasons. Jack Crompton got himself a doctor's note to escape. The former Luton trainer, who had been at Manchester United since the Munich plane crash of 1958, accepted the job but within days telephoned to say his doctor advised against him taking it. A duodenal ulcer was the stated reason.

The trimmed down Luton squad reported back for pre-season training with no manager in place. By now the board was frankly little more than a

joke in the eyes of fans. There was talk of a rebel 'ginger group' of disenchanted shareholders mobilising for a coup. Meanwhile, Mitchell turned to
the FA in his attempt to find a manager. England's Walter Winterbottom
answered the call and recommended Bristol City coach Bill Harvey as an
energetic forward-thinker who deserved consideration. Mitchell duly invited 42-year-old Harvey for an interview and, in the absence of serious competition, this relative unknown was given the job.

League points again proved elusive and Luton soon slumped to the bottom of Division Two in 1962-63. It proved a hard winter in many ways –
not least thanks to the weather. Britain was in the grip of a big freeze, and
hundreds of games were postponed. Luton were one of a number of clubs
who didn't play a single match between Boxing Day and the end of January.
Shortly after a costly fire in the main stand, more sparks flew at the club's
annual meeting, when the so-called ginger group put their head above the
parapet to propose a vote of no confidence. They were backed by a show
of hands at the meeting, but because Mitchell and his colleagues held the
majority of shares they were unable to wrest control from them.

As Luton slid inexorably towards the Third Division, the only reason
for optimism among Hatters fans was the good form of new recruit Ron
Davies, a Welsh centre-forward signed from Chester. But even Davies' regular goals weren't enough and with gates dipping below 8,000, Bill Harvey's
first season ended in disaster. Luton finished bottom with just 29 points
and were relegated to play in English football's third tier for the first time
in 26 years.

Despite relegation the board kept faith with Harvey, but as 1963-64 got
under way he had to sell Ron Davies to raise cash. As President John F
Kennedy was assassinated in Dallas, Luton were 21st in the table, having
won only four of 21 games. Just three years after dropping out of the top
tier, Luton looked to be headed for Division Four. The situation wasn't
helped when opponents and referees began complaining about the floodlights, forcing the under-siege directors to cough up a small fortune for
replacements. It meant money became even more scarce. For three successive summers fans had reflected that things couldn't get much worse at
Luton Town – but they were wrong. The club was heading for oblivion and
soon something radical would have to be done.

The only solution seemed to be changes in the boardroom. But the
AGM saw yet another failed attempt to overthrow the regime. The incum-
bents were virtually untouchable due to their big shareholding. Mitchell had
been on the board since 1934 and saw no reason to quit. Instead of conceding power to new faces, the board manoeuvred to co-opt two new
directors of their own choice. Mitchell stepped down as chairman, but
retained a directorship and resisted all criticism, denying accusations that

his reign had resembled a dictatorship. Many fans felt the board had been wrong to pursue the distant dream of a new super-stadium instead of investing in the ailing team. The Lewsey Farm project was by now looking doomed anyway, due to parking and transport issues.

Meanwhile, after several months without an effective replacement for Ron Davies, Chelsea teenager John O'Rourke arrived in December 1963 and proved an instant hit. The confident and stylish youngster banged in 22 goals in 23 games and helped Town scramble to the safety of 18th place. The horror of relegation to Division Four was staved off for the time being. A thrilling end-of-season victory over local rivals Watford saw a suc-cess-starved crowd react as if Luton had won the Cup, and the celebrations prompted the board to offer a contract extension to manager Harvey. In modern times it is hard to imagine a manager getting such treatment after finishes of 24th and 18th.

At the start of 1964-65, key man O'Rourke was scythed down by a tack-le, collecting an ankle problem that would plague him all season. The man-ager introduced promising young winger David Pleat, but the Nottingham lad's enthusiasm was not enough and things deteriorated again.

Pleat recalled his horror at finding a club in real decay after his arrival: 'The club was on the slide. All the older players had been kept going too long. There was no discipline. It was really bad. A lot of the players were out doing part-time jobs after training. I remember one afternoon I was on a bus coming down a hill into town and I looked out and saw two men in white coats carrying batteries around outside the Ford Motor Company. I looked carefully and saw it was [defenders] John Bramwell and Gordon Fincham. It was like this all the time. No one cared. They sat around drink-ing tea and having a fag and always shot straight off after training.'

With relegation to the Fourth Division again looking likely, hapless Luton were hammered 1-7 at QPR. Within a few days exasperated Harvey handed in his resignation. Once again, the board initially put footballing matters and team selection into the hands of a three-man committee, and again bided their time in finding a replacement. And when they did so, they turned to a semi-retired man of 64. George Martin had been in charge of Luton, Newcastle and Aston Villa after the war but had been out of man-agement for eleven years. Born when Victoria was still queen, Martin had quit the game to go into business while doing part-time scouting for Luton. Reluctantly, and after much persuasion, Martin agreed to try to save Town from relegation.

Martin was the fifth manager in less than seven years at a club whose decline was proving unprecedented in Football League history. The Fourth Division had been formed in 1958 and Luton looked set to become the first club to sink into it having come all the way down from Division One.

Martin began his 'mission impossible' in mid-February 1965 with Luton in 23rd place in Division Three. After watching a horrendous 2-7 home defeat by Shrewsbury, Martin inspired a brief revival, but a 0-5 hammering at Southend saw the slide resume. With a week of the season left, Luton had to win their last two games to save themselves. But, dreadful defending at lowly Scunthorpe saw goalkeeper Colin Tinsley being beaten three times in the first seven minutes and the writing was on the wall. Barrie Thomas racked up five goals and the game ended in a humiliating 1-8 massacre. Only 2,587 saw this record victory for the Lincolnshire club, which for Luton confirmed relegation and represented a new all-time low in the 80-year-old club's fortunes. No club had ever suffered such a spectacular and rapid fall from grace.

In the same week that relegation to Division Four was confirmed, the Lewsey Farm project was referred from the local town hall to Westminster and the seven-year saga rumbled on. By now a housing estate had been built next to the proposed stadium site and this clearly jeopardised Luton's plans. Eventually the whole sorry episode would come to a close when the stadium site was earmarked for a school to serve the new homes.

In the 1965 close season George Martin worked to rebuild pride but seemed to be fighting a losing battle. Not only were players embroiled in disputes over wages and club rules over where they lived, but winger David Pleat broke a leg in training. Goalkeeper Tony Read was tried out in attack. To use the parlance of the time, it was like Fred Karno's circus. None the less, thanks largely to the goals of O'Rourke, a promotion challenge was eventually salvaged from the wreckage in 1965-66. Ultimately Luton would miss out by the narrowest of margins – an inferior goal-average. Failure to go up was largely due to gaining just one point from the final two games, when a pay dispute blew up over promotion bonuses. The directors refused to accede to the players' demands and it appears revenge was gained by a distinct lack of effort in those vital final games.

The bonus row rocked the club, and an end-of-season tour to West Germany just prior to the 1966 World Cup was promptly cancelled. Once again Luton Town were in chaos. The three principal pay rebels – Woods, O'Rourke and Reid – departed in another major clear-out. But if Hatters fans spent the summer enjoying England's 1966 World Cup triumph and thinking Luton's long decline had now bottomed out, they were very much mistaken. The real nadir was in fact still several months away.

Despite the promise shown by emerging youngsters like Bruce Rioch and Alan Slough, Luton made a mediocre start to 1966-67, their second season in Division Four. By early November they were in the bottom four, attendances had plummeted to below 5,000, and morale was rock bottom again. The board was forced to act and George Martin, by now 67, parted company after less than two years as manager. Some players had objected to Martin's attempts to keep them in line, and 'player power' certainly helped oust him. For once, Luton were able to make an instant appointment and didn't struggle on without a leader. Their choice was their own former inside-forward Allan Brown, the erstwhile 40-year-old player-manager of non-league Wigan Athletic in the Cheshire County League. By the time Martin had cleared his desk and Brown was properly in place, Town were 21st in Division Four. This was a club falling apart at the seams. The Beach Boys topped the pop charts that week with *Good Vibrations*, but Brown could feel the negativity enshrouding Kenilworth Road.

And things would get worse before they got better for the new man. He'd been in charge for less than a month when he suffered the ignominy of being the man in charge when Luton astonished even their own long-suffering supporters by sinking to a new all-time low. The occasion was a visit to Lincoln, then slumped miserably in 92nd place in the League rankings – the only club below Luton. Somehow Luton managed to ship no fewer than *eight* goals that afternoon. This one-sided 'contest' was climaxed by a comical eighth goal when journeyman centre-forward Joe Bonson spotted Tony Read off his line and clouted a long distance effort into the unguarded net. The decay was complete. From top of Division One to rock bottom of the Fourth in eight years.

CRISIS 2 (1966-71)
The Insurance Men Run for Cover

The arrival of the so-called 'summer of love' of 1967 was a time of renaissance at Luton Town. Wealthy and charismatic businessman Tony Hunt became the hero of the hour, bringing to the Board of Directors a style and energy that blew away the cobwebs and signalled an end to the bad old days. Without delay, Hunt made money available to manager Allan Brown, who was able to build a new playing squad of some substance.

Since the 1-8 hammering by bottom-of-the league Lincoln six months earlier, Brown had manipulated his limited resources with commendable skill and garnered enough league points to steer the team clear of the reelection zone in the spring of 1967. They finished a humble 17th, but after the horrors of earlier, that was a start. Local lad Bruce Rioch had emerged as a star of the future, and once Tony Hunt and his business colleague Reggie Burr breezed into the boardroom in the summer, there was cause for genuine optimism. Luton Town's first great crisis – the slide from top to bottom of the league in eight years – had been overcome.

Following an extraordinary general meeting in July 1967, 'a massive reconstruction of finances' at Luton Town was announced. Action was being taken, the fans were told, to end the perennial shortage of working capital and to place temporary borrowings from the bank on a more permanent basis. An initial mortgage on freehold land, buildings and properties in Oak and Kenilworth Roads was arranged and further money would be available when required. It amounted to around £100,000 – in 1967 terms, big money as far as the hard-up Hatters were concerned. Share capital was increased from £2,000 to £11,000. It also emerged that £5,000 in bonus money would be shared among the players if they could get promotion. Miserly chairman Percy Mitchell and his failed Lewsey Farm project were consigned to history as Luton Town at last moved into the modern world.

The rebirth had been possible after Hunt and Burr, senior figures at the Vehicle & General Insurance company, were unanimously voted on to the Board. Former RAF fighter pilot Hunt told the *Luton News* he was one of the club's greatest fans, having lived in the area since the war. He had enjoyed playing for Luton Town Cricket Club in Wardown Park for a number of summers after the war and had also been a qualified referee in local football. Burr, his associate, was a Londoner and lifelong Spurs fan.

Hunt said he had been appalled to see Luton Town slide down to the Fourth Division in the early 1960s and admitted that at one point he gave up attending matches altogether. Now he wanted to help bring back the good times: his aim was to oversee the finances and to have the strength of mind to leave the managing of the team to the manager. It was clear his level of involvement would soon require him to become chairman, but for now that role was left to long-serving Tom Hodgson.

Hunt had started his working life as a 10-bob-a-week insurance clerk in 1939. Following his war service as a Battle of Britain pilot, he received a £400 gratuity and sunk this into a small bicycle insurance firm called V&G, which was purchased from a widow anxious to sell for tax reasons. Working with Burr and a third colleague, Lawrence Kershaw, Hunt became managing director and built the Bushey-based company to spectacular success as the nation's second biggest motor insurance group. Burr was another self-made man who had earlier built up the country's biggest pasta manufacturing company. At its peak, V&G would have 800,000 policy holders (private motorists), and its success was based on Hunt's pioneering plan to penalise bad drivers by offering a 'no claims bonus' to the good ones.

Hunt, who said he hated being labelled a millionaire, became wealthy enough to move his family into the magnificent opulence of Waresley Park, near the Bedfordshire-Cambridgeshire border. This 120-acre pile featured a huge white mansion, cricket pitch, tennis courts and near-Olympic-sized pool, with a Rolls Royce in the driveway. Hunt also had a penthouse apartment in St John's Wood, overlooking Regent's Park, and a villa on the Algarve.

With the new money in the coffers, Allan Brown was able to transform Luton's squad and create a new spine to the team. Among the new men who established themselves in the opening weeks of 1967-68 were centre-half Terry Branston, wing-half Billy McDerment, and forwards Ian Buxton and Keith Allen. Gates soared as the team made a solid start and then improved further as the weeks went by, with results at home particularly impressive. A 100 per cent home record was maintained until January (eleven straight wins) and the atmosphere was transformed as the promotion push gained momentum. The team hit the top of the table after a win at Brentford in February and from that point there was no looking back.

On the same landmark day that Enoch Powell made his famous 'rivers of blood' speech, Luton players were to be found sipping champagne and celebrating promotion after a 1-0 win over Halifax at the Shay Ground. The Division Four title was clinched in a 4-0 romp against third-placed Crewe with three games still to go. The goals of local lad Bruce Rioch and the leadership of Branston had been pivotal. Success had been such a stranger to Kenilworth Road in recent years that the jubilant fans even forgave the players for relaxing in the final three games, their lethargy no doubt due in part to excessive celebrations behind the scenes.

During the summer of 1968 the club splashed the cash on quality forwards Brian Lewis, Mike Harrison and Laurie Sheffield, and invested yet more on new changing rooms, a gymnasium and new team bus. The fans rewarded Hunt for his spending by purchasing season-tickets in unprecedented numbers. In every respect, Kenilworth Road was now almost unrecognisable from the gloom-ridden morgue of eighteen months earlier. Luton Town were back.

The optimism was justified. The 1968-69 season was full of thrills and spills and would see Luton narrowly miss out on promotion to Division Two at the first attempt, following a fabulous start. Allan Brown refused to copy the 1966 success of Alf Ramsey's wingless wonders, and opted for a bold 4-2-4 formation, with Graham French and Mike Harrison rampaging down the wings. Visiting teams were overwhelmed by Luton's all-out attacking style. Over the season Luton won 24, drew three and lost none of their 27 home league and cup games. It was a fabulous record and Hatters fans had never had it so good. Highlights included the opening day's 4-0 thrashing of Oldham, which is believed to be the first match attended by comedian Eric Morecambe (no wonder he became hooked), and the unbelievable solo goal by French in a stormy 4-2 win over Mansfield. French beat virtually the entire Stags team on his long loping run from one end of the pitch to the other before slotting home. As there appears to be no surviving film footage of this goal, it tends to get better every time it is described. However, club historian Roger Wash is not a man prone to hyperbole, and after more than 50 years of watching Luton he reckons there's never been a better goal.

Thanks largely to their home form, Luton led the Division Three table until mid-October 1968 but in mid-season the club was temporarily rocked by a change of manager. Allan Brown, the man who seemingly could do no wrong, was shown the door. His exit saga began when he was linked with vacancies at no fewer than four top-division clubs (Ipswich, Leicester, QPR and Nottingham Forest). Brown brushed it off as speculation, although good for his morale. But on the morning of Friday, 13th December he confirmed to an *Evening Post* reporter that he was to be interviewed later that day by Leicester, where he was on a shortlist with Jimmy Scoular and Frank O'Farrell. He insisted he had not applied for the job. The *Post* revealed that he had arranged his interview to fit in with Luton's travel plans that weekend for a game at Hartlepool. After meeting Leicester officials at a hotel, Brown would be collected by his skipper Branston, who lived in nearby Rugby, and the pair would drive to Doncaster railway station for the onward journey to Hartlepool.

In the event, O'Farrell was given the job. Brown put on a brave face, telling reporters he was not disappointed as he had never applied for the job in the first place. His next problem was dealing with Tony Hunt and the Luton board, who were only just finding out what their manager had been up to. That evening, Brown left his Hartlepool hotel for a solo walk along the ice-cold, windswept streets of the Wearside port to clear his head and think about his future. The next day the papers were full of news about the managerial merry-go-round, and this time Brown was being tipped for the Nottingham Forest vacancy.

Luton chairman Hodgson told the press he was pleased Brown was staying, but Tony Hunt was furious and took a different line. He felt Brown had shown blatant disloyalty by meeting Leicester and he wasn't prepared to let the matter lie. The match with Hartlepool ended in a 0-1 defeat and in his local newspaper column Brown wrote that he still had loyal feelings for Luton and hoped the rumours of his departure would now stop. It was a forlorn hope and it was too late to patch things up.

The knives came out at Town's board meeting a week before Christmas. By now, Hunt had already decided Brown must go and was in the process of attempting to persuade Alec Stock, recently sacked by QPR, to take over. Director John Bain summoned Brown and gave him the bad tidings the following day. Within an hour or two the news had leaked and reporters gathered, looking expectantly up at the first-floor window of the terraced houses which contained the club's offices. As the mob grew in size down below, a window suddenly opened and Brown leaned out to shout: 'If you are waiting for me, I've nothing to say.' The reporters screamed back a volley of questions. Brown said he had resigned but had no new job to go to, before disappearing to collect his belongings and say goodbye to players and staff.

Director Bain then told reporters the board had been under the impression Brown was at Luton to take the club back to Division One, but by accepting the invitation to meet Leicester had indicated his future lay elsewhere. The *Evening Post* carried out a quick *vox pop* and found people in the town centre were shocked that the successful Brown had been shown the door. Meanwhile, with his budgie Billy perched on his shoulder, Brown was surrounded by dozens of Christmas cards from Luton fans when he granted the *Evening Post* an interview in the front room of his little clubhouse in Westbury Gardens. He said he had had little option but to resign after hearing what the board thought of the Leicester episode. He said he was 'a bit shaken' and had no new job to go to, although aware of speculation connecting him to managerless Forest.

Brown had been the twelfth league manager to part company with his club in just five weeks. This was 1968, Britain was changing, and football was changing. Directors and fans were becoming impatient. Brown left to spend part of the Christmas holidays in his native Scotland, returning to

Luton to find himself at a loose end: 'It's the first time since I was 17 that I've had free Saturdays,' he reflected. He was pictured in the local paper cutting a rather lonely figure as he went for a run through local streets in an attempt to keep fit. On Christmas Day he was telephoned by Torquay United, a call which led to him becoming the Devon club's manager a few weeks later. Ironically he replaced Frank O'Farrell, the man who had been given the Leicester job.

Meanwhile, dapper 51-year-old Alec Stock had marched into Kenilworth Road on the morning of Friday, 20th December, the choice of Tony Hunt as Town's new manager. The erudite Stock was delighted to get back into football, for he had a point to prove after being controversially sacked by QPR a month earlier. The man whose mannerisms would later inspire the character 'Ron Manager' on TV's *Fast Show*, was about to become the best-paid manager outside the top two divisions. Stock recently led QPR into the top division for the first time, winning the League Cup at Wembley en route, but for the past eighteen months had been dogged by asthma and stress-related problems. Ordered by doctors to take three months off just as QPR made their bow in the First Division, his ruthless chairman Jim Gregory responded with the sack rather than sympathy. Stock was outraged after all he had done for QPR and was now desperate to put one over them by becoming a big success at Luton.

Stock revealed that his health problems stemmed partly from over-work and partly from war wounds suffered on French battlefields while serving with the Northants Yeomanry. He had been hit by a bazooka in the back and came home from the war partially deaf, which meant he couldn't hear a referee's whistle or other high-pitched sounds. But he assured Luton's Tony Hunt that he was hungry and well enough to take the reins at Kenilworth Road. He was charismatic, fastidious, and skilled at man-management, and QPR's loss was certainly Luton's gain. He would have the last laugh on his former club, for replacement Tommy Docherty lasted only 28 days at Loftus Road and Rangers slid to relegation, amassing a meagre 18 points.

Stock seemed pleasantly surprised by the quality of the Luton side he inherited. In his first game he marvelled at Bruce Rioch ('I haven't seen such shooting since Bobby Charlton'), and the impish Brian Lewis, who scored direct from a corner and claimed it was deliberate. The Hatters were eighth in the Third Division when he arrived and Stock had them in the top three within a matter of weeks.

A famous face lent his support to the promotion push in early 1969 when the nation's favourite comic Eric Morecambe returned to Kenilworth Road for the first time since a heart attack the previous November. After being cooped up indoors while recuperating, Eric enjoyed the narrow win against Walsall, and declared he would also go to the away game at Crewe four days later. His plan was scuppered when his doctor banned him from such a long trip, as he had a cold. According to his diaries, Eric enjoyed meeting fellow Luton fans at the Walsall game, and the hospitality shown in the boardroom afterwards: 'One lady talked to me about heart attacks. Her father had three, her husband four. I think she was quite pleased, but it got them both in the end. I had to laugh.'

The Morecambes (real name 'Bartholomew') first began supporting Luton after moving to a new home in Harpenden around the time Town won the Fourth Division title. Club secretary Eric Readhead recalled Eric's agent contacting the club to ask for a couple of season-tickets for 1968-69. On the opening day of the campaign, the wonderful atmosphere as Town hammered Oldham 4-0 in front of 15,000 saw Eric and son Gary hooked to the cause for life. By now Eric was 42 and a huge star, and it was pressure of work which led to the heart attack in the autumn of 1968 after a series of late-night shows at the Variety Club in Batley. It forced him to give up his 50-a-day cigarette habit and find new ways to relax. He told his doctors he would switch to smoking a pipe and attend more Luton games.

Tony Hunt, 48, took over as chairman in February 1969 as expected, replacing an emotional Tom Hodgson, who became president, to add to his previous roles as player, captain, director and chairman. The meeting endorsed several other key appointments, with Jimmy Andrews becoming Alec Stock's right-hand man and first-team coach, and a relative unknown, Harry Haslam, appointed with the unusual title of 'chief scout and entertainments manager'. Haslam, 47, was a former full-back with Rochdale, Oldham, Brighton and Leyton Orient, who in recent years had managed non-league sides Eastbourne and Tonbridge and served Fulham as chief scout. He was a cheerful fellow with good contacts in the game. Part of his brief at Luton was said to be 'selling the club' to a wider audience.

In his early time at the club, few could have guessed the impact 'Happy Harry' would end up having on Luton's history. Eventually his shrewd football brain would be put to good use, but in the early days he was more of a PR man. His tasks included organising a bouquet of flowers to thank long-standing fan Molly Miles for supplying the players with chewing gum before games and cakes at Christmas. He also sent chairman Hunt on an expedition to the local hospital with Easter eggs for the fan run over by a car on the way to a game. Eric Morecambe had brightened up the boardroom and hospitality areas, and now Haslam did likewise around the club's offices. Haslam certainly needed his sense of humour on the day in March 1969 when a group of Luton fans based in Denmark sent a package containing 14 trolls, accompanied by a letter explaining that the bushy-haired mascots were 'good luck trolls' to help Luton's promotion fight.

Even with the trolls, Luton narrowly missed out on promotion to the
Second Division in the spring of 1969. Having spent nearly all the campaign in the top four, the Hatters couldn't match the consistency of
Watford and Swindon, and ended up third. The Hornets took the title
despite a stormy last-day defeat at Kenilworth Road which was marred by
pitch invasions, injuries and arrests. Three sendings-off and major crowd
trouble in front of 25,000-plus meant it had been the most memorable 'M1
derby' yet. One paper called it 'a night of quite appalling crowd behaviour
and bone-jarring violence [on the pitch]'. The new and growing phenome-
non of football hooliganism was rearing its ugly head. Prior to the game,
Watford boss Ken Furphy accused Luton of having adopted unsophisti-
cated long-ball tactics in order to overcome Barrow 5-1. Trying to defuse
the situation, Alec Stock called this 'a bad mannered outburst'. It was
indeed hard to tolerate Watford accusing Luton of crude tactics: the words
pot, kettle and black come to mind!

The fans were flocking back to Kenilworth Road by now and the misery of the early 1960s was fading from the memory. Some fans went to
greater efforts than others to express their devotion. Stanley Evans was a
Rootes factory worker in the town who was getting close to achieving an
ambition to watch his Luton heroes on all 92 league grounds. He travelled
by two wheels to most games from his Alexandra Avenue home and for a
match at Colchester had used a push-bike for the 132-mile round trip. Soon
after that game his bike was stolen, so he invested in a moped. He had to
get three days off work to get to Workington, and on another long trip to
Bury made it by kick-off despite falling off en route.

Many fans were angered by the club selling talented Bruce Rioch to
Aston Villa in the summer of 1969, but the six-figure fee was a record for
a Third Division club and far too good to refuse. A fraction of the cash
was spent wisely, it would turn out, when Luton signed an unknown
teenage full-back from Fulham called Malcolm Macdonald. Harry Haslam
knew the player from their days together at Southern League Tonbridge,
and when Haslam joined Fulham to scout for their new manager, Bobby
Robson, he took Macdonald with him. The player started at Craven
Cottage as a speedy left-back in the reserves, but during an injury crisis was
tried in attack by the first team, thanks to the persuasive powers of Haslam.
Fast, strong and raw, he scored five times in thirteen appearances, but was
dropped by Johnny Haynes who had become a caretaker manager after
Robson was sacked.

Haslam left Fulham for Luton at that point, but kept in touch with the
unhappy Macdonald. He urged Alec Stock to take a close look at the
youngster when Luton and Fulham reserves met. Stock recalled: 'I first laid
eyes on Macdonald on a Saturday afternoon playing for Fulham reserves at

Luton. Harry Haslam and I had hurried back from our match at Tranmere the previous night because once again Fulham's retained list included some interesting names; once again I thought they were throwing experience away for nothing. The first thing that struck me about Macdonald, apart from his strength, was his speed.'

Macdonald would later explain how he escaped from his 'living nightmare' at Fulham to become a Luton player, revealing that Haslam came up with a cunning plan to get the player away. Haslam ordered the player to make an appointment with the Fulham chairman Tommy Trinder in which he must trot out the following speech: 'I've spoken to the manager, I've spoken to the secretary and now you're my final option. I cannot afford to live on the money you're paying me. I finished second top scorer last season and that seems to have been totally ignored. So either give me a significant rise or let me go to another club. The man who's caused me most misery here is Johnny Haynes, if you don't let me go, I'm going to stick him up against the wall and beat the living shit out of him.'

A nervous Macdonald apparently trotted out the speech as instructed and reckoned it must have been the first time that comedian Trinder was ever completely lost for words. He was ordered out of the office and left sweating on what would happen. Thinking he might now be in big trouble, Macdonald was told to report back to the office. After nearly three hours waiting, suddenly the wheezing asthmatic Alec Stock burst through the door, followed by Haslam, the latter covered in grease and mud. Their car had suffered a puncture rushing over from Luton and Haslam had been forced to change the wheel. A wink from the filthy Haslam assured wide-eyed Macdonald that things would be fine and the full extent of his plan finally dawned. Within an hour or so he was a Luton player.

Stock recalled: 'Malcolm had clearly become disillusioned with football and explained that Fulham didn't think he could play and that the great Johnny Haynes was making life difficult for him. He was earning £25 a week at Fulham, £10 of which went on rent for a flat for his wife and daughter. We offered him £35 a week and a clubhouse next to Kenilworth Road upon which we spent £200 renovating for him. He even got an £800-plus signing-on fee. He felt the sun shone out of Luton after that.'

Stock was persuaded by Haslam to try Macdonald on the left wing in a pre-season friendly with the Italian Under-21s at Kenilworth Road and on the strength of his performance he was given the No 11 shirt for the opening league game of 1969-70. Before long he was moved across to centre-forward and the goals began to flow. Stock noted the player's self-confidence and the fact that he was never afraid to miss, and told him to go out and get 30 goals that season. Despite his lack of experience, Macdonald ended up with 28.

Stock's first full season in charge started brightly. Town went straight to the top of Division Three and stayed there until mid-January. The newly christened 'Supermac' and Matt Tees became the attacking spearheads, replacing the departed Laurie Sheffield and Brian Lewis. Six wins and two draws from the final nine games ensured runners-up spot behind Orient, and Town were promoted back to the Second Division after six years away. Kenilworth Road had become a real fortress and at one stage during 1969-70 Town racked up 72 home league and cup games of which only one had been lost (and even that was the 1968 'promotion party' game when the result was meaningless).

By now, Macdonald was not only scoring goals galore, but keeping Eric Morecambe supplied with material for his TV shows. After turning up at a 'black tie' function in the Hatters Club wearing a hired suit that was far too big, Macdonald lurked in the shadows trying to hide from the spotlight. Unfortunately Morecambe's wife Joan insisted he join her for a dance. The sight of wildly flapping trousers on the dance-floor brought the house down and inspired Morecambe to write a number of sketches featuring ill-fitting clothing and plus-fours, later used on TV.

With the manager and chairman confident the club was close to return-ing to the top division, the vexed question of Town's stadium came up for examination. Tony Hunt reckoned the club needed a 40,000-capacity ground and could create it on the current site if they cantilevered the Main Stand over the neighbouring railway line and built a new double-decker stand at the Kenilworth Road end. The local council was having none of it, however, and threw up objections about parking and congestion. It was a blow to Hunt, who was soon to go into hospital for what was described as major surgery.

In the summer of 1970, to prepare for their return to the Second Division, Luton's playing squad embarked on a two-week tour of Spain, followed by a short trip to Blankenberge in Belgium for a friendly. It was while the team bus was waiting to leave Kenilworth Road for Belgium that Bedfordshire police phoned to say that winger Graham French wouldn't be joining them – he was in custody after a shooting incident the previous night. French had been playing the best football of his career recently, set-ting up goals galore for Macdonald and Tees, and his absence would be a serious blow. French led an unconventional lifestyle away from football, and this was merely the latest in a series of episodes which jeopardised his career. Thus far, his remarkable skills had seen him survive as a full-time player, despite the unprofessional manner in which he chose to 'rest and recuperate'. This time, however, he was in serious trouble. As it turned out, he would not only miss the bus to Belgium, but the entire 1970-71 season due to his latest misdemeanour.

When the shooting incident came to court, French would be described by the judge as 'an unsavoury man with synthetic glamour'. These seemed like harsh words to the Luton fans who regarded him the finest winger ever to hug the Kenilworth Road touchlines. He had become the Hatters' wildman of the flanks and more than one writer would coin the phrase 'the poor man's George Best' when referring to his antics. Such an accolade was way off the mark, of course – French's behaviour made Best look positively angelic. After all, was Bestie ever charged with attempted murder? Did he ever fire a revolver into a punter's chest from point-blank range? Did Best ever serve time at Her Majesty's pleasure and then emerge a few years later with a new name?

French, by now 25 and at the peak of his playing powers, may not have had Best's good looks, but as a youngster he showed similar potential, playing a dazzling role as England's youth team won the 'Little World Cup' in 1963. His defining moment was probably the sensational solo goal against Mansfield in 1968, referred to earlier. Those who witnessed that goal struggle for the appropriate adjectives and swear it was better than anything Bestie ever produced. French would soon have plenty of time to ponder his greatest goal when he was put behind bars.

French's wing-play was full of golden moments, but his outrageous behaviour off the park had seen him en route for self-destruction from the moment he made an enemy of Tommy Docherty after returning from the Little World Cup. The Doc wanted French to sign for Chelsea and went to meet him at Heathrow but, amazingly, was given the brush-off by a teenager whose reputation for arrogance and surliness was already well-deserved. When two large egos collide in such circumstances, something has to give, and Docherty immediately washed his hands of the young upstart.

Having earlier given French a first-team debut at sixteen, Shrewsbury were not best pleased to miss out on Chelsea's cash. Aston Villa then took an interest but were put off by French's reputation. It was Swindon who took a chance and coughed up £12,000 for him in 1963, but French soon made it known he was fed up with life in Wiltshire and he drifted to Watford where no-nonsense Bill McGarry insisted he slimmed down his fourteen-stone frame. After a few weeks of jogging around Cassiobury Park wearing two or three tracksuits, French failed to make an impact and was given a free transfer.

French returned to his native West Midlands, his career apparently in tatters, and joined non-league Wellington, where he became a local star, turning the wing-wizardry on and off like a tap and boosting the club's gates whenever he chose to play. In the local paper he admitted he'd been a silly lad in the past and had become a member of the 'party set', enjoying the swinging sixties to the full, but promised to repay Wellington for the house they'd provided for his young family and the faith they had shown in him. At this point ex-Luton winger Mike Cullen spotted him in action and recommended him to The Hatters. French's two Luton managers, Brown and Stock, usually extracted the best out of him, but bigger clubs were constantly frightened off by his reputation as a trouble-maker. After he retired, Stock would reflect wistfully: 'I still think about French a lot and dream about what a great player he could have become without his outside distractions.'

Luton teammates never knew what to expect next, with French's chaotic personal life causing him to miss training, turn up late for games and on one occasion hide greyhounds in the club's gym, where they chewed the equipment. He smoked menthol cigarettes, allegedly for medicinal purposes, and had the appearance of a hung-over rock singer, but with the ball at his feet was a genius. More than once he took the field still under the influence of the previous evening's refreshments. Malcolm Macdonald told the story of the game at Bury for which French turned up at the railway station early in the morning, clearly having not been to bed at all. After Town surged into an early 2-0 lead, French suddenly called out 'Excuse me lads' and threw up on the touchline. Not surprisingly, he was immediately subbed, but not disciplined because he had set up both goals, hung-over or not.

But it was at the height of his form, just prior to the start of the 1970-71 season, that French pushed things too far. First he refused a new contract and then didn't bother to turn up for training. Shortly after suspending the player, just as the team were leaving for Belgium, Stock got the call about French's arrest on a charge of attempted murder. The case subsequently went before a jury at Nottingham Assizes, who were told that a petty, sneering remark about an autograph in Luton's Caesar's Palace nightspot had set off a chain of violent events in South Bedfordshire. A man was shot in the chest and another beaten up with a knuckle-duster after a car chase. The person responsible for both attacks was French, said the prosecuting lawyer.

After the main charge was reduced from attempted murder to GBH, French and his gang (including a 23-stone bouncer known as 'Tiny') lined up in court to deny the allegations. The court was told French had recruited the gang to go on a revenge mission after the pub altercation. French borrowed a white Mini from a married woman he was on 'visiting terms' with, and lay in wait late at night for one of his victims to pass. After being chased and cornered, the man had his nose and ribs broken, with French allegedly using a knuckle-duster. French and his boys later located their other principal target at the Unicorn pub in Luton, in the shape of a man known as the 'King Joker' of the local housing estate. By this time the footballer was in possession of a .22 American revolver. French claimed the gun had only been for show, and it had gone off accidentally, but a ballistics expert made a nonsense of this claim with evidence that it had been in contact with the man's chest when the heavy trigger was pulled. The victim needed emergency surgery at a London hospital to have the bullet removed.

After the shooting there was a Keystone Cop-style getaway from the pub as French and his five substantial cohorts squeezed into their tiny getaway car while their opposite numbers hurled random missiles at them. French brandished the gun Hollywood-style as the little car chugged off. French denied the assault charges, although admitting possession of the gun, but was found guilty. Justice Melford Stevenson said there was little doubt the whole unsavoury plot had been organised by the footballer himself. He said French's 'synthetic glamour' as a local hero in Luton had influenced his hangers-on. French was sentenced to three years' imprisonment on a Friday morning in December 1970 as his Luton teammates were at the other end of the M1 preparing for a table-topping game with Sheffield United. But, even as the prison doors clanged shut, this was not the end of Graham French in a Luton Town shirt – but more of that later.

The absence of French, who created most of his scoring opportunities, did not faze Malcolm Macdonald once the 1970-71 season got moving. He started his second season as Luton's main striker in even more spectacular style than the first. Before the end of October, Mac had fifteen goals to his name and exploded onto the national consciousness with a hat-trick in the 5-1 hammering of Sheffield Wednesday at Hillsborough, which featured on ITV's *The Big Match*.

It proved a roller-coaster of a campaign. Alec Stock would later reflect that it turned into 'a queer season', with Luton hit by everything but the kitchen sink. As well as the drama of French's imprisonment, the club signed half-a-dozen quality players (no fewer than four in a daring raid on Old Trafford), there were thrilling home ties in both cups, and the team spent much of the season in the top four of Division Two. But, as is so often the case at Luton Town, the immense promise shown on the field would suddenly be overshadowed by a crisis off it.

In the wake of winning at Portsmouth in February 1971, which elevated Town to third in the table, came ominous developments in the business world, events that would have huge implications for the future of Luton Town. Fans were stunned to pick up their *Evening Post* and read quotes from Luton's swashbuckling chairman Tony Hunt, saying he did not know whether he would be able to stay at his beloved Hatters. He was reacting to the spectacular crash of his company, Vehicle & General. All efforts to save the huge insurance business had failed after its shares plummeted. The problem for Luton was that V&G shares had been underpinning the football club for the past three years.

The business world was rocked by news of V&G's collapse and the event was front page news everywhere. A petition to wind up the company was presented to the High Court and a crestfallen Hunt told reporters: 'I didn't know anything about this until Friday afternoon just after I had seen the [Luton] team off to Sunderland. It's come out of the blue.' He admitted it was likely to mean the end of his involvement at the football club. Fans were told an emergency board meeting at the club had been hastily arranged.

As the news emerged, the Luton squad was blissfully unaware of events, holed up in Jersey and enjoying a short mid-season break on local golf courses. Their peace was shattered by the news back home. Alec Stock recalled the fateful day: 'On the first night in Jersey I had gone to bed early and was having a lie-in, something I never managed to do at Luton when I was driving up the M1 every morning. I had the papers, a pot of tea and life was marvellous. I smiled to myself as I nestled back for an hour's read. The first headline in the *Daily Telegraph* hit me between the eyes like a sledgehammer "V&G collapse". I just held my head in my hands, for I knew exactly what that meant to the club and me. Life would never be the same again at Kenilworth Road.'

The press soon tracked down the Luton party at its Jersey hideaway, but found club director John Bain putting a brave face on things. He said he didn't think the football club would be badly affected by the V&G situation. If he truly believed that, he would soon be proved very wrong. V&G shares had been propping up the club's substantial overdraft and providing the collateral for the club to borrow from the bank and continue trading. As these shares were now worthless, so the mortgage on the ground and the overdraft were no longer properly secured. According to Tim Collings' centenary history of the club, Luton Town therefore found itself in a position regarded as 'unofficial receivership'.

The fall of V&G had been swift and dramatic. It followed a steady depreciation of its shares over a number of months and then a minor recovery in February. The collapse left around 800,000 motorists without insurance cover and thousands more finding their premiums would now be increased by a third. The *Financial Times* reported on its front page that 10 per cent of all British motorists had been left without insurance cover after by far the largest collapse by any motor insurance group. They said that of 6.4 million shares in the company, 590,635 were held by Finance Director and Luton Town director Reggie Burr, and 403,619 by Tony Hunt. It was reported that the Secretary for Trade and Industry, John Davies, was planning an inquiry into the affairs of V&G. The British Insurance Association

(BIA) was criticised for not intervening and saving the company, but this body claimed it couldn't afford the £11 million it would have cost to do that. The BIA said it would have been cheaper to refloat the company in the summer of 1970 when the Board of Trade first suspected it was in trouble. The crash had huge implications for the insurance world in general and the press called it 'the end of cheap motor insurance'.

Tony Hunt, the charismatic 'saviour' of Luton Town, was now cast in a different light. His movements over the weekend of the breaking news were reported as 'uncertain'. He didn't travel with the Luton team to the goalless draw at Sunderland, nor did he appear in the Roker Park directors box as originally planned. Shortly afterwards his secretary said a lunch engagement had been cancelled as he was going into hospital, but Hunt's besieged wife told reporters she didn't know where he was, or if he was going into hospital. Hunt was, it was known, still recovering from major surgery at a top London clinic six months earlier. His health problems had led him to recently stand down as Managing Director of V&G after nine years in the role.

Following a Kenilworth Road board meeting, it was announced that Hunt was retiring as club chairman with immediate effect – to be replaced by the club's erstwhile auditor, Robert Keens – but would remain a director. Reggie Burr stepped down as joint vice-chairman but would also remain on the board. The club said it would accept these retirements with great reluctance, and sympathy was expressed over Hunt and Burr's 'recent business catastrophe'. This news was announced in the Kenilworth Suite, a miserable looking Hunt standing nearby drinking coffee, but not taking part in the meeting.

Tony Hunt's entrepreneurial spirit was history, The Beatles had broken up, the swinging sixties were over, no more love and peace. Trouble was flaring in Northern Ireland, students were shot dead by police in the USA. Sixty-six football fans died in a crush at Ibrox Park. All around was trouble and strife.

It marked the end of a short but exciting chapter at Luton Town. The dashing partnership of Hunt and Stock had built on Allan Brown's good work and, thanks to the investment organised by Hunt and Burr, Luton had looked bound for a return to Division One. Now the atmosphere at the club was one of uncertainty and worry. Hunt responded on his time as chairman: 'Certainly it has cost me more than I anticipated – and I would warn any businessman who wants to do the same to make sure he can afford it.' Stock reflected: '[Tony Hunt] was a major influence on the rise of Luton Town. He was a personality, a man with a bit of style who allowed us to get on with running the club … Tony, who had been the blue-eyed boy only a couple of weeks earlier was suddenly the villain. And through it all only one director stood firm alongside me – Eric Morecambe. He knew where his loyalties lay. He knew Hunt had done so much for Luton.'

For a while there were genuine fears that creditors of V&G would descend on the football club to recoup their losses. Office staff fielded many phone calls from people who couldn't get through to the V&G headquarters at Bushey. It had a hugely unsettling effect on players and staff, whose future was suddenly in doubt, and it seemed to affect performances on the pitch. The promotion challenge didn't so much wither and die, it simply spluttered to an undignified halt.

Luton Town were certainly not alone in fretting about money and what the future held in that troubled spring of 1971. An associate of Tory Prime Minister Ted Heath was quoted as saying: 'Britain is like a destroyer heading full-steam towards the shore. There's only so much sea room, and it's running out fast.' The stock market was at its lowest level in four years, unemployment at its worst in 31 years (721,000 out of work, 70,000 of them executives). Inflation was running at nearly 9 per cent a year, while the economy was growing by a paltry 1.1 per cent. V&G had followed Rolls-Royce into bankruptcy and the nation's largest industrial complex, ICI, was about to impose 25 per cent cutbacks. The number of working days lost to industrial action was at its worst level since the General Strike of 1926. Even the Rolling Stones were emigrating to France to get away from it all. The only good news was Clive Dunn's *Grandad* being knocked off the top of the charts.

The Luton party flew home from Jersey, hoping to resume their promotion challenge in March 1971 regardless of the shadow cast by the V&G collapse. On the day their chairman stood down in a blaze of publicity, Alec Stock and his players had to prepare for a visit from Charlton Athletic. What they didn't need – the over-stressed Stock in particular – was another off-field drama to interrupt their usual routine. But that is exactly what happened at lunchtime on Friday 5th March.

Skipper Mike Keen was sitting in the Hatters Club bar after a light training session, sipping coffee. Suddenly the peace was shattered when someone with a loud hailer screamed: 'This is a raid, this is a raid.' Seconds later six people dressed in animal costumes burst into the room and made a bee-line for Keen. Astonished staff watched open-mouthed as the captain was bundled out of the bar and into a waiting mini-van. The vehicle sped off towards Dunstable Road and disappeared.

Alec Stock was quickly given the unwelcome news that his captain had been kidnapped and he reached for the phone. It soon became clear that Keen's abduction had been a stunt by students as part of their Rag Week. Whether the Luton skipper had gone willingly or not was not immediately clear. Either way Stock was not amused. He telephoned Luton College of Technology and was put through to the students' Rag headquarters. The conversation was not particularly friendly. A spokesman for the students announced afterwards: 'We have him [Mike Keen] securely in hiding. He is relaxed and smiling and will be released on receipt of a donation from the Football Club to Rag funds.'

Bearing in mind the unfolding collapse of V&G, rarely can a request for money from Luton Town have come at a more inopportune moment. The students were asked what would happen to Keen now that the furious Stock refused to pay up. Would he be released to play against Charlton the following day? The students avoided the question and said the next move was up to Mr Stock. The manager was asked for his views of the episode: 'I think they are the biggest load of rubbish God ever created and I hope this rag blows up in their faces. Friday is a very busy day for us – it's the day we win football matches. If we lose tomorrow you know who is to blame.'

Stock refused to hand over the £100 ransom and Keen was held for more than two hours. After the deadlock was broken, the students allowed waiting reporters and photographers into the house in Russell Street where Keen was being held. Unlike his manager, Keen was smiling and apparently unfazed. He was duly released and later, following considerable persuasion by the local press, Stock agreed to shake hands with rag organisers Jeff Barnes and Linda Platen although he steadfastly refused to pay the ransom. Keen was pictured in the *Evening Post* being manhandled by a woman wearing a large pig's head and a man with a large devil's head. The whole surreal episode was soon forgotten and Keen went on to have fine game against Charlton, setting up Viv Busby's goal in a 1-1 draw.

Following the news of the V&G collapse, Luton's form dived. They won just four of their last fifteen league games, ending up sixth and missing promotion to the top flight by seven points. Three defeats in a disastrous four-day Easter programme did the real damage. The last realistic chance of promotion disappeared on Easter Monday when title-chasing Leicester won 3-1 at Kenilworth Road. It was an occasion when all the recent pressure on Alec Stock became clear – at least in the eyes of director Eric Morecambe. The comedian recalled how, after this hugely disappointing game, he held open the boardroom door and bid a cheery farewell as Stock departed for home. Stock, not realising Morecambe was still looking on, crossed the landing outside the boardroom and gave an almighty kick to a chair, sending it flying. 'It was his private moment of pressure release', recalled Eric.

It was no wonder Stock felt frustrated by Luton's failure to get promotion. Events completely out of his control had combined to scupper any realistic chance of reaching Division One – and now the fine team he had assembled would probably have to be broken up.

The fall-out from the V&G crisis meant Luton had to raise nearly £200,000 very quickly – and the only way to do that would be to sell star centre-forward Malcolm Macdonald. It was heartbreaking for Stock, not to mention thousands of fans, and he would look back on this episode with sad regret for the rest of his life: 'I was very distressed when my Luton team had to be changed. It was a most excellent young team and so rewarding to Harry Haslam, Jimmy Andrews and I because it was built from nothing. When you watched them in training you thought to yourself – what a bunch of smoothies, I fancy us to do something this year. Had it not been for the V&G collapse I believe that team would have reached the First Division.'

Although the football grapevine speculated about Macdonald's future, the player himself seemed happy to stay at Luton. But by the time the season reached its closing weeks, Stock had spoken privately to him to confirm interest from three big clubs, admitting he would have to be sold whether he wanted to leave or not: 'The bank is on our backs.' The final game of the 1970-71 season saw Macdonald fire a hat-trick against Cardiff City, those three goals allowing Luton to qualify for the following season's Watney Cup. This late flourish enabled hard-up Luton to crank up their asking price for Macdonald from £150,000 to £180,000.

The player's final appearance in a Hatters shirt would be in a testimonial at Margate two days later, when he banged in another two goals. Despite a late bid by Chelsea, he joined Newcastle later that week. Local car firm Twigg's, in conjunction with the club, arranged for Macdonald to journey from Luton to Newcastle to sign in a chauffeur driven Rolls-Royce. At a stroke, the fee wiped out Luton's £173,000 deficit and saved the club from going under. New chairman Robert Keens was a relieved man and announced: 'I can now state the club's finances have recovered.'

Macdonald was stepping into a new world of superstardom, but for Stock it seemed like the beginning of the end. His health still occasionally troubled him, the daily drive from his Epsom home up the M1 to Luton was getting him down, and now all his work since joining Luton seemed to have gone to waste.

Stock was in a tetchy mood as he told reporters: 'There is nothing in this selling business for a manager. It's just the best way to lose your job – to sell your best players.' Stock even took an unexpected swipe at Luton supporters, who were distinctly unhappy about missing promotion and the sale of Macdonald. Stock said they should get behind the team more, and although the average gate of 17,400 was good, lately they had been too quiet.

Postscript

More than five years later, the blame for the V&G collapse was laid officially at the feet of Tony Hunt, Reggie Burr and Lawrence Kershaw, the
three main directors of the company. A Public Inquiry into the affair was
completed in 1972 but for four years its findings remained in the hands of
the Director of Public Prosecutions. No charges were brought.

'Mismanagement' by the named trio was blamed for the crisis, which
saw V&G 'over-reach itself' as early as 1964. The Inquiry lasted a month
and delved into allegations about leaked confidential information, negli-
gence by a senior civil servant and shady meetings in a Hertfordshire pub.
Among those who gave evidence was *Private Eye* editor Richard Ingrams.

CRISIS 3 (1971-76)
Sell the Accountant!

It seemed very cruel that four years of unremitting success at Kenilworth Road should be rudely interrupted by the V&G crisis, an event totally unrelated to football. Especially galling for battle-weary manager Alec Stock, who found himself under pressure to maintain Luton Town's progress even though the club now had no money and its big plans for the future were in tatters.

During the sparkling Tony Hunt era, Luton had risen from the bottom of the pile and achieved two promotions and two near-misses. Between Hunt's arrival in the summer of 1967 and the spectacular crash of his business empire in early 1971, Luton won 74 matches and lost just 28. Now as season 1971-72 loomed, the priority had to be to steady the ship and steer it safely through choppy transitional waters.

The new financial constraints scuppered plans to develop Kenilworth Road, at least for the foreseeable future. After the failure to find a new ground during the 1960s, the board had hoped to build a huge new edifice to replace the Main Stand at Kenilworth Road. This would house 10,000 seats and provide uninterrupted views of play, unlike the current stand, and there would be car-parking close by. This was not a pipe-dream, it was insisted, but a real necessity for the club's future. Despite initial opposition, the local council indicated cautious approval of these ideas. Now the V&G crash meant the club could not possibly afford to proceed with the £600,000 project.

Skint or not, the club scraped together funds to pay for the squad to fly to Portugal for an end-of season jolly on the Algarve in May 1971. One man missing was chief scout Harry Haslam, who was given Stock's office at Kenilworth Road and told to stay there until he had found a replacement for the recently sold Malcolm Macdonald. The Luton party stayed near the beach in Montegordo and a highlight of the trip was a cocktail party at the nearby villa of Tony Hunt. There was also a surprise in store when a message arrived from a UEFA agent, inviting the team to play a friendly against mighty Benfica.

As requested, Alec Stock stayed at the hotel to await details. But while the rest of the party were out enjoying themselves, Stock kicked his heels for hours as the agent failed to show. Once the man was tracked down, he blamed bad weather for his absence – but added that, in any case, Benfica had now decided they didn't want to play Luton anyway. Stock was predictably miffed, and other problems, compounded by heavy rain, turned the tour into a shambles. By the end of the week the bored players had no football to play and were holed up in their hotel as the Algarve suffered 'its worst weather in living memory', according to locals. The squad ended up sitting around playing Monopoly, keen to get back to sunny Luton. With nothing else to write, *Evening Post* reporter Roger Duckworth extracted a slew of 'exclusives' from Alec Stock as everyone sat around twiddling their thumbs.

Duckworth filed a number of startling stories: Luton Town were willing to take Graham French back when he was released from HM Prison, Stafford; Stock was soon to become chief executive/general manager with Jimmy Andrews promoted to team manager; the club would be jazzing up Kenilworth Road with cheerleaders and programme sellers in 'hot pants', which were all the rage that summer. One snippet that Stock kept up his sleeve was that Luton Town might be open to moving, lock, stock and barrel, to the new town of Milton Keynes, which was beginning to take shape twenty miles up the M1. Stock and director John Bain were said to have met with a representative of the MK Development Corporation for preliminary talks around this time. Little apparently came of the meeting, for the time being at least.

Against this generally unsettled background, the 1971-72 season set off with Luton hoping that cut-price captures Vic Halom and Gordon Hindson could fill the enormous gap left by Malcolm Macdonald. It was a vain hope. Goals proved hard to come by, and the reliable defence was also seriously weakened when big Chris Nicholl was sold ludicrously cheaply to Aston Villa in early 1972 to keep the bank happy. There was still talent in the squad, but the spark seemed to have gone. Town finished mid-table in Division Two and by the end of the season Stock decided he'd had enough.

The reasons for his disillusionment were manifold: he'd been forced to sell his best men but was still expected to challenge for promotion, he was fed up with the awkward daily commute from his Surrey home, he was suffering from ill health from time to time – and on top of all this had grown weary of the shenanigans in the Luton boardroom, where his only ally these days was Eric Morecambe. By 1972 Haslam and Andrews had taken increasingly more active roles in running the team in any case, so it was perhaps no great surprise when 55-year-old Stock called it a day. He formally resigned on Thursday, 27th April 1972, leaving chief scout Haslam to take charge of the team, assisted by Ken Whitfield, for the final game of the season, a meaningless 1-1 draw at Cardiff. The future of Stock's right-hand man, Andrews, was left unclear, amid signs of mutual disenchantment. Although highly regarded within the game as a coach, the former West Ham winger had suffered criticism at Luton that his methods were too defensive.

Stock said he'd known for a while he should give up, and it was just a question of getting the timing right. In the event his plans leaked out, so he had quit earlier than intended: 'For nearly three-and-a-half years I have been doing a round trip of 120 miles a day from my home in Epsom and due to the financial position of the club I have kept my nose to the grindstone for the last 22 months without a break. This is neither good for me nor the club and I had begun to feel more than a little worn out. It was often midnight or later when I arrived home, having left at 7am.

'We got out of dire financial trouble due to the calibre of the players and great credit is also due to my coach Andrews. The selling of players like Supermac makes life difficult for the staff who have to dash all over the country to try to replace them, and it is just not on! In this modern age of football when you have good players you hang on to them, and what worried me was the constant breaking of faith with supporters and the football public at large.'

Stock seemed genuinely sad at letting Luton fans down by having to sell the best players after the V&G crisis. He recalled a function at Aylesbury when a young fan pleaded with him not to sell Chris Nicholl: 'I said I would not [sell], but when the transfer did go through the boy must have thought I was a liar. Also, by selling your best players you are breaking faith with other players whose chances of win bonuses are lessened. It's a very bad thing in my estimation to let everybody down like this. Before my period with the club and for a number of years before that, the football world has always known that Luton would sell players and, as for the future, I feel that the first thing that has to be done is to kick that right in the teeth. I say this for the sake of good relations between the supporters and the club.'

Stock denied gossip about him being tapped up by other clubs, saying the only thing in his mind was to watch some cricket and relax: 'For months, I had a five-year contact with Luton lying on my desk but I never got round to signing it. Why? Because I knew that one day or another I would blow my top!' Chairman Robert Keens said that for once this was not a case of a manager's true reasons for leaving being 'screened' and he denied categorically any element of Stock being pushed out. He praised Stock for taking Luton back to Division Two and for standing by them during the V&G crisis when the club very nearly became 'a lost cause'.

Stock was praised for his work in establishing the new Supporters Club and his willingness to accept speaking invitations which kept him busy in the evenings after a full day in his office. After V&G collapsed he forsook his summer holiday to search for new players, such was his dedication. In addition to being manager, Stock had latterly held the job title of chief executive, which came about after Football League rules scotched Tony Hunt's original plan to make him Managing Director.

The players and staff had a whip-round and presented Stock with a pair of binoculars so that he could watch horse-racing near his Epsom home.

The Luton directors met in early May and, as widely expected, made Haslam manager. Haslam said he felt 'sickly pleased' by the decision, as he welcomed the challenge but not in the way it had come about: 'I feel like I have taken the Crown jewels, without ever having seen them,' he quipped, rather mysteriously. The board announced that Andrews had resigned with immediate effect for personal reasons. The 45-year-old Scotsman failed to elaborate, apart from saying it was the end of an era now Stock had gone, but the general feeling was that he had wanted the manager's job himself and was not willing to work under Haslam, who had never managed or coached at senior level before.

One of the new manager's first acts was to give free transfers to skipper Mike Keen and former Arsenal midfielder David Court. He then started an extensive search for new men. Coach Roy McCrohan left Ipswich to become Haslam's right-hand man. Meanwhile the boardroom, which had been something of a battleground lately, welcomed two new directors. Tony Hunt had by now departed altogether and in came Denis Mortimer, boss of a local haulage firm, who claimed he had watched the Hatters since before the war and they were his main love, even though he'd often watched Watford on alternate Saturdays. Mortimer's arrival stemmed from a meeting with director Bain at the 1970 Mexico World Cup. The other new face was Roger Smith, managing director of Luton company Tricentrol, who admitted he was a more recent recruit to the fan base.

The three charismatic 'stars' of a successful era had now all left – Stock, Hunt and Macdonald – but Luton fans had no need to feel pessimistic. Chairman Keens introduced a host of new fund-raising initiatives and Haslam spent wisely on the team, securing winger John Aston (man-of-the-match in the 1968 European Cup final) from Manchester United and record £44,000 purchase Rod Fern from Leicester. Haslam and McCrohan introduced an ultra-modern tactical ploy which involved a floating midfield of five men, a system labelled 'total football' when employed at the highest level by the likes of Holland. Haslam showed he was in tune with 'the Luton way' when he announced a policy of all-out attack and said that 'leaving the back door open' needn't be much of a problem. 'I much prefer a 4-3 win to 1-0, whatever other managers and coaches say,' chuckled the man known throughout football as 'Happy Harry'. It was music to the ears of most Luton fans.

Haslam was a novice at this level, but had many contacts within the game and was a great communicator. Born in Manchester in 1921, he had played a few games at full-back for Rochdale, Oldham, Brighton, Orient and Guildford in his twenties, but had his career interrupted by the war.

His non-league jobs included six years managing Barry Town, a spell at Eastbourne, and then nine years at Tonbridge. His breakthrough into the professional game came late – at the age of 47 – when he assisted Bobby Robson at Fulham. Haslam had been a jack-of-all-trades in football thus far, and his skills as a communicator were called upon when he led the Luton team on a summer tour to Turkey before the start of his first season in charge, 1972-73. Telephone communications between Turkey and Britain crashed during the trip and it was left to Haslam to send a series of postcards home to keep everyone informed of results and other developments. 'Weather hot, players fit, looking forward to the matches,' said one. Another arrived at Kenilworth Road, stating: 'If you have ever heard of organised chaos, then this tour could currently beat that.'

After two Town games in Turkey had been called off, action finally took place when Luton beat Besiktas 3-1. Then the trouble-torn tour collapsed in chaos. The party were coming home, said the postcards, after a showpiece game with Fenerbahce was abandoned after a brawl between the players. Vic Halom was sent off, a decision which so disgusted his teammates that they had to be persuaded to play on, and then fighting broke out following a foul on John Moore. After the referee gave up the ghost, police rushed on to separate the players. The referee had never officiated a senior game before and was 'so biased it was beyond belief', said one Luton official. In the first twenty minutes he blew for 28 'fouls' against Luton and only two against the home side. After this so-called 'friendly' the Luton list of walking wounded included John Faulkner, with a black eye after being kicked while on the ground, various players with stud marks all over their legs, and Robin Wainwright with a nasty wound near his groin.

Starved of details, there was considerable anxiety back in Luton, but eventually Haslam found a working telephone and called his wife Trudy to say nobody had been seriously hurt and they were coming home. For diplomatic reasons the players and officials were instructed not to comment about what had happened when they disembarked at Heathrow to be met by pressmen. It was a lively start to Haslam's managerial career but he kept smiling as usual.

As the Luton team flew back into London they were followed by athlete Dave Bedford, an occasional visitor at Hatters matches, who was fleeing a training camp at the Munich Olympics in a blaze of publicity. Runner Bedford was Britain's main gold medal hope at the forthcoming games, and dad Norman said he was coming home because he was being hounded and the pressure was turning him into 'another George Best figure'. Bedford would later return to Munich in time to compete, but flopped in both 10,000 and 5,000 metre races. The Games would ultimately be overshadowed by the terrorism which led to the death of eleven Israeli athletes.

As the 1972-73 season proper got under way, Haslam showed he could wield the big stick as well as joke around. When midfielder Peter Anderson slipped away without permission to make a phone call, thereby missing a train to Portsmouth, furious Haslam immediately axed him from the side. He wouldn't relent even when the player made it to Fratton Park before kick-off under his own steam.

As winter approached, Luton rose into the top four, and the promotion fight was boosted when Haslam hinted that Graham French, recently released from prison, might soon be ready for a return to senior football. French, still only 26, had been working hard in training and made his comeback at home to Colchester reserves at the end of November 1972. Also returning in that game was full-back Don Shanks, who had patched things up with the club after demanding his cards and walking out following a pay dispute. Twice the usual crowd attended the game and they created an 'electric' atmosphere, according to the *Luton News*, producing roars of encouragement every time French touched the ball. He did well and made three goals in a 5-1 win. Rookie Colchester full-back Dave Willingham tried to mark French, but was on a hiding to nothing. French's new-found commitment was illustrated the next day when he showed up on his own for training, even though it was officially a day off. On the same day that the two 'bad boys' returned to action, Haslam finally found a cut-price replacement for Malcolm Macdonald when he paid £50,000 for Barry Butlin of Derby. Butlin netted a powerful header on his home debut against QPR and earned the instant nickname 'Bullet'.

In his second match back, for the reserves at Northampton, French strained a muscle, but soon afterwards the *Evening Post* splashed on its front page the news that French would play in midfield for the first team at home to Millwall the next day. The supporters were delighted that the old rogue was back. Looking slimmer than ever and sporting his familiar dark-eyed enigmatic scowl, French was allowed to lead the team out and received a huge welcome from the 11,000 crowd. He performed superbly in midfield, tormenting the Lions defence, although he looked a little weary towards end of the first half.

French's dream return was made complete just after the interval when he raced from midfield to latch on to a pass, drew lanky Bryan King out of goal, and knocked the ball past him into the Oak Road net to make it 2-0. It brought the house down. Grown men were in a frenzy, but French acknowledged the dancing crowd with little more than a smile. According to reporter Roger Duckworth, the goal brought the biggest roar heard at Kenilworth Road for years and it was a truly unforgettable moment. Distracted by the ongoing celebrations, the Luton defence then allowed Millwall to score twice and rescue an unlikely point.

French hurried off afterwards without comment, leaving it to manager Haslam to explain apologetically that he had asked French to give an interview but the player was too shattered. French was seen departing in a natty white jacket, face flushed with elation and fatigue, brushing aside pressmen and stopping only to sign an autograph for a small boy. Director Reggie Burr was ecstatic: 'What did I tell you? At one time I was the only one who believed that Graham could still do it'. The comeback left French feeling shattered and stiff and he experienced bouts of stomach trouble, which prompted colleague John Moore to point out: 'Prison grub had taken its toll.'

Not all stories have a happy ending, however, and this was one of them. After a handful of appearances for Luton and a loan spell at Reading, it became clear French was a mere shadow of his former self and could not turn the old magic on and off at will. After trying his luck in the USA, things took a strange turn when he suddenly appeared in the Southport team in Division Four, using a new name – 'Graham Lafite'. His former mentor at Luton, Allan Brown, had taken the reins at struggling Southport and invited French to Haig Avenue for a trial. French was duly registered under the name 'Lafite', which was not a bid to start afresh with a new identity, but merely a whim, the name a play on words that had apparently amused the player. With little prior publicity, French/Lafite was slipped into the Southport team for a couple of games and helped inspire a mini-revival with occasional flashes of inspirational wing-play.

Again, however, he never looked fit enough for the rigours of full-time football and was soon released, announcing his intention to head for South Africa. Former acquaintances at Luton, including historian Roger Wash, have lost track of his movements in recent times, although several sources believe he was refused entry to Australia and ended up back on a council estate in his native West Midlands.

Life was rarely dull at Kenilworth Road over this period and, at the start of the calendar year of 1973, chairman Robert Keens revealed that, in addition to new, brighter floodlights, the team would be wearing a radical new kit in selected matches. After 50 years in conservative white shirts and black shorts, the club went to the other extreme and unveiled bright orange shirts with a thick black and white stripe down the left side. Director Eric Morecambe was largely responsible, saying that previously the team had 'looked like negatives' and now they resembled Liquorice Allsorts! The new colours were paraded for FA Cup trips to Newcastle and Bolton, and seemed to have a welcome effect as Town pulled off surprise victories and marched to the quarter-finals. The players said they preferred orange as they found it easier to spot colleagues quickly. The kit didn't help at Roker Park, however, for here injury-hit Luton went out of the Cup, beaten by eventual winners Sunderland. The Cup run went some way to compensating for the way the promotion challenge fizzled out in the second half of 1972-73.

Chairman Keens admitted that changing the kit and the floodlights had been the easy bit, and Harry Haslam now had to tackle the task of converting Luton into a top division side, even though there was no more money in the kitty. It wasn't the first time a Luton manager was expected to perform miracles in such circumstances, and it certainly wouldn't be the last. But, remarkably, Haslam succeeded. Middlesbrough ran away with the 1973-74 Second Division title but, squeezing into second place came Luton Town, promoted with a low tally of 50 points. It had been a largely unexpected achievement and the more down-to-earth fans wondered if Luton were really ready for the rigours of the top flight.

A 1-1 draw at West Brom in April 1974 had secured the point that clinched promotion and made Luton the first club to fall from First to Fourth Divisions and then rise all the way back again. It took a while to sink in. After all, this was a club that was virtually skint, pulled in average gates of under 13,000, sometimes wore garish orange shirts and had comedians Haslam and Morecambe on the sidelines. Middlesbrough were welcomed into the top flight as serious contenders, but Luton (and third-placed Carlisle) were regarded as anachronisms by the po-faced traditionalists. Promotion had come three years ahead of Haslam's 'five-year plan'. Eight men (Thomson, Anderson, Faulkner, Garner, Jim Ryan, John Ryan, Butlin and West) had played in nearly every league match, and a further three in more than half (Husband, Horn and Shanks), which underlined the value of a settled side.

The roots of a growing crisis were sown in May 1974, the same month the promotion campaign ended. Astute chairman Robert Keens went down with double pneumonia, a condition that would render him absent for virtually all the following season. In his absence, the 'makeshift' board made spending decisions which would leave the club in big trouble. The teenage Futcher twins, Paul and Ron, arrived from Chester for a combined fee of £125,000, and Peter Spiring from Liverpool for £90,000. Haslam's judgment was questioned over these signings, and although the Futchers would eventually prove a big success, rifts in the boardroom grew. With Keens not in full control, trouble was just around the corner.

So, after an eventful fourteen years away, Luton were back in the big time. The pundits who predicted a struggle for Luton and Carlisle would be proved right. By late November the pair were bottom. As Christmas loomed, Haslam was forced to try something new, so plunged Ron Futcher into the forward line, having called up his brother a few weeks earlier. Critics who felt the money had been wasted on these 17-year-old twins were forced to eat their words as results instantly improved. Town went agonisingly close to saving themselves, and were only relegated on the last day of the campaign when fellow strugglers Tottenham beat an unmotivated Leeds 4-2 to move a point ahead and condemn Town to the drop. The fightback had been gutsy, but with hindsight it is clear the excitement of the second half of 1974-75 masked the real consequences of relegation. The club had been living beyond its means and there would soon be a big price to pay.

Over the first half of that season Luton had only managed one victory, but in the latter half they managed twelve. The dramatic post-Christmas encounters included a cracking win over mighty Leeds, then the nation's most hated team. That result left Harry Haslam euphoric – until, that is, he read the match report in the next day's *Sunday Times,* which declared that Luton were 'simply not good enough' for the First Division. Chris Lightbown's report said the boost that helped them beat Leeds came from the fervent crowd. He continued: 'Luton is a strange, strange place to find a football club, let alone a First Division one. Almost alone in England, there is a violent, menacing feeling in the town that spills over into the ground. Luton have a vast following of boisterous youngsters who make a hell of a noise – a real novelty for a team in Luton's position. Add to that the fact that it is not a football area and you have a crowd that does not know when its team is beaten. That would come to nothing in the spacious vaults of an Anfield or White Hart Lane, but in Luton's overcrowded little ground, it can make for a mightily high atmosphere.'

The victory smile was wiped off Haslam's normally jovial face by these words. He called it: 'A blistering attack on the fans of this club – as well as the rest of the people of Luton.' He went on: 'The piece was written by a bloke called Chris Lightbrown [sic]. Whatever he knows about football he chose not to put into his report. Instead he attacked the people of Luton in a manner I have never seen in all my years in football. He must be a remarkably perceptive young man if he can detect this great feeling of violence in the ten-minute walk from the station to the ground.'

Such public anger was uncharacteristic – perhaps the pressure was beginning to tell on Happy Harry? Indeed, he appeared to throw in the towel long before relegation was mathematically certain, and his team very nearly made him look foolish by surviving. In his programme notes for the Leicester game on 12th April, written with Luton five points adrift of safety but with still four games to play, he said: 'It now looks as though we will [be relegated] and I would like to say how upset I am about it. I maintain that we will be back at the first attempt. I am just sorry that we couldn't have hung on.' After these almost defeatist words, Luton proceeded to beat Everton, Leicester and Birmingham to collect six points and very nearly cling to their status. Looking back, it is almost unthinkable that a modern-day manager would utter such sentiments until failure was mathematically certain.

By mid-1975 Haslam was being assisted by two young coaches who would later make a name for themselves in different ways. Former player David Pleat had returned to Kenilworth Road after a spell as boss of non-league Nuneaton, and also working behind the scenes (unofficially, due to work permit problems) was the man who would become English football's first foreign manager – the chain-smoking Urguayan, Danny Bergara.

Bergara explained how he ended up at Kenilworth Road: 'I arrived in Spain from Uruguay in 1962 as a 20-year-old striker. I spent about 10 years there and was top scorer for Real Mallorca for four seasons and at Seville for two years. But I had married an English travel guide there so, when I retired in the early 1970s, we decided to live in England. My manager at Seville, Vic Buckingham, told me that I didn't have a chance of becoming a coach or manager in England: English football was only for the British.' Bergara made plans for a new career in the travel trade but found that because of the 1973 fuel crisis travel companies were laying people off instead of recruiting. Thomas Cook's loss was football's gain: 'I'd bought a house in St Albans, very close to my wife's parents, and a cousin of hers put me in touch with Harry Haslam, who was managing Luton. He said bring your boots along, and we'll see what you can do. I played six games for their reserves and scored three goals, but I couldn't get a work permit. Foreigners were not allowed in English football then. Eventually they gave me a job as youth coach, but on paper I was a lorry loader, working for the chairman's company.'

From 1974 to 1977 Bergara would supplement his unofficial £40 wage packet by working for the FA, assisting staff-coaching courses. Later he was caretaker-manger of Sheffield United, coached England Under-18s and Under-20s and became the country's first foreign manager when taking over at Rochdale in 1988, followed by stints at Rotherham, Doncaster and Stockport.

Despite relegation from the top division in 1975, the only significant Luton departure was Aussie striker Adrian Alston, and with local boy Andy King emerging as a key player, the squad looked settled and ready to challenge for a quick return in 1976. At this point few fans can have realised the extent of the storm clouds gathering on the horizon. The first signs of trouble came when Haslam launched an ambitious bid to sign legendary Scots winger Jimmy Johnstone from Celtic, but was blocked because the board were unhappy over the wee man's wage demands. There had been little other spending on players for months, so such a development confirmed that money must be in very short supply.

The tongues began wagging when 'Jinky' Johnstone was spotted in the Kenilworth Road directors box during a goalless draw with Bristol City. The 31-year-old had given fourteen seasons' service to Celtic and was being offered a free transfer in recognition of his 515 appearances and 130 goals (he would later be voted Celtic's greatest ever player). Jinky told one reporter he would love to join Luton and would run his heart out for Haslam. However, as there was no transfer fee, the player's terms were high and it soon became clear the Luton board was split. Two directors were fearful of the player's off-field reputation and believed the club couldn't afford him anyway. They even threatened to resign if their opposition was out-voted. The over-riding issue, it seemed, was that because of a £350,000 overdraft following relegation, Luton were under pressure to cut staff and not increase it. The deal stalled amid much bad feeling. The fall-out sparked continuing unrest in the boardroom, leading to what some horrified observers described as a 'coup' by director Denis Mortimer.

The whole sordid mess became public when the *Luton News* splashed the latest developments on its front page of 13th November. They reported that chairman Len Hawkins had been stripped of his executive powers by a boardroom reshuffle, and was claiming a group of directors tried to get him to resign: 'They can't vote me out of office easily because I am the major shareholder and I refused to go,' said Hawkins. The club, meanwhile, confirmed rumours that the director now in charge was Hemel Hempstead transport firm boss Mortimer, previously Hawkins' vice-chairman, who had now taken the title chief executive, with Hawkins continuing as chairman on a non-executive basis.

Luton builder Jim Richardson had become director in charge of finances, and 31-year-old Jim Yates, the club's youngest-ever director, was put in charge of commercial affairs. Yates was head of an engineering company he built from scratch with his brother in Dallow Road, close to the football ground on the site of a former pig sty. The emergence of this new power-base, ostensibly to tackle a heightening financial crisis, not only upset chairman Hawkins, but also the club's most high-profile director Eric Morecambe. Citing the pressures of his TV work, Morecambe resigned from the board, but it was clear his main reasons for stepping down were connected with the upheavals. Hawkins had been a director for thirteen years and chairman for the past eleven months, and refused to resign and become a vice-president as requested. He said he would stay until due to step down two years hence.

Few believed Mortimer when he claimed there had been no boardroom split – especially after a second disgusted director announced he would be following Eric Morecambe out of the door. Brian Swain of the *Luton News* said he risked being banned from the ground for publicising the matter, but felt 'something must be said' about what was going on, for the club appeared on the verge of self-destruction. Swain reported that Haslam had at one point faced the sack for publicly confirming his desire to sign Jimmy Johnstone and for his keenness to hang on to young defender Paul Futcher, the club's most precious asset. The board had hoped to keep Morecambe's resignation quiet, but the news leaked out and was broadcast on TV and seen by a surprised Haslam and his squad as they lunched before an away game at Southampton.

Players Steve Litt, Graham Horn and Gordon Hindson had all been loaned out to save money, but apparently further cuts were still needed to satisfy the bank. It seemed inevitable that key men like Futcher and midfielder Alan West would soon be sold to reduce the huge overdraft. Talk of player sales and the bid to unseat the chairman left many fans focusing their ire on directors Mortimer, Yates and Richardson. Richardson received further flak when he was reported as saying Eric Morecambe would not be missed. This came to light in an extraordinary report in the *Luton News*, in which Richardson was quoted as saying that if Morecambe was to be given another role at the club it should not be as a vice-president' as proposed, but as 'club clown'.

Richardson complained bitterly about how the media had broken the news of Morecambe's resignation: 'Why [could it not be kept quiet]? What interest is Eric Morecambe to anyone? He is not a public figure. I don't understand why all the Sunday papers wrote about his resignation. Who wants to read that? I certainly don't. They must be hard up for news.' Reporter Swain said most people felt the comedian had been the best PR man Luton Town ever had, but got the reply: 'We don't need him, he's put no money in. He's not one of the workers here.'

Morecambe attended the next home match, against Oldham, and admitted that if necessary he would pay through the turnstiles to watch from the Bobbers Stand, for he remained fully committed to the cause as a fan. Such actions would not be necessary, as he was subsequently confirmed as a vice-president. Morecambe, however, felt compelled to answer the criticism by Jim Richardson in a statement:

'After I had stopped laughing at what dear old Jim had to say about me … my first thought was how sad the board of directors allowed him to say such things. My second thought was that they probably didn't know he had said it, so I will give them the benefit of the doubt. It's funny really, I have always liked Jim. I still do … he is a man with a great sense of humour – he always made me laugh. He is a man of humour, integrity, sincerity and lots of charm and wit, as you can see by what he said. If Jim wants me to be the 'club clown' I would accept the post with pleasure as I am happy just to be connected with the name of LTFC. Obviously I will continue to mention the team in my radio broadcasts, newspaper articles and TV shows, which according to Jim he has never seen. Maybe one of the board will tell him about it. I would like to take this opportunity to say a big thank you to Harry Haslam for all the hard work he has done for the club. I would also like to thank the team and names like Malcolm Macdonald, Chris Nicholl, Bruce Rioch, Viv Busby, Alan Slough, Don Givens and so many, many more for giving me some of the most exciting moments of my life. I will always remember them – and you too Jim! Signed: Eric 'The Clown' Morecambe.'

Morecambe might have been willing to laugh off the ill feeling, but the club remained in a mess. Three more directors followed his lead in quitting, leaving the nine-man board slashed to five. Richard Banks, director of a Sandy grain firm and V&G's Reggie Burr left, along with chairman Len Hawkins who changed his mind about staying till the bitter end. He'd been the major shareholder for thirteen years but had already been stripped of his power: 'I didn't want to resign but what could I do?' he complained. The board now comprised Mortimer, Yates and Richardson, plus Ed Pearson, a barrister and a company chairman, and Roger Smith, a Tricentrol executive currently working in the USA. Mortimer said the new-look board was determined to pull the club out of its difficulties, even though the overdraft of £350,000 was increasing week by week and attendances not breaking even. He gave Harry Haslam the dreaded 'vote of confidence' but did admit the board regarded the current playing squad as far too large.

To add to their woes, Haslam and assistant coach David Pleat were involved in an M1 car crash. Haslam's Vauxhall was struck from behind by a lorry near Hemel Hempstead when returning from a reserve game at Brentford. They escaped without serious injury, but poor Haslam must have wondered when the ill fortune would end. For Pleat, just making his way in the game as a coach, it was a case of riding the chaos and getting down to business as usual. He had recently received a routine call from a Hitchin schoolmaster who urged him to attend a forthcoming under-16 cup-tie against a school from NW London, with a view to viewing his own son and some of his other youngsters. Pleat went to the game and came away impressed by the skills of an overweight lad sporting an Afro haircut in the London team. The boy's name was Ricky Hill.

Hill was quietly invited for trials and – despite apparently being rather reluctant to make the trip up from Cricklewood – was soon slipped into the Town's reserve side as a raw 16-year-old to see how he fared against more seasoned players. Reporter Brian Swain noticed the youngster but was persuaded by Haslam not to write any glowing reports. Luton had still not properly got the lad signed up and didn't want to alert other clubs to his potential. Hill's mum Doris wasn't too keen on Ricky joining Luton, but she eventually relented. He became an apprentice and six months later came on as a 17-year-old first-team substitute against Bristol Rovers. With his first touch he made a goal for Brian Chambers, and with his next he scored a cracking goal. It was the first step towards legendary status at Kenilworth Road.

Meanwhile, the true seriousness of the club's financial crisis became clear in the first week of December 1975, when the club at short notice called a special shareholders meeting after an informal discussion between directors and the club's major creditors. The club's bankers were evidently no longer willing to increase the overdraft and there was no money in the kitty to pay staff and players. As well as calling the crisis meeting, directors had to hastily dip into their own pockets to pay that week's wages and running costs. These were clearly developments that threatened the very existence of the club.

The horrific extent of the problem would be revealed at the meeting on Friday, 5th December. As grim-faced directors gathered to face the music and dish out the bad news, manager Haslam must have felt more than a little smug. He and the team had definitely done their bit – for 48 hours earlier they had travelled to The Valley and trounced Charlton Athletic 5-1, thus recording one of the best away wins in the Hatters' history. Perhaps this unexpected result was a sign that here was a club definitely not willing to curl up and die.

Crisis day was chilly, grey and sunless. Dropping pins could be heard as chief executive Mortimer stood up and stated the bald facts with a minimum of preamble. He spoke in a soft monotone which seemed to heighten the tension in the room: Luton Town faced extinction through bankruptcy as the club now had debts of £724,025. The club's assets (i.e. mainly the ground, stands and houses, and not including players) had a book value of £571,452, but had recently been revalued at only £340,252. There was a trading debt of £340,000 and overdraft of £383,000. Chester FC were still owed money for the transfer of the Futcher twins nearly eighteen months earlier, and Liverpool for Peter Spiring, who'd signed a year ago. The bank, whose interest charges were running at £1,000 a week, had finally said enough was enough.

The crunch had come earlier that week, when the National Westminster Bank, after years of patience, refused to cash the club's weekly wage cheque of around £4,000. Four directors, plus their outgoing colleague Richard Banks, forked out five-figure sums each to pay these wages and other immediate running costs, but it was clear further drastic action was needed immediately to save the club. Luton Town could be days away from being the first League club to fold in mid-season since Accrington Stanley in 1962. Mortimer told horrified shareholders that the club's creditors had the power to demand liquidation of the club, but for now had agreed on one month's grace while something was sorted out. Their patience, he admitted, was based on the fact that negotiations were already under way with Royal Antwerp FC, who might buy midfield ace Peter Anderson. If that deal fell through, the game could be up.

Mortimer said various other ideas to stave off liquidation were being considered, including sales of other players, wholesale staff redundancies, the axing of the reserve team and a request that the bank accept ownership of the ground, stands and offices in lieu of the overdraft. A rallying call to the fans was planned, in the hope they would buy special 'supporters shares' of £1 each.

Anderson and Haslam spent the weekend trying to finalise the deal with Royal Antwerp. Mortimer said some or all of these plans had to be implemented or Luton Town would be no more. Figures from an audit had made it a near certainty that Luton faced liquidation but the transfer of Anderson and the creditors' patience would give them a little breathing space. The stunned meeting gave Mortimer the go-ahead to do 'whatever was necessary' to stave off liquidation.

The next step was to await news of Haslam's negotiations in Belgium. The club's future was in the hands of Happy Harry. 'It was one of the most nerve wracking weekends of my life,' he reflected. At the Esso Hotel in Antwerp, *Evening Post* reporter Roger Duckworth caught up with Haslam and Anderson and told them of events at the shareholders' meeting the previous day and informed Haslam that the club's future was now in his hands. As if that wasn't bad enough, Haslam soon realised he was in danger of losing any bargaining power regarding the transfer deal because the press ran the story that Luton must sell to survive. The crisis at Kenilworth Road even gained substantial space on the front page of *The Times*.

Antwerp's interest in Anderson was down to the efforts of recently ousted chairman Len Hawkins, whose personal contacts set up the deal. It was only after the latest press coverage, however, that the Belgians realised quite how desperate Luton were.

Haslam and Anderson went to an Antwerp reserve game on the Saturday afternoon and then watched the first team against Charleroi in the evening. Anderson's girlfriend also came along to join the talks, but forgot her passport and, according to a Luton official, was 'somehow smuggled through customs'. Haslam admitted he felt under terrible pressure and was fully aware that if he failed Luton could become another Accrington Stanley. A major point in his favour was that Anderson had performed brilliantly in his final Luton match (the big win at Charlton) which had been watched by Antwerp representatives.

Haslam originally requested £105,000 for the player, but Antwerp's powerful negotiating position saw agreement ultimately reached at less than £60,000. It was surely well below the player's true value, but would at least buy ailing Luton a little time. Back in England, the Luton players and staff were without a match that weekend and waited anxiously for news from Belgium. Livelihoods were at stake. Skipper Alan West was deputed to phone Haslam for updates and there was huge relief when the signing was completed. An exhausted Denis Mortimer called it 'marvellous news'.

The transfer did not end the crisis, but it did stave off the most urgent problems and prevented immediate wholesale sackings. Staff who thought they would be made redundant just before Christmas were reprieved. Also giving cause for optimism was the initial healthy response to the SOS appeal to fans. The 'Save Luton Town' campaign had a good start with donations arriving from around the country. More than £600 worth of £1 'shares' were sold in 48 hours. Company secretary Doug Lygo said money had come not just from exiled Lutonians, but from other clubs' fans who didn't like to see another club in trouble. Even former centre-forward Malcolm Macdonald had been in touch to see how he could help. The *Luton News* urged fans to buy more shares and 'forget the incompetence that saw Luton give away its cup final year profits to the taxman, and forget the many [other] failings of the past'.

The signs were promising, but there was clearly still much to do. To break even for the remainder of 1975-76, the club calculated it would need capacity attendances in the remaining eleven home league matches, plus a lucrative Cup run. As the current average gate was 10,800, this clearly was not going to happen, so the club would listen to offers for any players. Unfortunately the market was currently depressed and all that came in was a derisory £50,000-plus-player offer for Paul Futcher. It was rejected. Money had to be saved in any way possible, and secretary Lygo revealed that the practice of giving away complimentary match tickets to MPs and certain other dignitaries had now been stopped.

The crisis and its attendant publicity seemed to galvanise the team. It now embarked on an excellent run, winning seven games in a row and by the turn of the year had joined the race for promotion. After local youngster Andy King netted a wonder goal at Bristol Rovers to gain another two points, the skint Hatters had risen into the top six.

Behind the scenes, the club slowly got back on its feet. An independent supporters group called Friends of Luton Town was launched to help feed the fighting fund, and by early 1976 there was plenty of optimism as the club sought cooperation from three key areas: The Board of Trade (for permission to issue 100,000 £1 supporters shares); the club's bankers (a plea to reduce crippling overdraft charges); and the creditors (a request for a further period of grace). During January, lingering worries about the club's short-term future were banished when the manager announced cautiously in his programme notes: 'Certain pressures have now been lifted.'

Crisis, what crisis? The team was now winning and those scary days of December were quickly forgotten. The only obvious after-effect was the fact that the promotion bid could not be bolstered by new signings. If Harry Haslam could prevent player sales in the short term, the future seemed reasonably bright.

The sale of Peter Anderson had saved the club, but the loss of his midfield talents was skilfully minimised by Haslam. The vacant shirt was given to eager Ron Futcher, who reclaimed a regular place in the side with some success. Anderson, then aged 26 and at his peak, went on to spend several years playing in Belgium and then the USA, plus a short spell with Sheffield United before a two-year stint as player-manager at Third Division Millwall. He would be replaced at The Den by George Graham, and before long headed back to the USA to make use of his accountancy and business qualifications. Ultimately Anderson would become co-founder of Florida-based corporation Bayshore Technologies, becoming President and CEO.

Fan fervour from the fabulous 1950s

Chairman Denis Mortimer
navigated the club through
difficult, but largely successful
times (1976-84)

English First Division 1958/1959	Pld	Home					Away					Overall					Pts
		W	D	L	F	A	W	D	L	F	A	W	D	L	F	A	
Luton Town	10	3	3	0	15	5	1	3	0	5	4	4	6	0	20	9	14
Preston North End	10	4	0	1	12	5	1	3	1	9	9	5	3	2	21	14	13
Bolton Wanderers	10	5	0	1	16	6	0	3	1	5	10	5	3	2	21	16	13
Chelsea	10	5	0	0	22	11	1	1	3	8	16	6	1	3	30	27	13
Arsenal	10	5	0	0	21	4	1	0	4	10	10	6	0	4	31	14	12
Manchester United	10	3	2	0	18	7	1	2	2	8	7	4	4	2	26	14	12
Blackpool	10	3	2	0	9	3	1	2	2	4	6	4	4	2	13	9	12
West Bromwich Albion	10	0	3	2	7	9	3	2	0	18	6	3	5	2	25	15	11
Wolverhampton Wanderers	10	3	1	1	13	5	2	0	3	8	12	5	1	4	21	17	11

From top of the Football League in 1958 (above), to rock bottom in 1966 (below)

English Fourth Division 1966/1967	Pld	Home					Away					Overall					Pts
		W	D	L	F	A	W	D	L	F	A	W	D	L	F	A	
1 Stockport County	19	9	1	0	18	4	5	1	3	10	6	14	2	3	28	10	30
2 Southport	20	9	1	1	23	7	2	3	4	11	12	11	4	5	34	19	26
3 Wrexham	19	5	4	0	21	6	2	6	2	14	12	7	10	2	35	18	24
4 Barrow	20	2	7	1	18	11	6	1	3	19	18	8	8	4	37	29	24
5 Southend United	19	7	1	1	24	7	3	2	5	10	15	10	3	6	34	22	23
6 Tranmere Rovers	19	5	4	0	16	7	2	4	4	8	10	7	8	4	24	17	22
7 Aldershot	21	6	2	2	20	8	2	4	5	11	19	8	6	7	31	27	22
8 Chesterfield	18	5	3	1	12	5	3	2	4	12	14	8	5	5	24	19	21
9 Bradford City	19	7	0	2	19	8	2	3	5	12	17	9	3	7	31	25	21
10 Hartlepools United	19	5	1	3	15	9	3	3	4	11	14	8	4	7	26	23	20
11 Brentford	19	6	3	0	15	6	2	1	7	12	23	8	4	7	27	29	20
12 Crewe Alexandra	18	5	2	1	15	10	2	4	4	11	18	7	6	5	26	28	20
13 Newport County	19	5	2	2	15	7	2	3	5	10	16	7	5	7	25	23	19
14 Port Vale	18	4	3	3	13	12	2	3	3	6	10	6	6	6	19	22	18
15 Halifax Town	19	4	4	0	18	12	2	1	8	12	22	6	5	8	30	34	17
16 Barnsley	20	3	2	5	11	15	3	2	5	15	14	6	4	10	26	29	16
17 Bradford Park Avenue	19	2	3	5	14	14	3	3	3	14	20	5	6	8	28	34	16
18 Exeter City	19	3	3	3	11	11	1	5	4	9	16	4	8	7	20	27	16
19 York City	19	5	3	3	22	17	0	2	6	7	17	5	5	9	29	34	15
20 Chester	18	3	2	5	12	19	2	3	3	8	17	5	5	8	20	36	15
21 Rochdale	18	4	1	4	12	12	0	5	4	8	16	4	6	8	20	28	14
22 Notts. County	20	3	5	3	14	15	1	1	7	14	26	4	6	10	28	41	14
23 Luton Town	20	5	2	2	18	13	0	1	10	4	28	5	3	12	22	41	13
24 Lincoln City	19	3	5	3	23	18	0	1	7	5	19	3	6	10	28	37	12

Allan Brown enjoyed success at Kenilworth Road as both player and manager

A matchday programme from the golden days of the 1950s

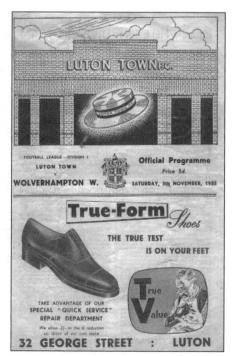

George Martin (left) and John Moore (below), stalwart Scots who both played and managed at Luton

David Pleat, a nippy winger whose playing career was eclipsed by his managerial achievements

Kay Mills was elected Luton Town 'Football Queen' to help lighten the gloom of the mid-1960s

Tony Hunt, charismatic
chairman whose V&G
company dramatically
collapsed in 1971

Director Eric Morecambe (left) with manager Alec Stock.

Promotion in 1968 signalled an end to eight years of constant failure

Mine host Tom Hodgson, a former player, director and chairman at Luton

A message from V&G in 1970. Within a year the company collapsed and nearly took Luton with it

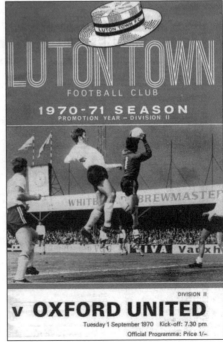

A bright new matchday programme following promotion in 1970

Eric Morecambe helps Harry
Haslam celebrate a Manager of
the Month award

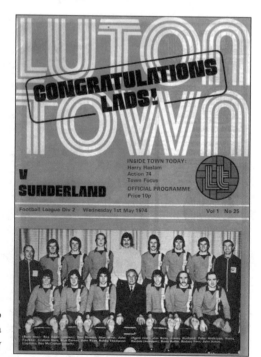

Promotion to the top
flight in 1974 came as a
big surprise to many

Kenilworth Road, in need of renovation in 1973

Jim Ryan, over 200 games on
the wing (1970-76) and 17
months as manager (1990-91)

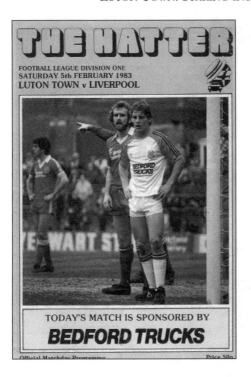

Halcyon days: 1982-83 was the first of nine straight seasons in the top flight

Architect Philip Dodd, appointed in 1983 to design a brand new stadium

The popular Futcher twins,
Ron (left) and Paul, Luton stars
of the mid-1970s

The news from May 1983 that shocked Luton fans to the core

A place for Luton fans to raise a glass to their most famous compatriot

Peter Anderson, the talented
midfielder sold in 1975 to save
the club from going bust

The controversial A505 relief road, built in 1987 within feet of Luton's main stand

Mike Watson-Challis (left) and David Evans, leading lights in the boardroom

Godfrey Ingram, a forward who later helped rescue Luton with the 2020 consortium

The Kohlerdome, a dream that fell by the wayside in 1999

Mike Newell, a goalscoring
forward and outspoken
manager

Luton's finest hour, victory over
Arsenal at Wembley in 1988

CRISIS 4 (1976-85)
When Concrete Cows Beckon

Having survived the 1975 financial crisis with Second Division status intact, Luton Town spent the rest of the decade striving in vain to mount a serious promotion challenge back to the top flight. As ever, money was in short supply to buy new players, but fortunately gems like Ricky Hill and Paul Price were unearthed and came through the youth ranks.

A year or so after the club was yanked back from the abyss, company secretary and commercial manager Doug Lygo gave a cautious progress report. He said the club had survived without a mass sale of players, even though the new share issue had proved so disappointing that directors had to purchase a large proportion of the stock to meet the target figure. He praised the sympathetic attitude of many of the club's creditors, who had accepted shares in lieu of money owed. He added: 'Although the first corner has been turned there are still many difficulties to overcome and the biggest danger is complacency. It is absolutely imperative that the club should reduce its overdraft to a level which it can afford to service.'

Inevitably, the books had to be balanced by player sales, and money was raised when key men like Andy King, John Ryan and Steve Buckley departed for top-division clubs. Harry Haslam had hung onto talented young defender Paul Futcher for much longer than most fans expected, so it was a crushing blow when news broke in November 1977 that the 22-year-old had been badly hurt in a car smash. He sustained life-threatening injuries and spent time in intensive care, but surprised medical staff by emerging to declare himself fit for a return to action within three months.

However, every silver lining contains a cloud when you support Luton Town. Within 48 hours of celebrating Futcher's return to action, Hatters fans' chins were back on the floor when popular manager Haslam quit the club. The genial boss had been in place for nearly six years and there had rarely been a dull moment. After the unlucky relegation and ensuing cash crisis of 1975, Haslam had worked wonders to oversee Second Division finishes of seventh and sixth, and when he left in January 1978 Luton were again on the fringe of the promotion race.

A rift had developed between Haslam and the board, and speculation about his future was rife throughout the winter of 1977-78. Just days before his eventual exit he'd tried to put the matter to bed, saying he didn't want to leave Luton and never had, even though there were 'one or two little local difficulties' behind the scenes. He dismissed talk that Millwall wanted him as manager, and Manchester United as chief scout. 'Things are now settled and I am staying, he told the fans who had read with dismay that the board was set to replace him with former Chelsea full-back Eddie McCreadie. Nine days later Haslam walked out to become manager of fellow Second Division outfit Sheffield United, taking youth-team coach Danny Bergara with him.

The Blades had been managerless for three months since sacking Jimmy Sirrell following a bad start to the 1977-78 season, and had been interested in Haslam for some time. The crunch had come after Haslam failed to get his contract extended at Luton, and had to sell ace full-back Steve Buckley to Derby. By now, Haslam and new director David Evans were not seeing eye to eye, to the extent that the manager reportedly even insisted on the new man being barred from the dressing room. Evans, a self-made successful businessman, wanted changes to the coaching and playing staff and Haslam decided he'd had enough. He gave Sheffield United the nod.

Chairman Mortimer shocked almost everyone by offering the vacancy to inexperienced coach David Pleat, who was thus persuaded to turn down Haslam's invitation to join him at Bramall Lane. Some called it a panic measure by Mortimer, but with hindsight it was probably the best footballing decision the chairman ever made. Although 33-year-old Pleat had only been senior coach at Luton for a matter of a month or so, his enthusiasm and knowledge had already made a big impression. He'd schooled himself thoroughly at Lilleshall after a playing career that was blighted by injury.

If Pleat had any illusions about the size of the task, they would soon be shattered. It took him six games to achieve his first win as a manager, and when he asked to take the team for a short midweek break by the sea, he had to settle for chilly Margate and not Majorca. The change of scene was supposed to promote team bonding, but when he told his shivering players to take a stroll down Margate prom, most of them shot straight into the nearest tea shop.

Pleat steered the club clear of relegation to the Third Division in his first few months, even though a major transition was under way, which meant only three wins were gained from the seventeen remaining games that season. Over the summer he got cracking with the task of building a side to play the sort of football he enjoyed – with a strong emphasis on swift counter-attacking, wing play, and plenty of flair. The opening day of his first full season in charge (1978-79) was a revelation. No fewer than seven players made their Luton debuts at home to Oldham, and after an uncertain first half in which they fell a goal behind, Luton scored six times in the final 43 minutes to mark the true beginning of the wonderful Pleat era.

In common with his predecessors, Pleat rarely had much money to spend and needed to sell at regular intervals, but between 1978 and 1982 he slowly created an inspirational team that narrowly missed promotion twice and then took the Second Division by storm, winning the title in May 1982 with a record 88 points and by an eight-point margin. Once the likes of Ricky Hill, Brian Stein, David Moss and Mal Donaghy had blended and hit full throttle there was no stopping them. The final piece in the jigsaw was the capture of skipper Brian Horton. First Division football was back at Kenilworth Road after an absence of seven years and the club appeared to be on a firm financial footing, thanks to innovative work behind the scenes by new chief executive John Smith.

Smith had arrived in 1979 from Leicester, one of a new breed of career football administrators, who was hailed by Pleat as 'the best in his field'. Smith's *modus operandi* was examined in depth by *Marketing* magazine, which revealed that Luton's new recruit was breaking new boundaries within football. Along with his colleague Mike Beevor, a former international athlete, Smith pioneered sponsorship and other marketing initiatives that funded Luton's climb back to the top division. When the Football League relaxed its rules on shirt advertising, Luton became the first southern club to take advantage, and players began wearing the brand name Tricentrol on their shirts as part of a £50,000 deal. The energetic Beevor, a talented middle-distance runner in his day, had originally been recruited to sell advertising space, but he branched out and introduced promotional ideas that did so well they were imitated elsewhere.

When John Smith spoke publicly to Luton fans it was usually to herald good news about events behind the scenes. But on Boxing Day 1980 all that changed. He announced that British Rail was to present a Bill to Parliament that would see some of Luton Town's land snatched via a compulsory purchase to make room for a new A505 relief road to Dunstable. The land in question was at the rear of the ancient main stand and was currently used for access, parking and hospitality. 'If this happens it will have serious consequences for the club and indeed, unless a solution can be found, we shall be forced out of existence altogether,' said Smith grimly.

Luton West MP John Carlisle raised objections to the plan and sided with the football club, saying it would damage the Hatters irrevocably by making it impossible to maintain vital hospitality suites, car parking and administrative areas. Smith said it was a kick in the teeth for the club, which had recently spent more than £300,000 on widespread improvements to meet new ground safety regulations. Worryingly, there were few positive or supportive noises coming from Luton Borough Council or Bedfordshire County Council over what appeared an increasingly serious threat to the financial and geographical future of the club in Luton.

As in the past, however, off-field concerns didn't affect the team's performance and, after they stormed to the Second Division title, manager Pleat was emotional as he chatted to writer Tim Collings behind the desk of his humble little office, which was actually the former bedroom in one of the Victorian terraced houses beside the ground. 'Congratulations to everyone, even to wonderful Watford [runners-up] for keeping us on our toes right to the end,' said Pleat. 'Well done D Mortimer. Well done [wife] Maureen. Well done every single person who has helped get the show back on the road since that dreadful financial dilemma. We have sold, juggled, coached and succeeded for Luton.'

Pleat's cavalier outfit took the First Division by storm in the autumn of 1982. Goals flew in from all angles, many of them admittedly into Luton's net, but the outcome was attacking entertainment of the highest order. Notts County were beaten 5-3, Liverpool were held 3-3 at Anfield (a match in which Luton fielded three different goalkeepers), an eight-goal thriller at Stoke ended 4-4, with David Moss missing a last-minute penalty, and nine goals were netted against Brighton in two games. In the first seven games of the season, no fewer than 38 goals were scored, 20 of them by the division's new boys. Anything could happen when Pleat's men took the field, and few First Division defences could handle the flair of Stein, Hill, Moss and new-boy Paul Walsh when they hit form. The club had secured a major sponsorship deal with Bedford Trucks and everything in the garden was looking rosy – apart from that relief road issue.

Fans could hardly bear to take their eyes off the action for fear of missing something, but the match programme for the Manchester United visit in September contained essential reading for those interested in the future of the club. Reproduced was a joint statement from the club, the borough council (LBC) and the county council (BCC): 'Representatives of LTFC, LBC and BCC have met to explore the possibility of a relocation of the club from Kenilworth Road to another site in Luton. The county council's proposals for the new A505 relief road affects the club's present premises, taking part of the present parking space and requiring the Kenilworth Suite to be re-sited. Discussions are continuing between the county and the club as to the full implications of the proposals. It would not … be in our interests merely to transfer the problems of football from Kenilworth Road to another site, and we shall be looking closely at that. Our concept will be something new, something which will, we think, stimulate the residents of Luton, and the surrounding areas in the same way it has stimulated us and those with whom we have had discussion already.'

A site at Lewsey Farm, a residential area beside the M1 and less than three miles north-west of the current ground, was generally regarded as the most suitable new home for the club at this point. However, local residents reacted with horror and turned out in force for a series of meetings to voice their disapproval. In early October it was reported that councillors were by now looking at a list of other potential locations, including Dallow Road, a short distance from Kenilworth Road, plus sites a little further afield at Leagrave Common, Stockwood Park, Stopsley Common, Warden Hills, Wardown Park, Wigmore Valley Park, Luton Hoo, the Vauxhall Motors' test track and land next to the new East Circular road.

The Luton Hoo estate had recently passed into the ownership of Nicholas Phillips, following the death of his grandmother, Lady Zia Wernher, and he was considering ideas for the future use of the mansion and its grounds. But he reacted with horror when approached about the possibility of the football club moving in as neighbours and declared it unsuitable in terms of traffic and accessibility. Lady Zia, a member of the former Russian Imperial family, was probably turning in her crypt at the idea of the Hatters playing where her walled garden used to be.

Tory MP John Carlisle said the issue represented the biggest dilemma he'd faced since being elected, for he had to decide whether to whole-heartedly support the football club and its plan to move, or to side with his constituents, who were so firmly against the Lewsey and Leagrave sites. The borough council was not much help, telling the club in November it could not provide any council-owned land for a new ground as all poten-tial sites they could come up with had compelling reasons against being chosen.

Frustrated, John Smith appealed publicly for help, saying Luton Town were being forced to move through no fault of its own. He urged fans to send in any ideas and comments and revealed that architect Philip Dodd had been appointed to design a state-of-the-art stadium which the club and its fans would be proud to occupy. It would be an indoor facility that would seat around 20,000, have an artificial pitch and a membership scheme that would bar hooligans associated with other clubs. It was radical stuff, but with no site earmarked, many fans thought it was pie in the sky. Talk of a new ground was nothing new at Luton and the bulk of the hardcore 13,000 supporters seemed apathetic to the growing threat that Smith warned of.

Within a week or two, land off Park Street on the Brache estate, owned by Vauxhall Motors, emerged as a site with genuine possibilities. Although it was not council-owned land, the council indicated it might be able to help the Hatters move here, but there were fears that if approved publicly the plan would generate opposition from the NIMBY brigade ('not in my back yard'). Sure enough, immediately word got out, a petition was organ-ised in the Park Town area politely telling the club to look elsewhere.

As the saga rolled on, with the club's hierarchy seemingly frustrated at every turn, the team continued to win new friends with its fine attacking football, chalking up splendid wins over Manchester City, Watford, West Ham and Brighton. It was only after a post-Christmas 1982 run of just one win in eight games that any relegation alarm bells began to sound. It was around this time that sad news arrived from thousands of miles away. Well-known comedian Marty Feldman, who grew up in Luton and was an avid supporter as a boy, had collapsed and died at the age of 49 while filming in Mexico City.

As the 1982-83 winter gave way to spring, Luton were no nearer finding a new home, but inching their way towards safety from relegation. Draws against Southampton and Stoke left Luton with six teams below them and only three games left. Another three points from the final three games would guarantee safety. If results went their way elsewhere, less than three might even be sufficient. Those three games looked tough on paper. The true seriousness of the situation only really hit home when the 40th game of the 42-match season ended in a 1-5 home slaughter by Everton. Injuries meant youngsters Garry Parker and Ray Daniel had to be plunged into the penultimate game at Old Trafford. Manchester United's 3-0 win meant the Hatters had suddenly plunged from 16th to second-from-bottom. Once the calculators had been put away, the situation was clear. Only a win at Manchester City on the final day would keep Luton up. Any other result would save City and send Luton down.

It turned into the most turbulent week in the club's history, for all sorts of reasons. In the days before the game manager Pleat had to put Division One survival to one side to comfort his wife upon the death of her father. Then came rumours that *Luton News* reporter Brian Swain had uncovered a sensational story that would shake Luton fans to the core. Sure enough, just hours before the team headed north to Manchester for the biggest game of their careers, Swain's paper hit the streets with the dramatic news. He wrote:

'I am convinced that Luton Town FC, disgusted with Luton council's failure to help it find a site for a new stadium within the borough, will announce shortly that it intends to move to Milton Keynes. And when chief executive John Smith makes the formal announcement he will explode a time bomb of discontent. At least one club official expects to resign or be sacked for opposing the plans, and several wealthy Hatters supporters have threatened to join a battle to stop the move taking place. Although most Luton supporters want their club to stay in the town and redevelop Kenilworth Road if necessary, it seems Mr Smith will announce that the club finds that situation impracticable. The club will lose a strip of land running behind the main stand including the car park and entrance to the boardroom and executive suites. Mr Smith maintains this will prevent Kenilworth Road's continued use as a stadium but some of his own employees are not entirely convinced. And one has told Mr Smith that he will risk being sacked by declaring his backing for any protest movement. Mr Smith was unavailable for comment this week.'

The report was unconfirmed but certainly gave hordes of Luton fans food for thought as they made their way up the M1 and M6 to Manchester. As if moving the club to a different county wasn't bad enough, the chosen home was to be a place widely derided for its soulless grid layout, its myriad roundabouts and its concrete cows. As Swain had predicted, the fans reacted with horror. But, for now, such matters had to be put aside and, fortunately, events at Maine Road would prove dramatic enough to overshadow the grim news. It turned into a day never to be forgotten when 'feeling for the club was as passionate as anyone could recall', according to Roger Wash's centenary history.

City were favourites to pip Luton to stay up, for they only needed a draw in front of their own fans. The circumstances lent the game the flavour of a cup final, yet with more importance attached to the result. Pleat took the risk of rushing injured players Paul Elliott and Brian Stein back into the side. The tension was unbearable and a 43,000 crowd suffered 85 agonising minutes of goalless deadlock before the decisive moment arrived. City keeper Alex Williams pushed out a low driven cross by half-fit Stein and Luton sub Raddy Antic cracked the loose ball home via a deflection. Cue an explosion of joy from more than 5,000 travelling fans and a frightening, almost palpable rage from the stunned home support. Luton held out for the last few agonising minutes and at the final whistle tears flowed and grown men embarrassed themselves. As commentator John Motson gabbled away, a Luton photographer galloped on the pitch to hug skipper Brian Horton, to be followed by manager Pleat, skipping along in his beige suit in manic yet childlike fashion. Many years later, a national paper would vote this moment one of the game's most compelling all-time images, an ambitious manager released from his chains in an unbridled explosion of joy.

Pleat's mad dance has since been screened many times, much to his dismay: 'My wife's father had died the day before and I was very emotional. It was an incredible finish and almost as though it was God-given. It was the unbelievable feeling of emotion that got the better of me. I didn't know what I was doing; I just ran silly. I didn't know who I was running to, but I went to my captain Brian Horton and not the goalscorer. We had worked so hard to get into the First Division the previous year.'

Little Luton dumping the big guns out of the First Division was akin to an act of cup giant-killing. The media loved it, particularly as the underdogs had entertained the country all season and didn't deserve to be sent back to Division Two so abruptly. Justice had surely been done. The camera zoomed in on Peter Swailes, City's outspoken chairman, who looked shell-shocked. Meanwhile, Pleat, an intrinsically quiet character, was lost to exhilaration. In the post-match interview with 'Motty' he almost crumbled into tears as he struggled for words: 'I don't know John, I'm a Lutonian. I'm a Lutonian.'

Later, having had time to gather his thoughts, Pleat described the unbearable tension of the week. He told one reporter: 'The night before, we avoided Manchester, instead staying in Staffordshire. So when we drove up we were accompanied by all the cars and coaches from Luton. It showed the players they were not alone. I was a mess emotionally. My father-in-law had just died, I'd had to leave my wife and two young kids dealing with that to go to Manchester. So when the final whistle went I just lost my head. I felt I was bouncing on air as I ran to my captain, Brian Horton. The police said we had to get away and they stayed with us to the edge of Manchester. They [the police] were United fans. When we got the beer and champagne out they joined in. [Our] bus hit a fan and our physio had to get off and treat him.'

Back down south, Luton supporters who had not travelled to Maine Road celebrated wildly, castigating themselves for not going. This writer knows, because he was one of them. Even important work commitments paled into insignificance when the events unfolded on the radio. The only consolation (if you can call it that) for the absentees was that we were first to hear official confirmation that Luton's directors were planning to move the club up the M1 to Milton Keynes. This was announced in dramatic fashion by BBC radio's five o'clock sports show, and was linked to the story of the club's amazing escape from relegation. How typical. The joy of one of Luton's finest hours was immediately being dampened by news of the gloomiest nature. They say ups and downs are part of supporting this club, but those few minutes on the BBC encapsulated it like nothing before or since.

The BBC had sniffed the Milton Keynes story from a Football League circular which stated that Luton officials had made preliminary enquiries about the possibility of moving to a different town in a different county. Such a move was unprecedented in senior football, certainly in modern times, but Luton had told the League the relief road plans and lack of local sites had left them no alternative. Even with Brian Swain's speculative 'leak' a few days earlier, the timing of the BBC's revelations seemed cruel – although it evidently did little to curtail some remarkable celebrations over the Maine Road result.

The Luton hierarchy must have expected opposition to their drastic plans, but probably not on the scale that transpired. Various factions quickly mobilised a protest campaign, and there was talk of boycotting home games during the following season unless the idea was scrapped. As the *Luton News* had hinted, not everyone working at the club wanted to move twenty miles to Buckinghamshire. Colin Ball, youth development officer and associated with the club for 33 years, wrote to John Smith to express his opposition and was asked to resign. Ball stayed put for a couple of months before quitting, admitting he could no longer work for the present administration: 'I find it hard to believe any football club could have acted like Luton has.' Sympathy came from the leader of the Tory majority group on Luton council, Vivian Dunington, who described moving the club to Milton Keynes as 'unethical'. He rebuffed criticism that his council hadn't done enough to find a new home for the club in its own community.

Opponents of the move launched a petition at the annual town carnival at the end of May, gained the support of John Carlisle MP, and wrote to the other 91 League clubs urging them to oppose the move. They also claimed the relief road plan didn't adversely affect the club as badly as the directors claimed. Meanwhile, Milton Keynes Development Corporation confirmed they had been in talks with Luton Town over a long period and that their overall plan for recreation in their city did involve a multi-use sports centre. Occupancy by a top league club like Luton would be perfect, it was said.

So did Luton Town's board really have no choice but to move away, as they claimed? Opponents believed this was not the case and called for the search to continue in Luton for a new home. The *Luton News* called in an 'independent expert' who identified the Laporte complex off Kingsway as a possible site, and also some General Motors land on twenty acres off Toddington Road as another. The paper accused the directors of opting for Milton Keynes purely because the backing of MKDC would help them create a financial structure that would make other clubs green with envy: 'Money is the name of the game,' suggested the leading article, not the lack of other options. The editor wrote: 'We must assume that the club is hell-bent on moving to Milton Keynes, they have received an offer they can't refuse. What is at stake is part of Luton's heritage ... the proposal to move the football club away from its supporters to another city in another county makes nonsense of the present geographical loyalties within the Football League. If Milton Keynes is allowed to buy its way into Division One, we predict a queue of business entrepreneurs seeking to do the same for their own towns. The League must prevent its membership from being manipulated in this way.'

Chairman Denis Mortimer admitted he would be sad if the club was forced to move out of Luton and was bitterly critical of local councillors and planners for not helping. He also said pointedly that no serious negotiations were currently under way with MK, and suggested that perhaps somebody had 'rather cleverly' got the MK issue into the open so as to provoke further discussions: 'It has got the fans to react, but [unfortunately] not the council. It has got out of hand. I can assure you no decision has been made.' His comments thus gave the fans a glimmer of hope that they weren't really about to lose their club – and this was all a ploy to get Luton council to pull its finger out. However, a spokesman for MKDC said they were about to embark on detailed discussions involving the club, which nullified some of what Mortimer had said. The *Luton News* went back to Mortimer for clarification and the chairman responded: 'I can assure you with my hand on my heart and on my wife's life, that no irrevocable decision has been made.'

A month after the end of the 1982-83 season the Football League management committee considered the matter. Having consulted other clubs, the committee said it had no objection to the move in principle, but would strongly be against any new stadium having an artificial surface, which had been part of the proposal. Before this meeting, the newly formed Save Our Soccer (SOS) group from Luton handed over an 18,000-signature petition opposing any move out of the Luton area. Twelve fans had travelled up to Lytham St Anne's for the occasion and presented the huge document to League secretary Graham Kelly. The committee's verdict was disappointing for the fans, but the fight had only just begun.

During the summer John Smith trotted out his message again – the club must leave Kenilworth Road or it would simply die. He said he was happy to meet council chiefs in the bid to find a site in Luton, but insisted negotiations would continue with regard to Milton Keynes: 'If we stayed here we would rapidly be on the verge of liquidation – just like we were [in 1975-76].' He added that he had no desire to be critical of the anti-MK brigade, and he only wished their vigorous campaigning had been evident earlier on when the club was attempting to earmark the Lewsey Farm or Vauxhall Motors land. By the start of the new season, a protest group calling itself Supporters of Luton Town FC (1983) had been formed to fight the MK plan. The battle was hotting up. The football club, only too aware of criticism of its poor communications with fans in the past, responded by regularly including lengthy articles entitled 'Luton's future' in the match programmes during the early part of the 1983-84 season.

Writing in the match programme for the visit of Sunderland in early September, chairman Mortimer set out the broad background to the current crisis, emphasising how the A505 relief road and related railway diversion scheduled for 1985 would downgrade the club to such an extent that its very survival was under threat. He said the club would press for substantial compensation if and when the work went ahead, but would have to relocate before the start of the 1985-86 season – hence the development of the multi-purpose covered stadium plans, which had been examined by 'independent experts of international repute' who judged them sound.

'Several suitable sites in Luton have been considered,' added Mortimer, 'including many belonging to Luton Council, but none has received support from the Council, hardly the balanced view to be expected from a council committed to a policy of supporting its local football club. A suitable site exists in Milton Keynes where the Development Corporation has offered its wholehearted support to the project. The club's acceptance of the Borough Council's invitation to discuss its future was an indication that the board is still willing to consider other solutions. The club is doing all it can to protect [its own] future and in so doing has the chance to provide football and the country with an exciting new development, the first of its kind in the UK, of which they will feel proud. The project will also offer considerable local employment, both directly, because of the development, and indirectly because of the new business attracted by these developments.'

Mortimer believed that relocation locally would benefit all, for it would secure the club's future, give the county council its new road, and the borough council would get a unique sports/leisure complex, which they had already acknowledged as exciting and imaginative, and which would provide badly needed employment opportunities, fresh income and new business. But Mortimer said the borough council had failed to respond in any positive way to proposals, and seemed content to allow Luton Town to 'wither and die'.

The club reportedly ran up considerable bills examining potential sites around Luton, but in each case, they claimed, compelling reasons against building a football stadium were encountered. As no council land was offered, various 'enabling developments' alongside the stadium would be necessary in order to fund the project (i.e. shops, hotel, sports centres, etc) and some of the sites examined were not suitable for this sort of major development.

As the Milton Keynes debate raged on, the Borough Council suddenly performed what some observers regarded as a U-turn. They invited the club to submit outline plans for a new stadium on the Vauxhall sports ground land off Park Street in Luton. Earlier in the year, prior to the local elections, the council had seemingly opposed this option, and this change of heart caused a surprise, especially at the football club. Had the about-turn been caused by angry Luton supporters pressurising their elected representatives? Or was it a ploy to call the football club's bluff, to find out if they had already made their mind up to go to MK come what may?

Before long, the local press reported that the club and council were now 'teetering on the edge of a historic agreement' over the site off Park Street, which was not boxed in by housing and had the newly opened east circular road as a link with the M1. In many ways it looked an ideal site for a football ground, but at a key meeting to discuss this, things again failed to gel. Club officials came away accusing the Tory group running the council of being 'as lukewarm as ever', although the Labour and Liberal members were in favour of the project. A *Luton News* editorial urged the people of Luton to get behind the plan, but the club still seemed reluctant to play ball, saying a planning application for Park Street would be a waste of time and money unless there was evidence the majority Tory group on the council would fully support it.

It did seem that the MK Development Corporation's ability to provide a ready-made site, complete with road access and services, was proving a big plus for the club – for it negated the need for a hotel and other commercial premises on any non-council-owned Luton site. Talks continued with Luton council, however, and at one point were described as 'tough, challenging but friendly' and for a spell it looked like the two factions might be inching towards possible agreement. To pay for the £27 million multi-sports stadium in Luton, a superstore's involvement would be needed, speculated the local press, and that was a major part of the problem.

Against this background of uncertainty it emerged that a consortium led by a lifelong Hatters supporter was planning a takeover of the club in order to prevent it going to MK. Headed by businessman Derek Hardy, this group's ambitions were dismissed by chairman Mortimer, who indicated that he simply wasn't ready to leave. Another (part-time) employee then quit the football club in protest at the MK plans. Mascot and escort organiser John Williams followed Colin Ball out of the Kenilworth Road door, saying that Luton schoolchildren wanted the club to stay put in their town and he therefore felt obliged to resign.

On 8th September 1983 the borough council's general purposes committee voted in favour of the Vauxhall site and recommended its approval to the full council – thus answering some of the football club's doubts about the commitment of the council's Tory members. This was followed by further promising news when local brewery giant Whitbread indicated it might be interested in helping finance a stadium within Luton. These two developments put pressure on the club to submit a formal application for the Vauxhall site – but John Smith was not to be hurried and he told the press his advisers would look at the matter and provide an answer in due course. It was not the answer most fans wanted to hear.

At this seemingly crucial juncture, two of the club's directors, including the chairman, were said to be away on holiday. It left many fans doubting the board's interest in pursuing anything other than the Milton Keynes option. That view was strengthened at the home match with Wolves (a

thumping 4-0 win), after which the club was accused of being heavy handed in banning protesters from taking their 'No to Milton Keynes' banners
into the ground.

A meeting of the full council at Luton Town Hall followed, and the old
building resounded to loud cheers from the public gallery when 43 of the
46 councillors voted enthusiastically in favour of urging the club to stay in
the town. They passed a resolution that the council would consider 'sympathetically and speedily' any application to build a stadium on the Park
Street (Vauxhall) site. John Smith listened to the debate and said his fellow
directors would consider the issue at their next board meeting. The club
certainly didn't seem as excited as the fans by events at the Town Hall.
Chairman Mortimer complained that the Park Street site was not ideal as
the council didn't own it and it also had a river running through it.

At the October home game with Aston Villa, the crowd was swamped
with anti-MK leaflets and the protest ring-leaders staged a peaceful demo.
Earlier there had been rumours that feelings were running so high that
many of them were determined to invade the pitch and stop the game. The
leaflets contained the home addresses of club directors and suggested that
fans write to them. At half-time a chartered plane flew over the ground
trailing a banner proclaiming 'Keep Luton Town in Luton' and was met
with cheers from below. Chants and abuse were directed at the directors
box before and during the game, which ended in a 1-0 home win.

Three weeks later the directors issued another lengthy statement which,
in essence, said that having been criticised for its poor public relations, the
board felt it would be nonsensical to now submit a planning application for
the Park Street site simply for PR purposes. It said that even though the
council promised to deal with any planning application 'sympathetically
and speedily', they had also made it clear they would not make any final
decision themselves, but refer it to Westminster after a public inquiry.

'In all our meetings with Luton council, and there have been many
[since] 1980, we have demonstrated the need for a mixed sporting and
commercial development ... however the latest council invitation is for a
sports stadium only, which would effectively deny us the substantial funding that commercial development would otherwise provide. The time has
come to resolve the club's future and so bring to an end the present continuing uncertainty and speculation ... Having tried unsuccessfully to stay
in Luton, the club has been forced to examine other options and unless the
council offers a satisfactory solution we cannot and will not lightly pass up
the very real opportunity which now exists for us at MK.'

If there were any lingering doubts about the club's desire to stay in
Luton, a letter from the board published in the *Luton News* and the programme for the Birmingham City visit extinguished them. It stated that the

recent 'about-turn' by the council had been too little too late, and the move to Milton Keynes was now the only real option: 'Although we know that there are those who are against the club moving out of Luton, we do urge you all to look at this matter realistically and against the background of all the circumstances. We also assure you that we shall do all that we can to preserve our existing goodwill and support, to retain the club's identity, and to keep you fully informed.'

Prior to the Birmingham game, fans opposing the move organised a rally on Pope's Meadow, which was attended by around 2,000. There were various speeches and then a slow procession to the match. The size of the rally reportedly prompted John Smith to remark: 'Where were the 18,000 who signed [the petition]?' It was now all-out war between the club and a large number of fans. A consortium of local businessmen was put together by a group who called themselves 'HALT' and said they were dedicated to keeping Luton Town in the town at all costs. They formally approached the club about a takeover but were told they would need £5 million, at which point their interest appeared to end.

The anti-MK lobby was certainly making itself heard and a boycott of home games appeared to be biting. Over the 1983-84 season as a whole, home gates were, on average, down by 1,500 per game, (a drop of over 11 per cent). Apart from games against London sides with big away followings, attendances at Kenilworth Road hovered around the 10,000 mark, despite the team reaching the heady heights (albeit only briefly) of third in the table over the Christmas holiday period. For a spell the sporting press speculated that manager David Pleat was being coveted by bigger clubs. Arsenal were said to be one, but the Gunners eventually appointed the more experienced Don Howe.

Many fans found it unpalatable that the 'only' option was Milton Keynes. It was widely thought, rightly or wrongly, that members of the board had business connections with the new city and were determined to go there come what may. The bad feeling between the club and its supporters reached a new all-time low and would remain that way for some time. The fans were adamant their club belonged to the town of Luton – not to the directors – and they voiced their anger via the forerunners of fanzines and organised rallies. Opinions vary on the impact of the call to boycott home games, and ironically the directors would point to the low crowds as one of the reasons they had to move.

By December 1983 the board certainly appeared to be responding to the age-old criticism that it didn't communicate well with the fans. It published news of ground plans in home programmes, and even reproduced a letter from the Mayor of Luton, Frank Lester, in which he expressed 'disappointment that our town is going to lose a part of its life and entity that has meant so much in terms of entertainment and pleasure to thousands of citizens for almost 100 years.' The mayor sympathised with the club's view that its current ground was inadequate, but said he was convinced the Brache site could have been usable. The board backed its case to move by quoting author and football stadium expert Simon Inglis: 'Until you have been to Kenilworth Road you cannot appreciate how cramped is 'cramped'. Compared with Luton's ground, Filbert Street [Leicester] is spacious, The Baseball Ground [Derby] is well situated, even Millwall might just feel a little less aggrieved (but only a very little) with their lot.' Luton fans were, of course, fully aware that their 98-year-old ground compared unfavourably with many others, but that was hardly the point. Home is where the heart is.

The protests didn't waver and in January 1984 chairman Mortimer pleaded with fans to believe that his 'dearest wish' would be to stay in Luton, or at least in the Luton area: 'But the club could die if it has to continue at Kenilworth Road [with its] Coronation Street image, with the toilet at the end of the garden and the bath in front of the fire. What a dreadful thought for the 1980s!' He added: 'It has always been my understanding that Luton is a town with a cosmopolitan background and perhaps this is why there's very little civic pride here. In consequence, neither the county council, Luton or South Beds councils have reacted to the opportunity that is passing them by. Their neighbours in MK have in fact offered us prospects that are difficult to refuse and exciting to contemplate.'

Having resorted to Simon Inglis's words earlier, the board then quoted passages from Anton Rippon's book *Soccer: The Road to Crisis* to help justify their motives: 'People live far more sophisticated lives in the 1980s and the prospect of standing or sitting at a football stadium in below zero temperatures is not so attractive for the modern fan who lives in a centrally heated home. His father, who may have been used to trudging to an outside lavatory at the bottom of the garden in the small hours would have been prepared to endure such hardships. People who go to football out of sheer habit are a dwindling breed. The cloth cap and muffler brigade of Priestley's *The Good Companions*, grow fewer in number each season.'

At the club's AGM in April 1984 the majority of questions from shareholders were inevitably about the Milton Keynes issue. To answer these, chairman Mortimer merely issued a short statement which ended: 'Unfortunately there is nothing useful I can add to the directors' past statements. Negotiation with all parties concerned are proceeding.'

An unnamed season-ticket holder appeared to support the board by arguing: 'The present Board of Directors literally picked this clapped-out club off the floor, re-financed it, took painful and difficult decisions to streamline and make it viable ... I join a queue for every home match on the A6 at Barton and it is obvious all those people won't mind a journey to a better stadium.'

Against this troubled background, the team plunged alarmingly, from third in the First Division on Boxing Day 1983, and gained only three wins from the remaining 23 games, but luckily had enough points in the bag not to be relegated in the spring of 1984. Pride briefly returned when Bobby Robson sprang a surprise by selecting both Brian Stein and Paul Walsh for their full England debuts against France. However, neither was able to make much of an impression and it turned into a disappointing occasion for Luton fans.

There was more gloomy news on the way for beleaguered Hatters supporters. First came the death of the club's most famous fan – comedian Eric Morecambe – who collapsed moments after coming off stage in Tewkesbury in May 1984. The man voted Britain's Funniest Man was only 58 and this had been his third heart attack, following others in 1968 and 1979. Second, quicksilver striker Paul Walsh was sold to Liverpool for a fee reportedly amounting to £763,000, a Luton record, and although it eased growing financial pressures on the club, fans were angry and deflated by the little man's departure.

Walsh had been a huge success since his move from Charlton, scoring 28 goals in two seasons and making many more for partner Stein. Walsh was even forgiven his lapses, such as the night he kicked in the doors at Tiffany's nightclub when refused entry. That indiscretion landed him in court and saw David Pleat summoned to the police station to take Walsh away dressed in only underpants and a blanket. As well as disposing of his star forward, Pleat was also encouraged by the board to sell popular full-back Kirk 'Basher' Stephens to Coventry, but he cushioned the blow considerably by securing the Sky Blues' experienced Ashley Grimes as part of the deal.

During the long hot summer of 1984, Luton found its own answer to the famous 1966 World Cup dog Pickles. Three Hatters fans were walking in the Skimpot area of town when their dog stumbled across a huge LTFC logo, which, it turned out, had been prised off the wall of the club offices and stolen some time earlier. The walkers returned the item to the club and received grateful acknowledgement in the opening match programme of 1984-85. The recovered treasure didn't quite match the Jules Rimet Trophy uncovered by Pickles eighteen years earlier, but for hard-up Luton it was good news nonetheless.

The Milton Keynes issue remained a talking point as the 1984-85 season started, but was overshadowed for a spell when the club regularly featured in tabloid stories about football hooliganism and the various unsavoury groups indulging in this pursuit. The club reacted angrily to this bad publicity and complained that the reports were keeping some law-abiding fans away from matches. It acknowledged that one or two incidents had occurred at Luton games, but called the reporting irresponsible and exaggerated. David Pleat estimated that around 4,000 possible spectators steered clear of the Watford derby in October 1984 (the crowd was only 12,192) because of press reports that major trouble was brewing. He refuted claims that the two neighbouring clubs' rivalry had become 'intense and nasty' and claimed there was a healthy competitiveness between them. The (allegedly) frightened absentees missed a thriller, with Luton coming from behind twice to win 3-2, Frankie Bunn netting twice.

Hooliganism or not, gates continued to drop at Kenilworth Road and the anti-MK brigade claimed the boycott was chiefly responsible. There were pitiful attendances of under 9,000 for two of the first three home games, and ultimately the league average for the whole 1984-85 season was less than 11,000, the lowest at Luton for four years. Only Stoke City, who finished bottom by an astonishing 23-point margin, attracted fewer paying customers in the top flight that season. After the victory over Watford, Luton went six games without a win and dropped into the relegation zone. A long, hard winter looked likely. In fact, the months of November and December became something of a watershed, with momentous events both on and off the field having far-reaching effects.

November 1984 began with the local paper splashing on its front page a report that David Lee – the Tory leader of the Milton Keynes Borough Council and a member of the MK Development Corporation – had confirmed a planning application from a consortium involving Luton Town had been submitted for a town-centre stadium. The Luton chairman Denis Mortimer's reported response was a little baffling and did little to clarify the situation, for he said he hadn't a clue what the position was, knew nothing about the plan, and wasn't even sure if the club had sufficient financial backing to be able to formally propose the move to MK.

Naturally this was greeted with incredulity by the press and Luton fans alike. Tom Hunt of the Supporters of Luton Town (1983) group said: 'It is ridiculous for Denis Mortimer to say he doesn't know what is going on within his own club. It is so obvious that they must have the financial backing. They would look awful if they put their ideas forward and then said they did not have the money ready.'

Kenilworth Road was not a happy place and the directors bunkered in the boardroom were now said to be quarrelling among themselves. This turmoil seemed to be confirmed with the news that chairman Mortimer had stood up during a board meeting and resigned, apparently fed up and exhausted by the constant bickering and personal abuse, not to mention regular vandalising of his car. The *Luton News* reported that huge debts, a threat of bankruptcy, and the chance that Milton Keynes might no longer welcome the Hatters to their town had all combined to spark the latest turmoil in the boardroom. The club was by now thought to be losing £6,000 a week and its overdraft had ballooned to £700,000. The bank was said to have set a deadline for the club to sort out its finances and this had brought matters to a head. From being a fans' hate figure, Mortimer now attracted sympathy, particularly when the *Luton News* identified him as the only director with serious doubts about moving to MK. His contribution over the years meant it felt rather sad for him to leave in acrimonious circumstances. He had been regarded as saviour of the club during its 1975 troubles and architect of the return to Division One. He had also been the man who appointed the relatively unknown Pleat as manager.

Mortimer quit both the chair and his directorship, and was replaced as chairman by a very different character in 49-year-old David Evans, a self-made millionaire and director at the club since the late 1970s. Evans was outspoken and ostentatious and drove a car that would be easy to find if the vandals so wished – it was a Rolls-Royce bearing personalised number plates 'DAVID 1'. A new board member was introduced in the shape of Terry Bailey, head of the Wallspan company, who was said to have chipped in a substantial cash sum, loans and guarantees to help stave off threats from the bank. Bailey had already funded the club's electronic scoreboard earlier, and was well-known in local football circles, having aided Barton Rovers, a club he once skippered.

While Luton fans held their breath to see what would happen next, speculation mounted over whether the recent turmoil, including the resignation of Mortimer, was because Milton Keynes did not want the club any more. Mortimer commented: 'To be accused of feathering your own nest after putting in so much time, devotion and finance to keep this club going was a bitter pill to swallow.' He said he had felt 'bitterly let down' when Luton council was unable to help with relocation and had quit because of personal abuse from fans, combined with a lack of realistic support from the club's bankers. The pressures had taken their toll after twelve years with Luton (nine as chairman), and he had made his decision while wearily driving up the M1 one Tuesday night in mid-November. He said he could not bring himself to sell Ricky Hill, Brian Stein or any other of the home-produced stars – and the bank had been unhappy over this. Only the sale of Paul Walsh earlier had staved off the crisis. 'I have carried people around on my back for so long at Luton Town that by now I should have round shoulders,' he commented rather obliquely.

Mortimer reflected that the anti-MK abuse had affected his health and he had 'not been able to take a decent car to a Luton game for two years for fear of it being vandalised.' He had also been embarrassed time and again by gangs swearing at him while he accompanied important guests to games: 'With my track record, I do not think they should have been so unkind – I was never a Milton Keynes addict.' Years later Mortimer would say 'unreasonable financial pressures' were placed on him, and this was the main reason for his walkout.

His successor, the hawkish David Evans, was quick to address Luton fans, promising he would keep Luton in Luton if the right situation arose. He dismissed as 'utter nonsense' the idea that the board wanted to take the club to Milton Keynes mainly because directors had business interests there. He admitted too many barriers between board and fans had existed in the past and he pledged the board would be more open in future. He described Mortimer's departure as a surprise and his own election as chairman as even more surprising. He had evidently long been interested in taking charge of a football club, for it was reported he had come within a whisker in 1981 of joining Crystal Palace's board, but had decided against. Although Luton currently sat in 21st place, he promised they would not be relegated for he was planning to make cash available for new players. To his credit, this was a promise he kept, and one which helped kick-start a golden era for the club and its fans.

Making funds available to the manager went some way to appeasing the fans and shareholders who had only recently tried to throw Evans off the board because of the Milton Keynes issue. On a show of hands at the AGM, Evans lost his bid to be re-elected as a director, but when the majority shareholders used their block vote this was easily overturned. Evans was a bullish operator, a plain speaker and not afraid to court controversy. His CV showed that in his youth he had been a talented sportsman, playing cricket for Gloucestershire and Warwickshire, and making six England youth appearances while on Aston Villa and Bristol Rovers' books. He went on to skipper the Club Cricket Conference on 38 occasions and led them on their first tour of Australia in 1975, and later had a stint as chairman of the Lord's Taverners and on the Middlesex cricket committee.

Born in working class north London, Evans failed his 11-plus but made his way in business via Tottenham Technical College and in 1960 founded an office cleaning company, which later grew into Brengreen Holdings. After securing a contract to operate Britain's first private enterprise refuse collection and street cleaning services in Southend-on-Sea, Evans' company amassed twelve similar contracts, including Milton Keynes, and the Brengreen group grew to operate via fifteen subsidiary companies, employing around 22,000 people. After joining Luton Town's board in 1977, Evans developed a taste for politics. He became a St Albans district councillor and three years after becoming the Hatters chairman would enter Parliament as Tory member for Welwyn and Hatfield.

Manager Pleat, who spoke highly of the retiring Mortimer, had what he described as 'useful talks' with the new chairman. He said there would be no panic buying of players, but there would definitely be some new faces soon. In typically straight-talking style, Evans admitted Eddie McCreadie had been his choice when Pleat got the manager's job back in 1978, but in the five years since then he had been won over. He now wanted Pleat to stay for a long time. Evans arranged the financing for Pleat to make crucial signings which in effect gave the team a completely new spine. In came former England centre-half Steve Foster, who had been unhappy at Aston Villa, Birmingham's powerhouse centre-forward Mick Harford, Walsall's clever little midfielder David Preece, and finally Wales and former Arsenal midfielder Peter Nicholas. The total cost was around £650,000 and this talented foursome helped transform Luton's stuttering season. As would only be appreciated by fans later on, this money came in the form of loans which would have to be paid back one day, reportedly with considerable interest.

Evans tackled the immediate problems at Kenilworth Road in up-front fashion, discussing things openly, appearing on radio phone-ins and publicly criticising the local councils. He would help reorganise the board into what was described as a more dynamic unit, including the presence of Lebanese businessman Mustafa Aleyan.

An early task for the new chairman was to study new proposals from Bedfordshire County Council which showed the proposed relief road was just feet from the present stadium, but with arrangements that would allow the football club to stay put without the loss of land. The plan included the rebuilding of the Kenilworth Suite on stilts over the railway line adjacent to the ground and a pedestrian walkway and coach park was also involved. The new road would sit below the back of the Main Stand, but the cost of around £1.3 million would all be met by the council.

The Milton Keynes saga then took a surprising turn – and one which gave Luton fans cause for hope. It was revealed that two 'rival' schemes were now on the table, each providing the new town with a major sporting complex. These two were effectively competing with the Luton Town bid. Furthermore, it was suggested that there was plenty of opposition in MK to certain aspects of the three plans – particularly the prospect that a Football League club might be on its way. It slowly began to dawn that Luton's application might well be the least popular of the various options in front of MK's councillors.

MK Council now indicated it wasn't keen on a football club, the Hatters or anyone else, landing on its doorstep. Local residents had, perhaps predictably, objected on the grounds of potential hooliganism in their neighbourhood. However, the MK Development Corporation was thought to be a different kettle of fish, and the football club scheme was still alive in their eyes. Evans said the club now faced 'an electrifying decision', for the MK plan was going before the MKDC in early December. Bedfordshire County Council's offer regarding Kenilworth Road also required a decision. Evans went on local radio and appeared to be saying that the county council offer would be taken up if it met their requirements, and some interpreted this as the Luton board cooling on the MK idea, perhaps fearing it was now dead in the water.

Meanwhile, just to confuse the situation further, a blueprint for a major leisure complex capable of housing Luton Town on the Brache Estate was thrown out. It had been put forward by a consortium independent of the football club, but had been backed by Luton fans. It had been the subject of a planning inquiry, at which the inspector said he was unhappy for a complex that could house up to 20,000 spectators under one roof being so close to Luton Airport, a potentially disastrous situation if an air accident occurred.

Back in MK, two of the three plans now on the table were accepted by MKDC, including the Luton Town one. MK Borough councillors then voted at a separate meeting unanimously against league football in their city. Further disturbing news for the Luton Town board arrived when Bedfordshire County Council said it could be three months before talks could progress on their proposals for Kenilworth Road. This prompted an angry response from Evans, who accused them of not being committed to keeping Luton in the town. In their defence, Beds said they had to consult local residents before proceeding.

Shortly before Christmas 1984, Evans published a letter to shareholders and season-ticket holders in the home programme for West Brom. He invited people to come and hear him answer fans' accusations that the directors had distanced themselves from fans during the recent saga. These meetings would put that right, he claimed, and he invited 'constructive criticism advice or assistance'.

Fortunately for just about everyone concerned, things were suddenly looking up on the field. David Pleat's wheeling and dealing with the money invested by Evans was beginning to improve results and had earned Pleat an extension to his contract. According to the *Luton News*, Evans and new director Bailey put up around £500,000 between them to fund the club's future, and provide new guarantees to the bank. Pleat used his windfall well and even found loose change to take the players on a short break to Iceland.

By a quirk of fate, the turmoil over the club's future peaked early in 1985, the club's centenary year, when the atmosphere ought to have been one of celebration rather than recrimination. Long-term fans might say this was par for the course with Luton Town. Ever since Mr H G Spratley had stood in April 1885 to oppose the formation of Luton Town FC in the council chamber of the Town Hall, the club had been plagued by disputes and controversy. Back then Spratley was shouted down and formation went ahead, but the current dispute was surely a sign of things to come.

D-Day, as far as Milton Keynes was concerned, finally arrived on the mild and cloudy morning of Friday, 1st February. With Luton preparing for a big home match with Spurs the following day, news emerged from one of the shiny modern office blocks in Central Milton Keynes that Luton's plan to move there had been formally rejected by MKDC in favour of the one submitted by Mowlem in conjunction with an American developer. 'It's a major stab in the back,' was the word from the Luton boardroom, but for most fans it was cause for jubilation. All the demos, the letter writing, and even the boycotting of home games now seemed worthwhile. Luton were staying in Luton.

Naturally, even this key decision didn't mean Luton's future was immediately clear, but it did at least seem likely that Milton Keynes was off the agenda for good. The Hatters plan was finally rejected as too 'grandiose' and raised too many objections and potential problems. (Subsequently, the 'winning bid' would also fail, with the National Hockey Stadium eventually erected on the site in question, later to be occupied briefly by refugees from Wimbledon FC). Luton's board reacted to the rejection by calling on Bedfordshire County Council to fund a £2.3m scheme (£1 million higher than already offered) to improve Kenilworth Road and allow the club to stay put.

If and when Luton Town would ever move to a new ground was as unclear as ever. Most fans didn't seem to care, however, and with MK off the agenda, they rallied round and ended their match boycott. Demand for cut-price season-tickets for the remainder of 1984-85 was high, and the attendance at the Spurs game the next day was a bumper 17,511, easily the highest of the season. The atmosphere was superb and with Pleat's excellent new signings all playing together for the first time, the resulting 2-2 draw provided a footballing feast.

As far as the fans were concerned, this superb game marked the culmination of a remarkable transformation. During the previous autumn, things had looked bleak. The club had not only looked bound for Milton Keynes but also for relegation to Division Two. The team sank as low as 21st, star defender Paul Elliott had broken a leg, and new signing Steve Elliott had not really clicked. Desperate measures, like obtaining veterans Micky Droy and Colin Todd on loan, had been called for. A host of other injury worries came along, including a freak accident when defender Stacey North dislocated his hip. Since those black days, Pleat had spent wisely on

Foster, Preece, Harford and Nicholas, and now the MK plan was dead. All of a sudden, the club's 100th season looked worth celebrating again.

Luton's ramshackle ground would have to continue as home for a while yet, but such worries were overshadowed when the club raced to the semi-finals of the FA Cup, their first appearance in the last four for 26 years. Ricky Hill put Luton ahead at Villa Park, but Howard Kendall's all-conquering Everton came back to win 2-1, helped by a couple of controversial refereeing decisions. The confidence stemming from the Cup performances overflowed into league games, and relegation was comfortably avoided. The feelgood factor even led to manager Pleat accepting a place on the board of directors, alongside chief executive John Smith.

Evans emphasised that the club remained committed to relocation unless amenities and facilities lost to the relief road were replaced 'in full', to the tune of £2.3 million. The AGM took place in March and was a far more amicable affair than previously, with Evans allowing the audience to ask plenty of questions.

Evans was certainly not letting the grass grow under his feet. By April 1985 he was talking of sinking £5 million into improving Kenilworth Road. The innovations would include a plastic pitch (only the League's second, after QPR), a new main stand, a roof over the Kenilworth Road end, the pitch being repositioned, a new boardroom complex on stilts across the neighbouring road, and executive boxes to replaces the popular Bobbers Stand. Evans made it clear these improvements did not mean they were deflected from their main aim of finding a new arena within a 25-mile radius of the town. Some of the plans had been prompted by dreadful scenes of hooliganism during the FA Cup quarter-final with Millwall, more of which in the following chapter.

While MK had been on the table, few improvements had been made to Kenilworth Road, and the cramped ground had became even more of an embarrassment at top-tier level. The directors were particularly ashamed of facilities they had to use when hosting VIPs from the bigger clubs.

The 1984-85 season ended late (28th May) but in winning style, and Evans signed off by pleading with the borough and county councils to get together and make one huge effort to find a site for a ground, preferably in Luton. He said the relief road saga was dragging on, sapping both energy and resources. The county council had broadly accepted Luton's argument for compensation, despite claims of exaggeration. He said the recent tragedy at Bradford City (56 people died when fire destroyed a 77-year-old wooden stand at Valley Parade) underlined Luton's warnings about safety issues concerning the relief road being built next to the main stand, which was partly of timber construction.

CRISIS 5 (1985-90)
Living in the Plastic Age

During much of the 1980s Luton Town enjoyed unprecedented success on the field, but they became one of the most unpopular clubs in the country thanks to the abrasive *modus operandi* of chairman David Evans. The team that manager David Pleat built during the winter of 1984-85 established the club as a top-division force, but the subsequent introduction by Evans of a plastic pitch and a ban on away supporters led to condemnation of the club in the media and from opposition fans.

Inevitably, opposing clubs used the pitch and the absence of their fans as an excuse for defeats at Luton. It was ironic that supporters around the county who had previously condemned or ridiculed Luton's ancient little ground were suddenly outraged when told they weren't invited any more.

Most of the vitriol was directed at Evans, who was an easy target thanks to what the *Guardian* called his 'car salesman's accent'. Evans was not a man to hide his light under a bushel and his rants 'seemed like the incarnation of Thatcherite brutalism' to anyone who didn't support Luton or the Tory party. Life at Kenilworth Road was never dull while Evans was in charge. During his five-year tenure (1984-89) as chairman the club won the League Cup, played at Wembley four times, and finished in the top flight's top ten for three seasons in a row.

Casting a shadow over this unprecedented success were off-field issues which mostly flowed from the appalling events of one night in March 1985. It was the night when Kenilworth Road suffered arguably the worst outbreak of hooliganism ever seen inside a British football ground. The riots had greater impact through being shown live on that night's BBC news bulletins. The occasion was an FA Cup quarter-final with Millwall, a fixture hastily staged just four days after Luton's victory over Watford in a fifth-round replay.

Millwall fans' reputation for trouble was, of course, well known, but what was not expected was the sheer number of thugs attached to other London clubs who chose the occasion to descend on Luton for a night of mayhem. For hours the town resembled a battleground. The match was not all-ticket, although this became an irrelevance when thousands forced their way into the ground unchecked. At that time there was room for 8,700 fans on the away terrace at the Kenilworth Road end, but according to one club official an estimated 10,000 spent at least part of the night in that area. A notable absence of Millwall's blue and white colours confirmed that many of the visitors were not 'conventional' football fans but trouble-makers from established gangs who regularly battled around the country. True Millwall supporters would telephone London radio stations the following day to confirm that much of the trouble had been caused by Chelsea, West Ham and Arsenal fans who had no interest in the game, merely the opportunity to fight. So-called 'firms' of a new breed of super-hooligan were said to be in attendance, including Chelsea's 'Headhunters' and West Ham's 'Inter City Firm' in addition to the 'Millwall 'Bushwhackers'.

Luton had seen hooliganism before – few grounds escaped it altogether during this era – but nothing on this scale. Your author recalls this as the only occasion he ever exited a Luton game before half-time – the decision to depart coming after the umpteenth pitch invasion was accompanied by flying missiles. I was certainly not the only Luton fan to make for the exits, convinced the game would never be completed. Journalist Dennis O'Donoghue remarked: 'It should have been a night of rejoicing for the town, as Luton [1-0 winners] reached the semi-finals of the FA Cup for the first time in 26 years. Instead, the champagne tasted like cider vinegar.'

The trouble started much earlier in the day and involved major damage and disruption in the town centre. Minibus after minibus, and white van after white van, came off the M1 and headed into Luton, noisy Londoners hanging out of windows and doors and yelling at the locals. All around the ground were unaccustomed sights such as unlicensed souvenir sellers and ticket touts.

Some 45 minutes before kick-off the away end was packed, people sitting on the scoreboard supports and the passageway cages that divided the huge terrace into three sections. The turnstiles had been smashed and the tidal wave could not be stopped. The Luton players emerged to warm up but beat a hasty retreat when they saw what was going on. Suddenly police and stewards alike were swept aside as hundreds of invaders began scaling the fences behind the goal, and raced toward the Oak Road end. A hail of missiles was directed towards home supporters. Before long many of the law-abiding crowd were heading for home. Appeals over the loudspeakers for the trouble-makers to return to the away end were interspersed with messages broadcast from Luton fans separated in the mayhem from their friends or relatives, all with one aim in mind – to get out and home while they still could.

Invaders seized the Bobbers Stand, ignoring Tannoy warnings that the game wouldn't start until they withdrew. They ignored an appeal from Millwall boss George Graham, and it was reported later that many failed to recognise him, further evidence that these were not genuine football followers. Fighting erupted, seats were ripped out and hurled on the pitch. The game kicked off in an unreal atmosphere, with some perched on top of the Bobbers Stand after scaling the floodlight pylons. Inevitably more pitch invasions followed, and the game was less than fifteen minutes old when referee David Hutchinson– a police inspector – took the players off for 25 minutes. After the restart, and Brian Stein's winning goal, police reinforcements largely prevented further invasions although seats and debris continued to be hurled around in the area of the Bobbers Stand.

Luton goalkeeper Les Sealey spent the second half with his back to the Millwall end. He was struck on the head by one missile and handed a knife to police, but fortunately received early warning from the referee that the final whistle was about to blow, and was halfway to the dressing room by the time it sounded. Luton coach Trevor Hartley was one of several officials manhandled as people fled the mayhem, the scoreline secondary to personal safety. One policeman trampled on the pitch needed mouth to mouth resuscitation from a fellow officer – a process that was seen to be interrupted by hooligans. More seats and fences were ripped apart and the appalling scenes were transmitted live on the late-night TV news, bringing the true horror of football hooliganism into millions of homes for the first time.

Next day a horrified Prime Minister Margaret Thatcher personally intervened. The chaos also helped ensure that England failed in their bid to stage the 1988 European Championships. What had been most disturbing, in many people's eyes, was how 400 police officers at Kenilworth Road had been overwhelmed by events.

The morning after the riots the national and international media gathered at battered Kenilworth Road where club executives met for four hours. Chairman Evans was away on business in Singapore but his message was phoned through to the ground loud and clear: rather than subject the town and its football fans to such appalling violence again, Luton Town would [from now on] simply refuse to play any match likely to produce trouble. This statement, read out by chief executive John Smith, made clear that if Luton and Millwall were scheduled to meet again in the near future, Luton would simply refuse to play. They would take the consequences. 'It's time someone made a stand,' insisted Smith.

It was sickening how the thugs had overshadowed Luton's excellent run to the FA Cup semi-finals. TV presenter and long-standing Luton fan Nick Owen recalled his sadness at seeing Luton's young manager Pleat looking downcast after the game, at a time he should have been celebrating one of his finest hours.

A member of a Luton-based hooligan group known as 'the Migs', who would later have his memoirs published, reckoned a major factor in the trouble was the decision not to make the game all-ticket: 'Luton had [by then] become one of football's favourite battlegrounds, Millwall had a reputation as the worst firm in the country and hooliganism was at an all-time high. On the night ... they would be travelling just 30 miles for an FA Cup quarter-final and yet nobody in authority saw the threat. What were these idiots thinking?' He added it had been obvious hooligans from just about every club in London had come for a night out and a fight, taking advantage of the unusual situation of a big match that wasn't all-ticket. He said the Kenilworth end was packed, fuller than anyone had ever seen it, and that included elderly fans who'd known 30,000 gates in the 1950s. Fighting in the homely little Bobbers Stand was also completely unprecedented, for this was an area occupied normally by 'old men and divvies'.

Luton were thus unwillingly thrust into the national limelight for several weeks, the high profile TV coverage and intervention from an angry Mrs Thatcher ensuring a full investigation. The FA commission announced its findings a fortnight later, rebuking both Luton and Millwall and insisting fences must go up all around Kenilworth Road to prevent pitch invasions in future. David Evans was resolutely against this, for it would hamper the view of law-abiding home fans. He was provided with the perfect excuse to advance his scheme to prohibit all away fans, which had taken shape even before the Millwall riots. 'We will fight the fences ruling and will not punish our fans for something that was not their doing,' he said.

While Evans and the board were pondering the way ahead, Pleat was keen to spend more club money on strengthening the team. The threat of relegation in 1985 had been seen off with seven wins from the final eleven games, and now Pleat had his sights set on St Mirren's prolific goalscorer Frank McAvennie. The board invited McAvennie and his entourage to a hotel on the edge of Luton. A deal was done, but, according to the player, the whole thing fell through after he took a dislike to the Luton's chairman who clipped him around the ear!

McAvennie revealed later: 'I'd become St Mirren's top scorer from midfield and clubs started taking notice. David Pleat got hold of our [home] phone number and was always talking to mam and dad. Eventually a deal was done between Luton and my club but not with me. I had to fly to London to meet David – we were on first-name terms by now – but when he introduced me to his chairman, a [soon-to-be] Tory MP, he clipped me on the back of the head and said welcome. I didn't like that and wouldn't sign.' And so, despite their trip being funded by Luton, McAvennie's party talked to West Ham, who were also keen, and he joined them instead. One wonders how many goals McAvennie might have scored for Luton had David Evans not been quite so demonstrative.

British football was at a low ebb in mid-1985, thanks to the disasters at Heysel and Bradford, which came soon after the Millwall riots, but Luton were not letting the grass grow under their feet, so to speak, and duly installed an En-Tout-Cas synthetic playing surface during the summer.

Costing £335,000, its ten-week installation was funded by club sponsors Bedford Trucks. The surface was said to be less bouncy and more grass-like than QPR's much-criticised Loftus Road plastic, and would be a valu-able source of income from being hired out to local organisations – it was hoped to revolutionise the concept of how football stadia are used outside of matchdays, said the board. The Football League's second plastic surface was merely the first of a number of new Luton Town club initiatives, including an away fans ban that would come later.

Luton fans have mixed feelings over the Evans revolution, but those of us who suffered the fear and horror of the Millwall riots sympathised with his determination to create an environment where it could never be repeat-ed. There were doubts expressed about the plastic pitch, and another issue for concern was the decision to double the price of the match programme to £1, making it the most expensive in entire Football League.

Chief executive John Smith was not exaggerating when he described it an 'extraordinary close season' at Luton. He said that the Government's intervention after the Millwall Cup-tie had led directly to an alcohol ban and publication of the Popplewell Report, and had drawn PM Thatcher into the hooliganism arena: 'We have managed to persuade the FA to change its decision over Millwall [regarding fences], thereby exonerating our own supporters. Nevertheless we are all on trial this season.' He also pointed out that the A505 relief road plan still 'hangs over us like a guillo-tine, waiting to chop our life blood', particularly now that the Popplewell Report insisted on stricter safety guidelines.

Another initiative for Luton's centenary year was an attempt to promote better relations with Watford, following recent hooliganism attending the so-called 'M1 derby'. For many fans this was largely a waste of energy, as fostering antipathy between local rivals is an integral part of being a foot-ball fan, and always will be. Telling us that managers David Pleat and Graham Taylor were good mates wouldn't change anything.

What might have been more fruitful was a better relationship between the club and Luton Borough Council. Council leader Viv Dunington arranged a meeting in October 1985 to try and restore a relationship that had soured since the Milton Keynes saga. Dunington said the council was re-examining some of the sites previously considered for a new stadium, to see if they could meet the recently changed criteria. John Smith welcomed the news but warned: 'It will take a strong political will to see it through. After the last relocation discussions ended in 1982-83, the effect was ulti-mately to split the club. This must be avoided this time.'

Meanwhile, the talk in the football world was of a 'super league' being on the horizon. David Evans was asked how he felt about the way most pundits excluded Luton Town when this sort of thing was discussed. He pointed to recent results in the autumn of 1985, including a 7-0 thrashing of Southampton and a 3-1 win at Tottenham, and hit back: 'The exclusion of a club like ours would be ludicrous to say the least. We may not attract the crowds that the team deserves, but that is the only weakness in our argument should such a league ever be formed.'

By December 1985 Luton Town had climbed as high as seventh in the table, thanks largely to good results on their plastic pitch. A working party was also exploring the possibilities of a multi-purpose covered stadium in Luton. Chairman of the group was Eric Fountain, director of public affairs at Vauxhall Motors, and there was optimism that this time all the talking would result in positive action. In the meantime, the club had to maximise income from Kenilworth Road. It was proposed to dismantle the Bobbers Stand and replace it with a row of 28 'executive suites', which would provide corporate hospitality at matches. The plan would clearly generate new money, but the loss of the characterful Bobbers Stand didn't please the fans, particularly the season-ticket holders who were told they must give up their seats and be shunted behind the Oak Road goal to make way for the 'prawn sandwich brigade'.

Next on the Evans agenda was the 'members only' system that would effectively bar away fans from matches at Kenilworth Road. The chairman was quick to defend his controversial plan: 'I am not prepared to allow Luton Town's future to be put in peril by hooligans visiting our home in the guise of away supporters. It is therefore with considerable regret after the recent experiences that no away supporters will be allowed into our stadium next season [1986-87]. This season we have experimented successfully with home fans only in the main stand, except for the cup-tie with Bristol Rovers, when once again 50 away supporters out of 600 seats allocated caused so much havoc before the game that 300 of our regular season-ticket holders left the ground before kick-off. Under no circumstances will I allow the regular supporter who is the lifeblood of our club to be harassed in the manner which was experienced during most home games last year. We at this club are prepared to be radical to underline our belief and determination to provide a true family football club.'

The club was truly 'making history', admitted the board, and in addition to the controversial plastic pitch, the away fans ban and the new executive boxes, the speed of change would accelerate when the quaint club offices (housed inside former terraced houses) were demolished, and a roof erected over the Kenilworth Road end. 'All supporters will be under cover and there will be end to the Colditz-like environment, making for a new and less hostile atmosphere,' claimed John Smith.

A major unplanned change over the summer of 1986 came when David Pleat accepted an invitation to manage Tottenham, replacing sacked Peter

Shreeve. Luton had finished the previous campaign ninth in Division One (second-best in the club's history), above Tottenham, but chairman Evans' desperate attempts to persuade Pleat to stay were realistically never going to succeed. After eight tremendous years in charge (in which he improved the league position every single season), Pleat was genuinely sad to leave his spiritual home, but as an ambitious man he could hardly be blamed for wanting a crack at the Spurs job. Evans didn't seem to see it like that, and Pleat's departure was not a smooth affair.

Many fans were prepared to wish Pleat well in his new role, but most of the goodwill ran out when he promptly came back to raid Kenilworth Road for defender Mitchell Thomas in a deal that had to be settled by tribunal. Pleat's replacement was a surprise appointment from within, the redoubtable coach John Moore landing his first senior managerial role. The Scot quickly made the astute appointment of ex-Fulham manager Ray Harford as his right-hand man.

The new membership scheme inevitably got off to a stuttering start in 1986. Tales abounded of cunning attempts to circumvent it by fans of other clubs, and of bemused 'neutrals' turning up for matches and being unable to get in. Fewer than 9,000 attended the first home game, although opponents Southampton had never been a big lure, but the board was determined to persevere with the scheme and prove it was the right way to eliminate hooliganism. Unfortunately, their inflexibility saw the club expelled from the League Cup. After being paired at home with Cardiff, the club tried to evade competition rules by not making tickets available in advance, instead asking home fans to buy their tickets and show their membership card when they entered, with no guest tickets available. The Football League refused to accept this and, when the club refused the offer to play the tie on a neutral ground, they were kicked out altogether. John Smith called it a victory for the hooligans and slammed the FL management committee's short-sightedness and failure to use its discretion.

Smith also found himself engaged in media battles with critics of the scheme. One newspaper suggested as many as 2,000 Newcastle fans would ignore the ban on away fans and simply turn up, expecting to get in. But Smith reported that just eight visitors were subsequently turned away, and a similar number at the railway station. He spoke of a new 'friendly' atmosphere inside the ground since the ban started. This was true, but the downside was that matches were noticeably quieter than before, and there was often a lack of big-match atmosphere.

Inevitably, the ban was viewed by many as a fundamental affront to the genuine fans who follow their team around the country. Attempting to defeat hooliganism was one thing, but even some Hatters fans felt this was a step too far. It was clear that Luton were becoming almost a pariah, with nobody having a good word to say about the plastic pitch either. When Liverpool were beaten 4-1, manager Kenny Dalglish seemed to suggest they'd been beaten by the pitch and the lack of their fans, rather than Mike Newell's brilliant hat-trick.

Chief executive Smith alienated the club even further from the mainstream when he resigned his place on the League's management committee. He said his position had become impossible: 'I would be expected to vote for the wishes of all First Division clubs – against the best interests of Luton Town.' He then announced that work on the new A505 relief road would begin before the end of 1986-87 season, and that agreement had been reached with the county council on compensation, but admitted that the changes necessary behind the Main Stand would have considerable impact on facilities, parking and access.

Like many Luton supporters of the time, I struggled to defend my club against the derision of colleagues who followed other clubs. As soon as the name 'Luton' was mentioned, the subject of plastic pitches and the away fans ban would come up. The plastic suited Luton's quick, short-passing game and brought the best out of the deft, skilful players. However, if you like blood and thunder in your football, plastic was not the thing.

Nevertheless, John Smith strongly defended the surface. He reckoned many journalists had a 'fixation' about the plastic, implying that results would be different had the games been played on grass, a stance that devalued the fine work of Moore and Harford. He said tests had been carried out on pitches from Wembley to Wigan, covering all aspects of ball roll, bounce and resistance to players' movements. The results showed the only real difference between Luton's synthetic surface and many grass pitches was that the playing qualities were actually superior at Kenilworth Road. Furthermore, these qualities were guaranteed in frosty February and muddy March, which wasn't the case elsewhere. 'Don't worry about the plastic – there is undoubtedly greater home advantage for Liverpool with their 40,000 cheering Liverpudlians, or for Oxford with their steep slope, or for Manchester City with their wide open spaces,' said Smith.

Defending the membership scheme, Smith said an independent survey produced an overwhelming vote of confidence from [some of] the 28,000 Luton fans reportedly signed up to it. He admitted it had put the club at loggerheads with many others but pointed out: 'For 1987, if the improvement is maintained, we will be looking at ways of admitting small controlled groups of visiting supporters which could be integrated into our home crowd. But we will not return to fences and segregation, nor would we jeopardise the security now enjoyed by our supporters.'

Chairman David Evans was by now preparing to run for Parliament in the nearby Welwyn and Hatfield constituency, and Luton's recent stand against hooliganism must have won him plenty of approval from his party leader Margaret Thatcher. Her Sports Minister, Richard Tracy, visited the Leicester home game in January 1987 to see the membership scheme in action ('now that it has settled down'). He praised what he called Luton's very valuable experiment and pointed out that there were signs that other clubs were thinking about following suit.

At a public meeting for fans and local residents in early 1987, Evans repeated his pledge that the club would not move from the Luton area and added that the working party believed Stockwood Park was the only feasible place in the town itself. He recognised that such a move would be a sensitive issue, and added that Sundon, on the town's outskirts, was another possibility. Shortly afterwards he applauded recent initiatives involving the Football League and the Government, whereby '50 per cent' membership schemes were approved as a first step towards 100 per cent schemes. He said the evolving system could involve true fans applying for an identity card which in future would allow any member to attend any ground in the country, a scheme that would be monitored by fans themselves.

Evans scoffed at clubs who disapproved of his innovations: 'It is interesting to note that the same clubs who oppose synthetic surfaces and members-only schemes were once opposed to floodlighting for ten years of bitter argument when they tried to persuade smaller clubs that playing under lights was unreal and unacceptable. Will they ever learn?' He couldn't resist a final swipe at the 'big clubs' when he added, cheekily: 'I have no doubt that in the final weeks of the season, [Luton] will not only sustain our challenge for the league title, but if the ball runs for us, even win it!'

The 1986-87 season was highlighted by three memorable FA Cup-ties on the plastic – brilliant victories over Liverpool and Arsenal, and a quarter-final thriller with Everton which ended all-square. Three of the most memorable games in living memory for home fans. As a Luton supporter, there is nothing better than beating the big guns, particularly those who don't lose gracefully. Liverpool – in particular their dour manager Kenny Dalglish – had a good old moan about the 'unfairness' of the playing surface, but the bottom line was that his and other well-paid superstars were simply unable to match the skills, pace and application of the Luton players. And if big men like Mick Harford and Steve Foster could thrive on the plastic, why should it be such a problem for the superstars of Anfield and Highbury?

Just as Luton were failing to make another FA Cup semi-final, there was talk that the FA would soon order that all future cup-ties be played only on grass. It was clear the simmering dislike of artificial surfaces was unlikely to recede. It was now becoming a case of 'when' Luton would revert to grass, not 'if'. Meanwhile, the long-term future of membership schemes and fan segregation were issues that would be overtaken by events such as the Hillsborough disaster in 1989 and the subsequent Taylor Report.

Luton may have been brave and controversial innovators during the David Evans era, but the fundamental problem of lack of income wouldn't go away. In April 1987 the club announced that fresh investment had been found in the shape of new board members Brian Cole and Mike Watson-Challis. Evans confirmed he would be resigning soon as chairman, a development which coincided more or less simultaneously with his election as MP for Welwyn and Hatfield.

Against this volatile background, rookie manager John Moore did a sterling job, leading the team to a best-ever finishing position of seventh. The chairman reflected on a remarkable year in the life of Luton Town, which began with the loss of the manager, chief coach and physio, but saw what he called 'the comprehensive humiliation' of Liverpool in two home games and a remarkable 0-0 extra-time game at Anfield, after which came Dalglish and his 'pathetic' excuses: 'And who can describe the satisfaction and complete feeling of justice being done when we totally and completely outplayed Tottenham Hotspur?' enthused Evans. 'Their manager and chief coach took the defeat in a way one would expect in view of them having been trained and schooled at Luton, which is more than can be said for their chairman, who had obviously caught a bug from Dalglish.'

The first year of the away fans ban had not been a success financially, with gates slightly down on the previous season, but in terms of the safety and well-being of home fans it was described as a 'resounding winner'. There had been no arrests at the ground at all, compared to nearly 300 over the previous two seasons. St John Ambulance said they dealt with only sixteen casualties all season (all of which were people fainting, suffering upset stomachs or slipping on steps), against 96 the previous year, which included serious issues such as knife wounds. Police and club officials agreed the ban might be relaxed a bit in the future, but for now was working well.

The two new club directors would both in time become chairmen. Watson-Challis was relatively elderly. His wife Sheila was well known in the business world and had founded the Blue Arrow employment and recruitment agency. He was described as a sports-lover who was also a freeman of the City of London, Lord of the Manor of Debenham, and president of St Albans FC. Cole on the other hand was just 45, hailed from Letchworth Garden City and had followed Luton since boyhood. He was founder of Cleandustrial Services Ltd and now ran his own company Cole Management Services.

Even the summers seemed to be busy at Luton Town these days. 1987 was no exception. In mid-June, just five days after chairman Evans won a seat in Parliament by holding the Welwyn and Hatfield constituency for the

Tories, manager Moore declared he was quitting. Moore, a straightforward, no-nonsense figure, said he had not been comfortable with the high-profile nature of managing a top-division club, and was also said to be unhappy about his style of play being criticised as more negative than Luton teams of the past. Moore felt happier coaching than managing, he said, but turned down the club's offer to revert to that role, as he didn't want to tread on the toes of the new manager, his assistant Ray Harford. Many fans found it hard to believe that a popular manager who had led Luton to their best-ever league finish could simply walk away with no job to go to. But it was true. After taking a holiday, Moore reported to his local job centre and was eventually fixed up with a double glazing company. Cue a shaking of heads all around. It could only happen at Luton.

Moore publicly thanked the fans, particularly the one who came on the pitch after the final home game of 1986-87 to present him with a bottle of whisky in recognition of his contribution. Moore's eagerness to escape the media spotlight became rather more understandable barely a fortnight later when his predecessor, David Pleat, was the subject of unwelcome tabloid intrusion, which would ultimately lead to him leaving Spurs. Reporters from the 'red tops' descended on Luton and camped outside the Pleat bungalow on the edge of town, prompting his wife Maureen to appeal to be left alone, as their son was preparing for exams.

Just days before the start of what would prove to be arguably Luton Town's greatest-ever season, 1987-88, the subject of a new stadium reared its head again. The working party examining potential sites reported that a 355-acre former cement works and quarry close to the Bedfordshire village of Upper Sundon was now the leading candidate. In addition to a covered stadium containing no fewer than 90,000 seats, plans for the site included extensive shopping, hotel and leisure facilities, we were told. Developers Brookmount called the project Sundon Springs and painted an exciting picture, but matters were at an early stage and the announcement failed to generate much interest among fans, who felt they had heard it all before. Friends of the Earth described the quarry as a rare and precious spot, with wonderful biodiversity and splendid views, so it would come as no surprise when the county council later blocked the plans.

Luton were allowed back into the League Cup for the new season, but their controversial ticketing arrangements would still cause a stir when they were paired with Coventry in round three. The compromise was to play the tie at neutral Filbert Street, where the Hatters won 3-1 and progressed into the last sixteen. This would be just one of a remarkable tally of eighteen cup-ties this season, with the Hatters striding to Wembley *four* times – for the final of the League (Littlewoods) Cup, the Full-Members (Simod) Cup, and the semi-finals of the FA Cup. The fourth occasion was the Mercantile

Credit Centenary Festival at Wembley in April. It was a thrilling first campaign for new boss Harford, who also found time to guide his side to ninth in the league table. Throw in a 7-4 win over Oxford in February, and you have the ingredients of an unforgettable season, the like of which we are unlikely to see again. The club's finest hour, of course, came on the April afternoon when Arsenal were beaten 3-2 in the League (Littlewoods) Cup final, an occasion so momentous it would be marked by a friendly 're-match' twenty years later at Kenilworth Road. The final has been celebrated in detail in many other publications, so won't be relived here.

Chairman Evans settled into his new role as a Westminster MP, but his political ambition didn't entirely keep him out of the football headlines. He became embroiled in a legal row with boxing promoter Frank Warren in the summer of 1988 after top attraction Nigel Benn (the 'dark destroyer') failed to show for a money-spinning promotion on the artificial pitch. Barry McGuigan was also on the bill, but the absence of Benn was said to have halved the attendance and the row took a year to settle.

In the early weeks of 1988-89 Evans proposed the formation of an official supporters club, saying the time was right following lobbying from fans. Employee Bill Tomlins was given the role of liaising between the new supporters club and the football club, and relations between the parties continued to thaw following the freeze of recent years. With players like Roy Wegerle turning on the style, it would prove another fascinating season, albeit with a poor away record threatening relegation, which was only avoided by three points. Highlight was another appearance in the League Cup final following a 5-0 aggregate hammering of West Ham in the two-legged semis. Goalkeeper Les Sealey's moment of madness at Wembley – he clattered into Nigel Clough to concede a penalty – sparked a 1-3 defeat and left the furious chairman vowing 'Sealey will never play for this club again.' He never did.

Sealey had been a great servant of the club and some fans were unhappy at Evans dirtying his hands in team selection in this way, particularly as Evans had recently taken steps that were potentially calamitous for the club's future. In February 1989, while most fans were distracted by the cup run and fine league wins over Southampton and Everton, the board took the radical step of selling the Kenilworth Road stadium and land to Luton Borough Council.

The £3.25 million deal was said to include a seven-year leaseback at a peppercorn rent, meaning the Hatters would not be left homeless. We will have a new ground in seven years, and even if not, we would be protected tenants, promised Evans. Part of the reasoning was to pay off loans to the club made by Evans and other directors which incurred interest charges of around £300,000 a year. In addition, selling the ground 'would concentrate minds' and speed up the process of finding a new home, assured Evans. This is how the board justified to fans their decision to sell the club's 'crown jewels'. The statement appeared in the match programme:

* The sale would protect the land for the local authority when the club relocates;

* The Joint Working Party, including the Council, would have seven years in which to achieve relocation. This firm time-span would help 'focus minds';

* At the end of the seven-year period, the club would be protected by the Landlord and Tenants Act of 1954;

* The cash received would save the club several hundred thousand pounds in bank and loan interest;

* Directors' loans will be repaid.

Shareholders were informed of the sale at an Extraordinary General Meeting on 16th March, a week after a Supporters Club meeting was called to discuss the matter. What really rankled was not so much the loss of ownership of the famous old ground, but the revelation that the directors loans of recent years apparently involved huge interest repayments. Put in simplistic terms, the directors appeared to be profiting from the football club. Evans had been praised in 1985 for injecting the cash that helped build the successful Pleat team, but now he wanted his money back, and more, the fans moaned.

The sale of the ground duly went through. At the same time, partly in an attempt to establish the value of the Kenilworth Road site, outline planning permission was granted to the council to provide public open space and 109 housing units on the site. Evans expressed confidence that the sale had been in the club's best interests, but many fans feared that he was simply recouping his loans (with interest) prior to jumping ship to concentrate on his new Westminster career. Luton Town was still a club in debt, but now its only saleable assets were the players.

It was not long after Kenilworth Road was sold that the Hillsborough disaster occurred in Sheffield, prompting Luton's managing director John Smith to comment: 'The way forward is to dismantle fences, reduce police levels, get rid of segregation of fans, thus paving the way forward for clubs to provide new and enlightened facilities for fans, with supporters standing side by side. If we do not act now, the game will die and the hooligan will have won. At Luton we will commence discussions now with all the responsible authorities, including the local authorities, the police, the supporters club and the members to open a debate on not only our future, but the future of football.'

David Evans stepped down as chairman as planned in the summer of 1989. He ended a colourful era in the club's history by becoming embroiled in an undignified row over the departure of midfielder Ricky Hill, a first-teamer for fourteen years and one of the most popular Luton players of all time. Hill was left in limbo when Evans blocked the free transfer which would have allowed him to sign for Le Havre and join former Hatter Brian Stein in French football. Hill said he had been expecting a 'free' and on this basis had arranged the transfer, but Luton's board insisted Le Havre pay a £110,000 fee. The hard-up French club backed away, and the deadlock was only broken when Luton dropped the fee to £50,000, a sum Hill reportedly paid himself out of his signing-on fee. The outcome was that Hill ended his Luton career in bitter circumstances, which seemed a shame.

Evans' chairmanship at Luton coincided exactly with the most successful five-year period in the club's history. But, as ever, the horizon was clouded by money worries. John Smith also stepped down as managing director to become a vice-president, while Bill Tomlins was made chief executive/general secretary. Looking ahead, new chairman Brian Cole acknowledged that fellow club chairmen had voted to ban plastic pitches from the top two divisions within two years and vowed: 'We shall be looking for compensation and exploring all the natural rules of justice.' The general ban on away fans would continue, he said, but admitted there might have to be changes after the Taylor Report was published.

The new regime surprised everyone by then paying a record £850,000 for Danish international striker Lars Elstrup. However, with strike partner Mick Harford out through injury, Elstrup struggled to settle and was also hit by injury himself, only looking the genuine article later in his Luton career. The 1989-90 season proved to be one of struggle, and we were back on familiar territory in mid-season when the 'for sale' signs went up. Wegerle left for QPR for £1 million, then Harford for Derby for around half that amount. The bank had got tough, the fans were told, but the sale of the iconic Harford in particular was a bitter pill, even though the board was probably right to think it was a good deal for an injured 30-year-old.

The various upheavals were nothing new, but they peaked spectacularly in January 1990, with the Hatters second from bottom and looking near-certs for relegation. Chairman Cole decided the time was right for a change at the top. Ray Harford, the only manager ever to land one of the 'big three' domestic trophies, was shown the door. Much was made of a quote from the chairman in which he said Harford was departing partly because of his 'lack of charisma' and inability to communicate with the fans. This was manna from heaven for the sportswriters, who sent the story around the globe that Harford had been sacked for 'not smiling enough'. It was one of those stories that contained a grain of truth, but was a gross exaggeration. The real reasons for the sacking lie behind the issues of money, transfers and disappointing results.

Harford, who would die of lung cancer in 2003, was not really the dour character he'd been painted. He would actually be remembered by many for a wicked sense of humour, something he regretted he didn't always show: 'I wish I could be funny in public but it's not me,' he once said. Despite a lugubrious and often melancholic demeanour, Harford knew how to laugh at the absurdity of the football world. But he was definitely not the sort to dance along the touchline like Barry Fry, and Luton fans remembered how he looked unusually cool and composed even during the frantic, sweaty Wembley cup celebrations of 1988. Harford revealed later he had actually been very emotional after Brian Stein's last-minute winner, and his stony face was actually an attempt to stem the tears after spotting his family in the stand. He added: 'I thought all [the chairman] wanted was a decent team that could win matches, but he wanted me to wear a clown's nose and juggle at half time!' Harford would, of course, go on to coach Blackburn to the 1995 Premiership title and attract wide admiration within the game, Alan Shearer describing him as the best coach he ever worked with.

This writer recalls playing alongside Harford in a charity match in Essex, during which Ray strolled through the game at centre-half, patiently organising and encouraging the keen amateurs like myself. As often happens in these 'all star' games, some of the lesser figures get carried away, and when Perry Groves' father – a pub landlord playing for the opposition – got a little too full of himself, Harford took it on himself to quietly carry out one of the fiercest yet subtle 'tackles' I have ever seen. No bones were broken, the crowd didn't even notice it, but the job was done. Quiet but effective, that was Ray Harford.

Events at Kenilworth Road, not least the sale of Mick Harford (no relation to Ray), had roused fans' anger once again, and within days chairman Cole decided he'd had enough of the hassle. He stepped down, to be replaced by director Roger Smith. Cole had lasted barely six months. He was not the first, and certainly wouldn't be the last Luton chairman to call it a day after coming under fire from fan-power. Luton supporters have never been the sort to keep their dissent to themselves. By now the club had tumbled out of the FA Cup, humbled 1-4 by Second Division Brighton. Harford's assistant Terry Mancini had been put in temporary charge, but the dire display at the Goldstone Ground meant this was his only 90 minutes as Luton manager. Coach and former winger Jimmy Ryan was promoted to the manager's chair and given the daunting task of trying to fend off the mounting threat of relegation.

A possible club buy-out, led by Ray Pinney (a director for the past eight months) and the former club chairman Denis Mortimer, floundered and led to Pinney quitting the board. Asked to explain the wreckage behind the scenes, a spokesman would only say coyly: 'Ray Pinney had been involved in discussions with chairman Roger Smith relating to the long-term future of the club, but had now quit due to mounting business pressures.'

The failure of the Pinney/Mortimer coup meant that the £500,000 required to purchase Israeli striker Ronny Rosenthal, was no longer forthcoming. The player was on trial at Kenilworth Road from Standard Liege, but without the new money he had to be released and was eagerly snapped up by Liverpool. Rosenthal went on to play and score regularly for the title-chasing Reds, and Luton had to plough on with the inexperienced Kurt Nogan and Iain Dowie as their main strikers.

Despite the problems backstage, Ryan instilled some fighting spirit and did well in difficult circumstances. He somehow scraped together three wins and five draws in fourteen matches during his first three months in charge, but by mid-April 1990 it looked as if this would be insufficient to save Luton from the drop. All of the last three games had to be won to even have a chance of survival. As the team hadn't strung together two wins in a row so far this season, let alone three, the chances of staying up looked depressingly slim.

But, just when it mattered most, the team turned on the style to beat Arsenal 2-0 at Kenilworth Road. A week later, Crystal Palace were the visitors. After 89 minutes the game was goalless and Luton were seconds away from relegation. Then a cross by Jason Rees was bundled home by Iain Dowie and the points were won. Confidence now surged through the team as they travelled to Derby on the final day, accompanied by 5,000 fans in search of the win that would see 'mission impossible' accomplished – as long as relegation rivals Sheffield Wednesday lost at home to Nottingham Forest on the same day. Forest were mid-table and had nothing to play for, and Ron Atkinson's Wednesday only needed a single point to survive – so Luton's chances were still in doubt even if they won at Derby.

It was an unforgettable afternoon in unseasonal heat. A 30-yard blockbuster from Breacker beat Peter Shilton inside two minutes and Luton's great escape was on. Transistor radios carried the news that Wednesday had fallen behind and the tension was cranked up. The huge Luton turnout roared their team to a 3-2 win, (only their second away win all season) and Forest did their bit by thumping the Owls 3-0. Poor Ron Atkinson couldn't believe it. Ryan's heroes had escaped on an afternoon that surely equalled the Maine Road thriller of 1983 for sheer tension.

The joy overshadowed fears stemming from a special three-page 'crisis report' which was published that week by the *Luton News*, detailing the extent of the club's off-field problems. If anyone doubted that Luton Town was (yet again) in bad shape, this report spelled out the situation. It was said that the seeds of the problems had been sown four or five years earlier when the club spent freely, using money loaned by directors who were backing a dream. The payback had come more recently when the directors sold the ground in order to claw back that money, complete with interest. The players recruited and given new contracts during the David Evans era had been a talented bunch who contributed to unprecedented success, and the state of the Kenilworth Road ground had also been much improved – but it all came at a huge price, which was only now being paid.

Vice-president John Smith defended those directors who had used the sale of the ground to recoup their loans with interest. He said they had risked their cash on what they knew was a dodgy investment, and had recouped less interest than they might have from a building society. He added that directors had financed other items at the club for which they had not been repaid.

Of the £3.25 million raised by the sale of the ground, only £1.26m remained after debts were paid off. And with staff costs and salaries totaling £3 million for that year, this would soon be eaten up too. It was clear there would have to be yet more player sales unless a 'Mr Big' unexpectedly turned up. With David Evans moving on, new investors and owners were sought: 'We are looking for someone to take control who has a genuine interest in the club and who is right for the club. Money alone is not the deciding factor,' said Smith, adding that the immediate bottom line was that £1 million was quickly needed. Fans took this as a sign that young winger Kingsley Black would be on his way to a bigger club.

Chairman Roger Smith revealed that the club had enjoyed income of £5 million in the past three years. That was spent on staying in the top division and improving the ground, as well as big signing-on fees for new players and those signing contract extensions: 'We went for a bigger and better squad. With hindsight we might have overdone it – but with the right motives. Directors are supporters too and wanted the club to do well. Eight years in the First Division is a remarkable achievement for a club like ours.'

Smith also had an answer for the fans who dismissed the whole thing as another mess and demanded the board resign: 'If we did, there would be no club. It's not just the money we put in – we also have to be guarantors for the bank overdraft the club needs to keep going. If we leave, the bank forecloses and Luton Town ceases to exist. We are ready to step down for the good of Luton Town FC, but others have got to take up the commitment, as we have done.'

While all this was going on, three groups of businessmen were said to be studying the documentation relating to the sale of the major shareholding in Luton Town. Whether any of these consortia included a true 'Mr Big' remained to be seen. The fans had heard it all before and doubted it. The new owners, whoever they might turn out to be, would have to invest a minimum of £1 million immediately and then take over as guarantors for the bank, as the ground could no longer be used as collateral. The chairman said he was willing to talk to anyone interested in coming in but warned that 'time is getting short'.

As we waited with bated breath to see who the new owners would be, details emerged of a possible new ground at the Stopsley end of town, on Butterfield Green. A study document went before Luton council's general purposes committee in mid-May. It discussed how a new stadium might be part of a major development in Stopsley that might update and extend the current Regional Sports Centre which was starting to show its age. Town director Henry Richardson met fans to talk the matter over, but it became clear that there was considerable opposition from locals. Nobody wanted a football ground on their doorstep, it seemed. There was little evidence that Butterfield Green would succeed where other schemes had failed.

A week after Butterfield Green hit the local headlines it was announced that a deal had been done and new owners were in Kenilworth Road. The cheers from the Baseball Ground 'miracle' had barely subsided when we learned that David Evans had officially sold up. The new Luton Town supremo was Peter Nelkin, 43, a North London property developer, who supported Arsenal. Nelkin had taken control, along with his business partner David Kohler, a 31-year-old chartered surveyor, with an initial investment of £1.8 million securing a 60 per cent shareholding. As a result of the shares changing hands, Evans departed immediately and directors Pearson, Cole and Bailey would follow later in the summer. Directors Richardson and Watson-Challis retained their shares and were staying.

Many fans didn't know how to react. Given all the doom-laden warnings of recent times, it seemed like a positive step, although Nelkin was at pains to point out that he was not a big spender with bottomless pockets. Nelkin and Kohler got a cautious welcome and there were certainly mixed reactions as Evans rode off into the sunset. Always a controversial figure, as his subsequent political life would underline, Evans had overseen the most exciting era at Luton Town, but that had not made him universally popular.

Evans would ultimately spend ten years as MP for Welwyn and Hatfield, enjoying a colourful reputation as what his opponents liked to call 'a right-wing motormouth'. His outspoken views meant he was never far from the headlines. On one occasion, for example, he had to apologise to the so-called 'Birmingham Six' after claiming in an interview that they were guilty, even though they had been cleared by the Court of Appeal. Some years after leaving Kenilworth Road he sold his cleaning business for a reported figure of nearly £20 million. By then Evans was past retirement age and with this sort of cash might have been welcomed back at Kenilworth Road, but showed no signs of wanting a return to his old stomping ground.

CRISIS 6 (1990-99)
The Dome that Never Was

Luton's new owner promised the fans he would be a 'hands on' chairman and would work hand-in-hand with escapologist manager Jim Ryan to build a team capable of winning things. But, as far as the supporters were concerned, there was little evidence for renewed optimism at Kenilworth Road under the Peter Nelkin regime. Indeed, if anything, the club was now in a less secure position than ever, for it no longer owned its ground and was in the full control of two property developers. And although Nelkin and Kohler were presumably savvy enough not to expect a ticker-tape welcome from the fans, they cannot have remotely anticipated the sort of grief that would soon start coming their way.

Luton Town's ninth successive season in the top division of English football, 1990-91, saw Jim Ryan steer the side to the safety of mid-table by Christmas, an achievement all the more impressive given that two more regulars had departed (midfielders Danny Wilson and Mick Kennedy) without being replaced. Indeed, Ryan had to make do with what he had for many months, and the first twenty league matches of 1990-01 featured not a single debutant, which is remarkable given the high profile departures of recent times.

Thus it was with horror and much gnashing of teeth that the fans greeted the news that yet two more established stars were to be sold. In October 1990, after the Hatters had hit the heady heights of sixth, home-grown full-back Tim Breacker departed for West Ham. Later in the season, striker Iain Dowie, whom Luton had converted from a raw non-league centre-forward into a dangerous target man, would follow Breacker to Upton Park, the two sales bringing in around £1 million. This might have balanced the books, but Luton fans were livid. There were no adequate replacements in the squad for Dowie, and following his departure the team went seven league games without victory. This sent them tumbling into the bottom three and an inevitable battle against the drop.

For the third campaign in a row, survival would be dependent on results on the season's final day. It looked 'mission impossible' for the popular Ryan to save Luton yet again, for the accumulated sales had left him with the weakest top-division squad Luton had ever possessed. Nevertheless, thanks to Sunderland's defeat elsewhere and Luton recording their first win in more than two months (2-0 against Derby), another great escape was engineered. Ryan's reward – within hours of the champagne celebrations – was the sack.

Over the ensuing days it emerged that a change of manager had already been approved, but, for one reason or another the chairman had delayed the axe until the last ball was kicked. Former boss David Pleat – sacked in early 1991 by Leicester – had been spotted at Luton reserve games and the rumour mill suggested he was being lined up to take over. The whole affair was a shambles – somewhat typical of Luton Town, it might be suggested – and one bizarre story doing the rounds was that Ryan had been shown the door straight after the final-day victory partly due to an incident involving the chairman's family.

Mrs Nelkin and her daughter were reportedly told to stay away from the home dressing room before kick-off that day because Ryan didn't want his men distracted by outsiders. The pair were said to have left the ground in tears, a situation the chairman wouldn't tolerate: 'I thought to myself, who is chairman here? And I admit I was very cross. My daughter has been going into that dressing room before every game, and the manager didn't even tell me she was not being allowed in this time.'

Supporters and players alike were stunned by Ryan's sacking and didn't know whether to laugh or cry. A great day in Luton's history had been soured by the departure of a popular figure, with the general opinion being that Ryan had been extremely hard done by. It was tempting to ask why the club was being run in such a way that board members' families expected the privilege of being able to wander in and out of the dressing rooms in the first place. At best, this type of thing seemed unprofessional, and at worst, a symptom of the malaise at a poorly run club. Of course, the apocryphal dressing room incident played probably just a small part in the chairman's thinking, but it only served to give the fans more fuel in their war with the men in charge.

Brian Swain of the *Luton News* reported that the board had intended to announce Ryan's departure at a quieter point during the summer, but their intentions leaked while the 'booze flowed' after the Derby win: 'The story that Ryan was out and Pleat in went round the club bars after being handed down from the sponsors' lounge. Events speeded up because of press speculation on the Sunday morning [Ryan's birthday].'

The players were as shocked as the fans by events, and there was a torrent of protest letters to the local press, including one from former goalkeeper Tony Read, by now publican at The Old Bell at Greenfield. The *Luton News* called it the biggest rumpus among fans since the Milton Keynes controversy. Nelkin explained: 'This decision was not taken lightly, but there was a clash of personalities between us. You can't ask Jim to change, and I won't … there will be a virtual re-launch of Luton Town this summer with the new grass pitch, away fans back, a new stand, and now a new manager as well.'

Legal action by the shocked Ryan was reportedly averted only when a pay-off was agreed. Alex Ferguson then offered him a senior coaching job at Old Trafford. Ryan's 16-year-old son Neil had been due to sign for Luton as a trainee but was so upset by the treatment of his dad he began looking elsewhere. David Pleat, lurking in the background, knew all about the quirks of Luton Town, but even he must have worried about the perceived nest of vipers he was returning to. Wisely a few weeks were allowed to go by before he entered the manager's office again, after five years away at Spurs and Leicester.

If Messrs Nelkin and Kohler thought the Ryan episode would blow over quickly, they were wrong. Abusive and threatening phone calls went the way of the chairman, and the depth of feeling prompted David Kohler to offer a humble attempt at an explanation: 'Telling Jim he had to go was the hardest thing I have ever been involved in. With hindsight we ought to have done it much earlier in the season, perhaps before Christmas. But Peter and I were inexperienced. By March we knew the decision ought to be made, but it was too late by then. We were on a hiding to nothing but we kept quiet [in March] for the good of the team and the club.'

A new era was starting at Luton, even though the perennial problem of empty coffers was nothing new. The 100 per cent membership scheme was terminated – the club having lost an estimated £1.5 million through missing travelling fans. The plastic pitch was ripped up for good, with the Football League coughing up £100,000 compensation for lost revenue [hire-out fees], and a brand new stand was under construction next to the main stand. But on the down side, admission prices would be increased, which intensified the ugly mood. No wonder new director Peter Collins' first words in public were an admission that he was 'going into a lion's den'.

During the summer new manager Pleat put his thoughts on paper in his usual articulate fashion. He speculated optimistically about 'putting troubles behind us'. He must have been joking! Just around the corner was more mayhem: the club's record signing and top scorer was about to walk out and leave the country, and the chairman was about to resign, crumbling under a torrent of abuse and protests from fans.

After Peter Nelkin bid a tormented farewell, Roger Smith was promoted for his second spell as chairman. Nelkin's partner Kohler decided to tough it out, remaining as chief executive. He could barely hide his anger, however, stating: 'A group of so-called Luton fans decided between themselves that in their opinion Peter Nelkin should resign in the best interests of the football club. They undertook a vendetta against [him] and his family using various tactics such as letters, abusive phone calls and death threats, carried out over a number of weeks. I have in my possession proof that [his] phone number has been sent to various people in Luton. The abuse is far beyond that which any reasonable person should be made to endure and as a direct result of this Peter resigned as chairman of the club. The knock-on effect of this was to plunge the club into yet another financial crisis which has taken up the majority of my time, caused me many sleepless nights and a cancelled holiday. The ultimate conclusion could leave the Board with no option other than to sell a player. Is this what they wanted?'

Many fans, convinced that Nelkin had not been the man to take Luton forward, found Kohler's words hard to stomach. Why should the resignation of an unpopular chairman force the sale of another star player? If Mr Kohler was right, and chief asset Kingsley Black was about to be sold, the acrimony would surely intensify further.

In the words of the cult film *Withnail and I*, poor David Pleat had found himself 'entering the arena of the unwell'. He bravely stuck his head above the parapet to assure everyone: 'My feeling for Luton never went away.' He demanded a degree of autonomy from his new employers and brought in experienced Colin Murphy as his assistant, and then set about surveying the wreckage. A brilliant coach with bags of experience at all levels, Pleat would inevitably find himself hopelessly constrained financially, but must have expected this: 'We must put the recent discord behind us. Football changes are always controversial and invite much debate in clubs and pubs by people who care about football … at Luton it is clear the club has been impossible to run effectively with the changes of the last four or five years. The club has a reputation for playing good football and hopefully now that we have a grass pitch again we will attract a TV game or two and earn a few bob that way. We are the David facing a Goliath in most games. But don't forget David won the big one!'

Pleat welcomed the latest new era by reminding everyone that players, staff and directors come and go – but supporters are there for the long haul: 'One day, when the current management and coaching staff are long gone, there still has to be a flourishing Luton Town, a club for the true supporters to watch and enjoy. Everyone must work with that in mind.'

The size of the task ahead, to keep Luton in the top flight beyond 1992, was amply illustrated by Pleat's bleak assessment of his players. Out of the 28 he'd inherited, only five or six were what he called 'manly, experienced league players'. How the game has changed in the top division. Today top-flight clubs have huge squads which can be rotated, and in some cases two entire elevens of top quality men can be selected. Back in 1991, Pleat was evidently preparing to take on Manchester United, Liverpool and Arsenal with half-a-dozen players and a group of novices. He had the extra pressure of knowing that, if relegation was not avoided, Luton would be out in the cold when the new Premier League launched in 1992.

So the last thing Pleat needed at this point was to lose the services of a proven goalscorer. But record signing Lars Elstrup was not a happy man, and instead of signing a new contract decided he wanted to return to former club Odense in Denmark, even though they admitted they couldn't afford a realistic fee. Pleat demanded a showdown with the 28-year-old international, but must have known things were going pear-shaped when the player turned up 24 hours late. Elstrup's message was that if Luton failed to co-operate with his wishes he would simply quit football for six months, return to his former job in a Danish bank, and then join Odense later for nothing. Elstrup had bagged 17 goals the previous year for Luton, and losing his services was bad enough, but even more galling was the fact that he had cost a reported fortune of between £650,000 and £850,000. The matter was reported to the FA and to UEFA, and eventually a cut-price £250,000 was banked by Luton from Odense, which at least gave Pleat a little to spend in the marketplace.

Meanwhile, back in Luton, Pleat had to wheel and deal to strengthen his team. The Elstrup cash went on striker Phil Gray from Spurs, and more became available when local boy Kingsley Black finally departed for Nottingham Forest for a bumper £1.5 million. Selling the best players for big fees had now become an annual event at Luton, seemingly the only way to keep the club afloat. Mick Harford was welcomed back at the age of 32 for £325,000, while young defender Matt Jackson was sold for an initial £600,000, with more to follow. Pleat also scraped together another six-figure sum by selling the quartet of Dave Beaumont, Sean Farrell, Graham Rodger and Darron McDonough.

Given the profits he'd generated, it was a bitter blow later in the season when Pleat pleaded for £300,000 to sign loanee goalkeeper Steve Sutton, but was rebuffed by the board. This incensed the fans. Yet again relegation loomed and the heroic Sutton looked just the man to save them, but the board wouldn't budge. Sutton's eventual departure led to a poignant scenario with the team bus dropping him off near his Midlands home, leaving Pleat to watch ruefully as the player trudged sadly into the distance.

Whatever his inner feelings, Pleat avoided the temptation to bad-mouth his employers. Instead, he said carefully: 'We were all unhappy when Steve Sutton got off the bus on the way home from Leeds. He has been a first-class influence on everyone during his three months at the club and it is a source of great regret that the Board were unable to cope with an acquisition that would have been beneficial.'

Sutton wasn't the only one waving a sad goodbye. General manager/secretary Bill Tomlins was shown the door as the club trimmed its costs behind the scenes. All in the best interests of the club, said David Kohler, but the disharmony was clear to see. Kohler explained that the club had to reduce costs to a 'bare minimum', so it was perhaps no surprise when the end of 1991-92 saw the club fail in their annual late escape from relegation. They tumbled into the Second Division for the first time in ten years on what proved another dramatic last day.

Luton would survive only if they won at Notts County, and Coventry were beaten by Aston Villa. The Sky Blues did their bit by losing 0-2, but, despite taking an early lead, Luton toiled in vain at Meadow Lane and went down 1-2. It was all a huge anti-climax and made a thoroughly depressing trip back down the M1 for thousands of travelling fans. The new money-laden Premier League would start in three months' time and Luton would not be part of it. The tears of relegation had barely dried before radio stations and the local press were inundated with bitterly angry fans giving reasons for the decline.

They included a statement from the official Supporters Club which pulled no punches: 'The [football] club has alienated supporters across the spectrum, from executive box holders to life-long terrace fans … we have been accused of having a personal vendetta against Mr Kohler but this is not the case. Our complaint is that the present board, by their own admission, lack the financial muscle to compete at Premier League level, and as this should be the aim of any progressive club, they should seek a purchaser, without strings, for the good of Luton Town FC before it is too late and we disappear into obscurity.'

Among all the uncertainty and unpredictability of Luton Town, one thing remained (and remains) constant: The most saleable players will be sold. And sure enough in the summer of 1992 Mark Pembridge departed for £1.25 million to Derby and fans' favourite Mick Harford left (for a second time), joining Chelsea for £300,000. Disillusioned fans began taking bets on how little of that cash would be spent on replacements.

David Kohler and his board claimed they were acting in the best interests of the club, and the sales were entirely necessary, but this only served to intensify the anger supporters felt towards the men at the top. The manager was also said to have serious misgivings about the general situation, and Pleat leaked veiled quotes to the press saying as much. The 'Kohler Out' placards and chanting became commonplace on match-days in 1992-93.

The disaffected fans stepped up their noisy protests during a miserable 0-3 home defeat by Bristol City in the first home game of the new era in the second flight. After ten years at the top, the fans expected better than this and were convinced their club's decline was down to bad management at board level. Kohler labelled their behaviour 'distressing, depressing and unintelligent', adding: 'The minority who behave in this way clearly do not understand how perilously close the club has sailed to financial disaster in the last decade and how important it is for them to join with the club's many loyal supporters in helping keep the ship afloat.'

As the new season began, news emerged that Sizematch, the company that Messrs Nelkin and Kohler had formed in order to take control of LTFC, was to be the subject of High Court action. An injunction had been served on Nelkin to prevent him selling his share of Sizematch, and it was reported that Kohler planned to buy out his former partner. After the Tranmere home game in September there was another 'Kohler out' demo, and afterwards the man himself was pictured in the local press in a Range Rover with personalised number plates, driving past the very same 'Kohler Out' banner he'd ordered to be taken down during the game. He said abuse from fans wouldn't force him out of Luton – but a genuine buyer for the club would.

The *Luton News* speculated that a takeover was imminent. Sizematch's shares were being sought by businessman Keith Haslam, son of the former Town manager Harry. How close this deal came to fruition remains unclear. The fans were desperate for change and seized on the news of Haslam's interest with enthusiasm, presumably encouraged by the link with old favourite Harry. At one home match printed flyers were distributed, proclaiming 'Haslam in! Kohler out!' These documents amply illustrated how the row was getting personal. One of the questions for which the writers demanded answers was how the football club could afford a company Range Rover for Mr Kohler to drive around in, yet still be so skint that they were forced to plead for donations towards a £2,000 drying machine and £3,000 spiker for the pitch. It seemed like a reasonable question in the circumstances.

Kohler said if he bowed to the calls to resign, he would simply pull the plug and the club would go under. But he would gladly go if anyone would buy his shareholding. 'If it makes [the protestors] feel any better, they are entitled to vent their frustration. But I still don't like it. The truth doesn't change. Time and again I have met groups of supporters and told them the facts. When I talk to them face to face they seem to understand. Yet still people talk about others waiting in the wings to buy the club. Where are they? Who are they? I am ready to sell, but for sure there is no Jack Walker [Blackburn Rovers' benefactor] around here. We are losing £850,000 a year and that money has got to be covered by selling players. It's been like that for years at Luton, since long before I came. Our finances are now almost right. We have no overdraft at all – the bank won't let us have one. But we have got to get that yearly loss figure down.'

Some of the Managing Director's points were hard to dispute, but few fans were comfortable with his view that if he walked the club would fold. He expressed his fears for the club's future in an interview in the *Daily Mail*.

According to the local press, such negative publicity did not meet with the approval of Pleat, who, until now, had generally kept diplomatically quiet about the chaos around him. For his part, the under-siege Kohler tried to lighten the mood by wearing a 'Kohler Out' T-shirt at his office.

Team morale was also low. The troubles off-field were reflected by indifferent results on it. Experienced midfielder Chris Kamara asked for a move in the autumn of 1992 and then, in a surprising development, striker Steve Claridge was sold back to Cambridge United (for a profit) just four months after his arrival. Claridge had not been playing well, but the reported reason for his sale was to raise cash urgently needed for a tax bill.

Claridge later confessed that his short stint at Luton saw him play the worst football of his career. He scored just twice in seventeen games and found it hard to adjust to Pleat's passing game, following the stifling long-ball tactics of his years with John Beck at Cambridge. In his autobiography *Tales from the Boot Camps*, Claridge reflected: 'I stress that the problem was mainly with me, rather than Luton, who are a great little club. There were … particular problems with them at that time. I had come to a club where players were getting £1,500 a week and asking not to play because they wanted a move … the club had got too used to losing; it didn't hurt them enough … I believe I have always been able to hold my head up in any town I have played in, because I have always given my best, but Luton was probably the place where I let myself and everybody else down.'

Claridge wrote in *The People*: 'I went to Kenilworth Road when the club was not so much on a slippery slope, more a toboggan run. Players were laughing in the bath after 5-0 defeats, ducking out of headers, "bobbing" tackles and asking the manager if they could be excused from playing on the Saturday. David Pleat, a proper football man and someone I get on with very well, had very little control of the frauds and I wasn't helping matters by playing the worst football of my career. I'd just come from the long-ball lunatic at Cambridge and the culture shock was like going from a boot camp to Butlin's.'

The autumn of 1992 proved to be a battleground at Kenilworth Road. The beleaguered Hatters suffered their next body-blow when promising defender Darren Salton sustained injuries in a car crash that would end his playing career. The centre-half, who had recently made his Scotland Under-21 debut, was returning from a game of golf in a car driven by teammate Paul Telfer when it was in a head-on collision with another vehicle on the A507. Telfer wasn't seriously hurt, but 20-year-old Salton was left in a coma with severe head injuries. A passenger in the other car died.

Salton later attempted a long battle for fitness but eventually switched to coaching after it became clear his playing days were over. He had been regarded as likely to win full Scotland caps, something which car driver

Telfer did achieve – he would play for years at top level. Salton never begrudged his pal his success and they remained friends, but Scotland boss Craig Brown noted that Telfer did suffer: 'Paul went into his shell after that. He's a religious boy and didn't ever want to play football again. Then he realised that it was his living and that he had to get on with it. But he wanted to do so as quietly as possible and we respected that decision.'

Although Luton slumped to the foot of the table after Christmas 1992, they went on an unexpected run of seven league games without conceding a goal, equalling a club record of 69 years. Phil Gray started scoring regularly, helping the club avoid a second successive relegation. Defeat on the final day at Barry Fry's strugglers Southend left them safe, albeit rather too close to the trapdoor for comfort.

Pleat's expertise undoubtedly prevented Luton sinking through the divisions during this troubled period. He did remarkable work in the transfer market, despite having very little to spend. He persuaded Southampton to write off the £575,000 they'd paid Chelsea for Kerry Dixon and allow the striker to return to his home town for free. Dixon, rejected as a lad by Pleat in the 1970s, scored goals and mentored the emerging John Hartson. The young Welshman scored on his debut against Nottingham Forest and his presence compensated for the loss of leading scorer Gray, who was sold to Sunderland for £800,000 to balance the books in the summer of 1993.

Although Watford were beaten on the opening day of 1993-94, Luton then embarked on a run of eight league and cup games without a win. The anti-Kohler brigade returned with a vengeance. This unhappy spell even included twin 0-1 League Cup defeats by lowly Cambridge, for whom old friend Steve Claridge scored both winners.

The protesting fans seemed to have got their way when Kohler used the manager's column in the match programme to announce his departure. Kohler revealed he had agreed in principle to sell the club to the ex-Fulham and Millwall striker John Mitchell and business partner David Ellingham. Those clamouring for Kohler's exit celebrated, but others were more circumspect, particularly when scrutinising his hedged words. Nothing had been signed or completed, and this made him feel like he was 'writing an obituary before a death has been recorded'.

Kohler continued: 'My three-and-a-half years at Luton have certainly not been dull … the club is in a far better position now than it has been for a long time … the business has undergone a metamorphosis to enable it to compete and survive the very tough world of football.'

These words didn't impress his most bitter opponents, who didn't feel that limping along near the bottom of football's second tier for a second successive season represented progress. Leaving aside the club's entrenched poverty, the fans pointed to the 1992 relegation after ten years at the top, missing out on the birth of the Premiership, wholesale player sales, and the realistic fear of further demotions. These indicated major decline, not progress.

Kohler admitted: 'It has sometimes been ugly. Regrettably there has been a small and vindictive minority of individuals, fuelled by evil motives, who did nothing to enhance the club's or their own images.' Three days later his office was one of several at Kenilworth Road to be trashed in a break-in. It is not known whether this was the work of the anti-Kohler brigade or simply by a 'common or garden' burglar. Despite his long goodbye in the programme, the proposed sell-out to Mitchell and Ellingham dragged on and eventually died in its own silence.

In the course of that 1993-94 season – which proved a real curate's egg football-wise – the club announced two new directors who were both long-standing Luton fans. Cliff Bassett, boss of club sponsors Universal Salvage Auctions, and Chris Green were said to have eased the club's immediate financial worries. More cash arrived when Pleat led his team to an FA Cup semi-final at Wembley, where they lost 0-2 to Glenn Hoddle's Chelsea. The Cup run featured a replay win over Kevin Keegan's Newcastle and a 3-2 thriller with West Ham in which Scott Oakes grabbed a hat-trick. The lowly league position was temporarily forgotten, and the smiles got even wider when Pleat went on national TV to recreate his infamous celebration dance of 1983 at Manchester City: 'I just think that if you enter into the spirit of these things people are less likely to take the mick,' he said by way of explanation. 'I knew I had kept the shoes but I was surprised to find I could still fit into the suit.'

After his hat-trick against the Hammers, Oakes had the match-ball signed by teammates. Veteran Kerry Dixon, not expecting another trip to Wembley at his age, gratefully wrote: 'You have made an old man very happy.' It was Luton's fifth Wembley appearance in six years. 'It was crazy,' Pleat recalled of that semi-final. 'People were treating the match like it was the final. It should never have been played at Wembley. Okay, so it was the semi-final, but it went to people's heads. There were arguments among the directors about tickets for the Royal Box. There was a big fuss about the pre-match press conference. I picked the wrong hotel. It all went drastically wrong.'

Relegation that spring of 1994 was avoided by a mere two points, but the football world recognised Pleat's invaluable work in stemming the tide. That summer Spurs sounded him out about a return to White Hart Lane, this time to become general manager, but to the surprise of many he stayed put. The fourth season (1994-95) of Pleat's second term at Luton saw a mid-table finish – the first time Town were not involved in a relegation dog-fight for seven years. What did not change, however, was the club's selling policy. Centre-forward Hartson left for Arsenal for a monster fee of £2.5 million, a record for Luton and a British record for a teenager. It was a superb piece of business in many ways, but losing such a rare talent never goes down well with the fans, however big the fee. As a result, David Kohler remained Mr Unpopular.

In the spring of 1995 Kohler launched the project that will forever be associated with his name, the immodestly named Kohlerdome scheme. It involved an application to construct a £30 million, futuristic leisure-sports complex on the edge of town, close to Stockwood Park and Junction 10 of the M1. It was submitted jointly by the Kohlerdome Corporation with Whitbread plc, and involved an indoor 20,000-seat stadium, incorporating a range of entertainment, sporting, leisure, sports retail and administrative facilities, together with a restaurant and hotel. The stadium would have a dome-shaped roof and a movable grass football pitch. These two features meant the stadium could be used for all manner of events all year round, and the pitch removed to allow the grass to grow naturally in the fresh air to then be moved back in.

This site had already been identified as the only realistic option within the borough boundary, after no fewer than twenty others had been examined with Luton Town in mind. Luton Council listed the rejected sites as: land south of Cutenhoe Road [later known as Capability Green Business Park], Wigmore Valley Park, Stopsley Common, Lewsey Park, Leagrave Common, Dallow Hills, Wardown Park, Warden Hills, Vauxhall Sports Ground [The Brache], Butterfield Green, British Gas site Dallow Road. Those outside Luton were Houghton Hall, Laportes Sports Ground, Skimpot Road, Vauxhall Testing Ground, Sundon Springs, Elstow Storage Depot, Brogborough [former Ridgmont brickworks, nr J13], former AWD site, Dunstable and Milton Keynes.

Kohler's opponents sneered at the idea of incorporating his own name into the stadium, but others applauded his ambitious plans and praised the man's doggedness in the face of all manner of difficulties, not least a mountain of red tape. And not only did many Luton fans rail against him. A new group known as FAST (Fight Against Stadium Transfer) mobilised, distributing leaflets across south Luton and complaining that an unwanted shopping complex was part of the project. Kohler refuted this, saying the only retail outlet at his dome would be a Luton Town club shop.

Kohler staged an exhibition in the town's Arndale shopping centre and gathered thousands of signatures supporting his project. Within weeks the council voted unanimously to recommend the scheme to Environment Secretary John Gummer, which Kohler described as overcoming the first important hurdle: 'We have council backing, the majority of support in the town and my job is now to make sure we get the land and the funding, and

I feel they will be easier tasks than the planning.' The plan had to go before the Environment Department because it went against the Luton Local Plan. Once considered in Westminster it was referred onwards again, this time to be the subject of a Public Inquiry. It meant more delays, and a frustrated Kohler admitted: 'I'm not surprised but am disappointed.'

By now, developers Wyncote, appointed by the Luton Hoo estate which owned the land in question, had submitted a rival plan. This involved a new ground for the Hatters, smaller and less spectacular than the Kohlerdome, plus a large food retail outlet, which would be the 'enabling development' for the whole caboodle. However, the retail aspect was the very thing that led to it being refused planning permission. Kohler stressed that Wyncote had come along with their plans without reaching any agreement with the football club.

When it was announced that the Public Inquiry into the Kohlerdome would not start until July 1996 (the application had been submitted fifteen months earlier), a frustrated Kohler put his shareholding in Luton Town up for sale at £3 million. He held private talks with Milton Keynes about the possibility of building his dome there instead, and admitted that the delay in staging the inquiry had left the club in limbo – until probably January 1997 – which was 'too far away to even contemplate'. He felt an obligation not to allow the club to become homeless and would continue to explore every opportunity. 'I have also stated that I am ready to sell if someone else comes in ... but there is no one interested in buying.'

In December 1995 Kohler confirmed he had met borough councillors in Milton Keynes to present plans for the 20,000-seater dome and would attend the council's leisure committee meeting in his capacity as a property developer. Worryingly for Luton fans, this meant the threat of the club moving to Milton Keynes appeared back on the agenda. Kohler commented: 'It's a bit like Sainsbury's building one in Luton, one in MK and one in Watford ... if the theory works you can do it anywhere. I have always said that Luton Town should stay in Luton and I'm still doing everything I can to put Luton Town on the land by Junction 10 of the M1. But I would not allow a scenario to occur where Luton Town was kicked out [of Kenilworth Road] with nowhere to play, and there was a stadium up the road in MK where they could play. Whether I am still the owner of the club, if and when that scenario occurs, I don't know. We'll have to cross that bridge when we get there.'

The dome received an initial thumbs-up from Milton Keynes' leisure and community services committee. Kohler explained the original aim was to build it on the edge of Luton, but the concept of a stadium with movable grass pitch and variety of uses could work anywhere. He added: 'I have always said that LTFC should stay in Luton but at the present time the plan to move to J10 is looking less likely. J10 is where we ought to go as a football club and the fact that I am looking at a development scheme somewhere else is nothing really to do with the relocation of Luton Town, unless LT [becomes] homeless.' The MK committee agreed in principle to support the scheme, and, subject to the results of an impact study, develop a Lottery Fund proposal in partnership with the Commission for New Towns (CNT) and the Kohlerdome Corporation.

A 1995 edition of *Management Accounting* magazine examined the motives of Kohler, for he had originally paid £600,000 for a business (LTFC) which had been so close to liquidation. The magazine concluded that he had bought the club partly because of property development and partly so he could be involved in football. There's an element of ego, an element of 'I'll show them I can do it', he admitted. The magazine looked back to the era prior to Kohler's arrival at Luton and offered a succinct summary of the club's plight:

'By excelling in the [1988] cup competitions, Luton played in virtually every match that it was possible for the club to play in [that season] but maximum income had been achieved by heavy spending, financed by burdensome loans. For [Luton] to suffer losses of around a million pounds after such a successful season was clearly a signal of serious trouble ahead. Soon afterwards repayment of loans was demanded, together with outstanding interest payments. To avoid liquidation the club was forced to sell the freehold of its ground and, in the years since, a stream of talented players have been sold to keep the club afloat.'

During the summer of 1995 turmoil in Luton was not restricted to the football club. At Marsh Farm, one of the possible new homes for the club, riots broke out in which police were injured and property wrecked. It brought yet more high-profile negative media exposure to a town already struggling badly with its image. Polly Toynbee of *The Independent* wrote: 'They'll tell their grandchildren about it some day, the three hot nights when Marsh Farm was ablaze. Maybe some of them have great-grandfathers who helped to burn down Luton Town Hall in 1919, angry soldiers home from the war to find nothing fit for heroes. But they had a coherent objective, while now there is only nihilism with a dash of hedonism.'

Against all this uncertainty, perhaps the last thing the chairman needed at this point was to lose his manager. David Pleat was approached by Premiership Sheffield Wednesday in the summer of 1995 and agreed to join them, presumably weary of the troubles at Luton and eager for another crack at the big league. A row blew up over compensation from the Owls and it went beyond a war of words when Luton applied to the High Court for an injunction after Pleat walked out with a year of his contract still to run. Kohler said he was prepared to extend the legal battle in order 'to set an example' on behalf of smaller clubs who get bullied by the bigger boys. The row rumbled on across the summer and was eventually settled by arbitration before the start of the 1995-96 season.

Youth coach Terry Westley was the surprise successor to Pleat at Luton, and this young enthusiast from Suffolk tackled his new role with gusto, buoyed by the luxury of money to spend by the Luton board. The sales of John Hartson and Paul Telfer had raised almost £4 million. Former local bank clerk Mrs Cherry Newbery was promoted to club secretary and faced a hectic introduction dealing with the signings of a string of new players, including Bontcho Guentchev, Gavin Johnson, David Oldfield, Graham Alexander, Darren Patterson and Steve Davis. They would be followed in the autumn by goalkeeper Ian Feuer and Danish pair Johnny Vilstrup and Vidar Riseth. It seemed a major transformation, and for a while those who criticised Kohler's tight purse-strings were silenced.

On paper the new squad looked strong, but for one reason or another things simply failed to gel. By mid-December Town had won just four of 22 league games and were bottom of Endsleigh Division One. After a 0-4 humbling at Portsmouth, Westley was out, becoming the fifteenth managerial departure of the 1995-96 season. Kohler said: 'I feel very sorry for Terry. I wanted him to do well but we've spent more than £2 million on players and are bottom of the First Division. Something clearly is wrong and something had to be done before it was too late.' Westley's assistant, the former Ipswich coach Mick McGiven, was also shown the door.

One legacy of Westley's short tenure was his introduction of family friend Matthew Upson to Kenilworth Road. Upson would later be sold for a huge fee and go on to play for England. Westley later admitted that bringing through youngsters like Upson gave him his greatest satisfaction from football, and he didn't particularly want to repeat his experience of management after events at Luton: 'I went to Matthew's competitive debut for England up at Middlesbrough. I was standing there and tears were rolling down my face, his mum was beside me and she was crying as well.'

After the failure of rookie Westley, Kohler went for an experienced outsider. Former Charlton, Middlesbrough and Bradford City boss Lennie Lawrence became Luton's fifteenth different manager in the 30 years since the war (Pleat and Martin did two stints). Results improved for a while, but alarming late lapses kept Luton near the bottom and they were relegated alongside Watford. A spell of 26 years in the top two divisions came to an inglorious end with unhappy fans jeering Scott Oakes, Tony Thorpe and Bontcho Guentchev, skilful players all, but perceived as not working hard enough for the cause. In Oakes' case he would be on his way in the summer anyway, signed by his old mentor Pleat at Sheffield Wednesday for about £500,000. With hindsight this would represent excellent business for

Luton, for the enigmatic Oakes' career failed to take off and he eventually faded from the professional scene.

The summer of 1996 saw the Kohlerdome Public Inquiry kick off at Luton Town Hall. Kohler presented his case on behalf of the football club, at pains to point out that 89 per cent of the Luton public surveyed were in favour of his brainchild. The Government-appointed inspector listened to submissions from the borough council, the highways authority, neighbouring councils, protest groups, and developers Wyncote, working on behalf of landowners Luton Hoo. Kohler gave a progress report to the media: 'It's not like a cricket or football match where there's a scoreboard to tell you how you are doing. However to coin a footballing phrase – we haven't let any in yet. With regard to Wyncote, I would adopt the attitude of the barrister representing the Highways Agency when he commented on the information given by them. He said their information fell woefully short of what one would reasonably expect in such circumstances.'

The club and the borough council at last appeared to be singing from the same hymn-sheet. Kohler praised the council for their support and noted that they had resolved, in certain circumstances, to use their powers of compulsory purchase to bring the Kohlerdome to fruition. There seemed cause for optimism for the fans, at least those who didn't mind seeing their club play indoors on a movable pitch. The official Supporters Club addressed the Inquiry and backed the bid for a new home. There was further good news for Kohler when the Department of Transport gave the go-ahead for widening of the M1 between junctions 6a and 10, to four lanes in each direction. One of the Highways Agency's main objections to the dome at the Inquiry had been possible congestion. They proposed that it should not be built before any widening of the motorway.

To his credit, Kohler kept fans abreast of developments by way of updates, some of which he injected with a touch of humour: 'Our future is in the hands of a planning inspector … it's all very much like a court case, certainly in terms of the fees for the barristers. It is unusual for a public inquiry to deal with two schemes, one put forward by ourselves and one by developers [Wyncote] appointed by the landowners [Luton Hoo], and what they are proposing is a smaller, traditional, four-stand-green-pitch stadium that I don't believe fulfils the ambitions of Luton Town.'

The Inquiry took a break of several weeks for the club and Wyncote to submit an 'Environmental Statement'. Kohler explained that this was necessary because the Campaign for Rural England had suddenly complained to the European Commission in Brussels that the club had not produced any environmental statement, and the DoE agreed this must be done straight away. Kohler, fed up with slow-moving bureaucracy, was not best pleased by this interruption but accepted it philosophically.

Just as the inquiry reconvened, there was an 'off the ball' kerfuffle when *The Guardian* newspaper uncovered what they called a Parliamentary row surrounding the plans. The paper reported that Kohler had been urged to report a local Luton MP to the Parliamentary Commissioner for Standards for possible 'irregularities'. The article said that after Luton council had given the go-ahead for the Kohlerdome, the MP in question pressed the Environment and Transport Secretaries [John Gummer and George Young] to call in the plans and force the Public Inquiry which was now under way. This had allowed the 'rival' plan for a stadium plus retail outlet to be reopened. And the rival plan was said to have attracted the interest of a supermarket chain which allegedly used this MP as a consultant. The MP denied this link was irregular and said he worked for a department of the supermarket chain unconnected with development plans.

With difficulties mounting, envious eyes were cast northwards when work started in Huddersfield on the new McAlpine Stadium. Reading's move from Elm Park to the new Madejski Stadium was also in progress. Meanwhile, Lennie Lawrence's team were bidding for an instant return to Division One and as the Public Inquiry drew to a close the Hatters powered to the top of the division after a last-gasp win at Millwall. Top at Christmas. Luton fans had not had such cause for celebration for years.

Competition was tight at the top, with Luton battling alongside Dave Jones' Stockport and the notoriously hard-to-beat Bury. Despite conceding only one goal in their final five league games, Luton had to settle for third spot and a first-ever tilt at the play-offs. Opponents would be Crewe, who had finished five points behind and been hammered 6-0 at Kenilworth Road. The division's two best footballing sides went head to head and over the two legs it was Crewe who ultimately squeezed through 4-3 on aggregate. A promotion chase was something Luton supporters had not experienced for fifteen years – and in some cases they got a little carried away. For example, loyal fan Sue Miller was invited on to Richard Littlejohn's ITV football show *Do I Not Like That* and revealed to the surprised host that to commemorate Luton's success and her recent 40th birthday, she'd had the club's badge tattooed on her left breast.

As the chairman had predicted, the momentous General Election of May 1997 did indeed delay the Public Inquiry decision-making process. Kohler did not rest on his laurels, though, for he repeated his transfer coup of selling a Luton youngster to Arsenal for a huge fee that astonished the football world. Last time he'd prised £2.5 million out of the Gunners for John Hartson, and now he negotiated a £1 million down payment, with more to follow, for Matthew Upson. Centre-back Upson had played just two minutes of football for Luton's league team, coming on as a sub near the end of a home game with Rotherham nine months earlier, but his CV included skippering Luton's youth team to the FA Youth Cup semi-finals. Arsenal coughed up after Kohler warned that Newcastle were also sniffing around. For once, most fans agreed that this was a deal that could not be turned down. They were not so pleased, however, when the selling continued and Ceri Hughes joined Wimbledon and Kim Grant went to Millwall.

The General Election brought a Labour landslide and the end of eighteen years of Tory rule. This meant the decision over the Public Inquiry would now be made by a new regime. Among the raft of ousted Tory MPs was former Luton chairman David Evans, after ten years as Member for Welwyn and Hatfield.

While waiting for news from Westminster, Kohler said that he saw the funding of the Kohlerdome scheme as relatively straightforward: 'But we are in no way underestimating the difficulties in purchasing the freehold, despite the council having resolved to pass a compulsory purchase order. There are still a number of hurdles to overcome and I have always stated that before our stadium can be a reality there are three key elements required – planning consent, land acquisition and funding.'

In the late summer of 1997 the Inquiry inspector finally reported to the new Secretary of State, John Prescott. In response to a letter of complaint from Luton Town, the Department of the Environment apologised for the delays. Submission of the report by the inspector had been slowed by bouts of ill-health and other duties that the inspector was unable to avoid. Kohler arranged to meet new Sports Minister Tony Banks in a bid to publicise the plans and to get the decision hurried along, but the death of the Princess of Wales caused all ministerial engagements to be cancelled. In place of Banks, Kohler was visited by the new Luton South MP Margaret Moran, Luton council leader Roy Davis, and Football Trust chief executive Peter Lee. Kohler didn't get the VIP he wanted, but went ahead with a demonstration of how the movable pitch system would function.

Kohler's frustration at these delays was mirrored by manager Lawrence, who was suffering from the worst injury crisis in memory at Kenilworth Road. It contributed to some dreadful results, including a 2-5 home defeat by Wrexham, when coach Trevor Peake was forced to play at the age of nearly 41, and a 0-4 home loss at the hands of Watford. When Watford's fourth goal went in before half-time, the atmosphere turned poisonous and police and stewards had to move into position to prevent a riot. Luton fans had suffered much in recent years, but this humiliation was one disaster too far. Poor Lennie Lawrence must have feared for his life as the baying mob turned their ire on him and hammered with fists and feet on the roof of the home dugout. When things calmed a little in the second half, the Luton fans cheered themselves up by singing 'It only took ten years', a reference to Watford's first local derby victory in that time.

Just before Christmas 1997, with Luton third from bottom of Division Two, the *Mirror* reported that Lawrence had been summoned to explain to his directors why the team had gone six home games without a win. 'Of course he is under pressure,' said David Kohler. 'We all are – from me at the top to Lennie Lawrence in the middle and the players at the bottom. We have a team which, on the face of it, is good enough but which makes horrendous errors. The view of the board is that we are all in this together. [But] sacking the manager just lets him off the hook.' It was a new angle on the traditional 'vote of confidence'.

As 1998 dawned with no sign of any decision on the Kohlerdome, the chairman continued to press for a resolution. He was told by one official: 'We understand your concern to see a decision issued quickly given the football club's situation and the time the procedures have taken. We are aware of the importance that the club attaches to the success of the proposals to secure its future. However, it is also important that we reach the right decision and that we take a fair and balanced view of the issues which are complex … please be assured that we are taking every effort to ensure that the decision is issued as quickly as possible.'

Kohler moved quickly to quash talk of a takeover at Kenilworth Road, following press reports of an outside bid. He called a press conference and announced: 'Nobody has contacted me and, anyway, I don't want to sell. We're hopefully very close to getting planning consent for a new stadium and I'd be the biggest idiot in the world to want to walk away from it now, having done seven-and-a-half years of hard work to put a future for this football club together. I have a dream, and I aim to prove those people wrong who told me that I couldn't deliver. I want to turn around to those sceptics and say there it is, I have delivered.'

A month later Kohler came under more fire, this time for selling prolific Tony Thorpe, just as the relegation fight was hotting up. Big money or not, the sale seemed suicidal. Kohler retorted that the club was losing £40,000 a week: fans were wrong to think the board didn't care where the club was heading. 'I always seem to be pontificating about money, but unfortunately the modern game centres around that commodity.'

These words did little to appease the protestors. In early March 1998 Kohler woke to find the drive outside his Hertfordshire home had been vandalised. That day got steadily worse for all concerned, for a few hours later Luton played out a dismal 0-0 home draw with lowly Wycombe. Town were clearly missing Thorpe, who had gone to Fulham for £800,000 to cover the losses Kohler kept talking about. Thorpe had scored 48 goals in the past eighteen months and would be sorely missed. Although Lawrence must have been furious to lose him, he disapproved of fans attacking Kohler's home: 'That's out of order. It's fair enough to give us a bit of stick

in the ground but if it goes to your home, that's wrong – there is no justification or excuse for that.'

Thorpe's absence, at least in the short term, was compensated when
David Pleat recommended that Luton 'borrowed' young striker Rory Allen
from Spurs. Lawrence accepted the tip-off and Allen hit six goals in eight
appearances to help steer the Hatters clear of the drop.

1998-99 started with much-vaunted French signing Herve Bacque failing by some distance to materialise into a new Tony Thorpe. Nevertheless
Lawrence somehow kept Luton in the top six over the first few months. By
now the Kohlerdome appeared to be wobbling after the new Secretary of
State cancelled proposals for widening the M1 between Junctions 6A and
10, pending a wider review. Kohler stayed positive, however, insisting the
dome would come, but his patience appeared to have reached breaking
point by November. It had now been four years of waiting, and he wrote
a special message in the Chesterfield match programme: 'Dear Supporters.
We had considered delaying the start of the game by four minutes today to
make our point, but we decided that this might affect your enjoyment of
the game. We have therefore decided to make a peaceful protest with the
reverse of this sheet with the number '4' on it to demonstrate our frustration. The reason is to highlight the four-year delay in the Government
deciding on our new stadium plans. These are the main issues –

(1) Why? If we have one of the worst grounds in the country!

(2) Why? If our proposals were unanimously approved by Luton
Borough Council!

(3) Why? If the inspector at the public inquiry recommended that planning permission be granted for the new stadium!

(4) Why? If we are prepared to accept a smaller capacity until the M1
has been widened!

Why has it taken so long for the Secretary of State to make a decision
in favour of the new stadium? The club would be very grateful if, on the
instructions of the public address announcer, at about one minute before
kick-off, you would hold up this sheet with the '4' facing outwards for
about 30 seconds. The Board thank you for your support.'

Unfortunately, Mother Nature stepped in and inclement weather caused
the match to be called off. Kohler admitted afterwards he was struggling to
come up with new ideas to hurry things along: 'I'd stand in the middle of
the M1, or sit on the runway at Luton Airport, if I thought that would help,
but that would be unsafe.'

Kohler added that until planning permission was approved the club
would continue to sell players. This did not help the beleaguered Lawrence,
who told the *Luton News*: 'I don't own the club, but it's not in Luton Town
FC's interests for anybody to go at this stage. Short-term salvation is at

hand with the [Worthington] cup run and medium term salvation is at hand as long as we've got a chance of promotion. Long-term salvation is in the hands of the government and the decision over a new stadium.'

At long last, in the closing weeks of 1998, the Secretary of State's decision was released. Permission for the Kohlerdome was refused because of the traffic implications for the M1, although it conceded that a smaller stadium might be acceptable. The ruling came as the chairman was preparing for a surgery in hospital, and he reflected ruefully later: 'Picture the scene – I am in hospital having a very private part of my anatomy shaved in readiness for a hernia operation. Our lawyers have asked the Department of the Environment when we are going to get the final decision on our project for a stadium at Junction 10. And as the lather is slapped on and the razor raised, my mobile phone rings. It's the lawyer. Our application has been refused. Now is that sick, or is that sick? Fancy them pulling out their fingers just as I went into hospital. I suppose the timing was a coincidence.'

He said his first reaction was disbelief, followed by anger, and he would now seek a judicial review of the decision from the High Court. He felt his submission had contained all the information required for approval of a smaller stadium too, and didn't think he should have to start again with a new submission. The inquiry inspector had come down in Luton's favour, as had the democratically elected Luton Borough Council, so for permission to be refused 'Someone unelected and unaccountable has got it in for our football club, and I will not accept it, and neither should you! The latest decision is scandalous. As I have repeatedly said before, the fight goes on. We are all entitled to justice. And we will get it. We will get our new stadium. It will happen!'

Legal action followed, but it was clear morale was low at Kenilworth Road by this time. There was trouble at every turn. Skipper and defensive rock Steve Davis returned to Burnley for £750,000, after reportedly turning down 'the best contract offer Luton ever made'. Results in the league began to worsen and the club went out of the FA Cup at home to Hull, the bottom club in Division Three. By now, the fans were calling for Lennie Lawrence's head as well as the chairman's.

Another angrily worded flyer was distributed to supporters, this time by the unofficial Loyal Luton Supporters Club, its contents described by Kohler as libellous. A few days later Kohler attended the High Court for his judicial review of John Prescott's decision, having won an expedition order to get it heard quicker than anticipated. Part of Kohler's argument to Justice Dyson involved evidence that showed the M1 would not become much busier simply because of the Kohlerdome. Using the address database of supporters, the club calculated that just 800 cars would use the M1 to get to the dome on matchdays, the rest arriving from elsewhere.

Two days later, with the High Court outcome still pending, Kohler pledged to resign as chairman and also sell his majority shareholding. It was said an unlit 'petrol bomb' device, along with matches and a threatening note, had been pushed through the letterbox of his home near Radlett. Enough was enough, and he promised he would leave the club 'after my business affairs are put in order'. Police were called in to investigate.

Fellow directors Chris Green, Cliff Bassett and Nigel Terry issued a joint press release: they were 'astounded' that their chairman had opted to quit without consulting them, and it was important that the disposal of his controlling interest in the club was resolved as soon as possible.

Kohler told reporters: 'I've been involved with Luton Town for a quarter of my life and have always tried my best to act in the interests of the club. What happened is an act that any reasonable person must deplore. As a husband and father of three children, the youngest only five weeks old, my primary responsibility is to them. The police have viewed this petrol bomb as a warning. However, I am not prepared to use my family as a shield or place them in any circumstances that could endanger them.'

Four days after the petrol bomb incident, it was announced the High Court appeal had been turned down. According to a matchday programme editorial: 'A sad weekend for Luton ended with the High Court putting the boot into the club's plans for a new stadium. And with chairman David Kohler set to leave Kenilworth Road for good, as soon as he can sort out his financial involvement, it looks as though we are back to square one, operating in a hopelessly inadequate stadium and with no other known suitable site available in Luton. The Kohlerdome dream is over.'

The judge had also rejected Kohlerdome plc's offer to scale the scheme down to 12,000-seat capacity, but added that the club could, of course, put in a completely new planning application for a smaller stadium if it chose.

Kohler's departure from Luton Town was not quick. Three weeks later, amid reports of a clash of opinion between the directors over the value of his majority shareholding, he returned to his office at Kenilworth Road. He explained: 'I am still chairman of Luton Town until I can settle my business affairs, and that means getting someone who is financially able, and willing, to take on the club. I had decided to stay away after announcing my intention to resign as chairman, but with no progress made on the sale front I have taken the view, with some prompting from my family, that the club was like a ship without a rudder.'

Boardroom disagreement over the Kohler shares rumbled on through March 1999, whereupon director Cliff Bassett eventually decided on drastic action. As the main creditor, owed a reputed £2 million, he was in a position to call in the Receivers, and did so on 23rd March, thus putting Luton Town into Administration.

Luton supporters unfamiliar with the workings of the business world wondered if this was the beginning of the end. Accountants Buchler Phillips sent their representative John Kelly into Kenilworth Road and we braced ourselves for the inevitable fire-sale, with the transfer deadline just days away. With the very future of the club in the balance, the match programme for the visit of Gillingham was pored over. Fortunately, the detailed explanation of recent events at the club was written by local journalist Brian Swain, and not by an accountant, and was therefore clearly set out in language the ordinary supporter could understand.

Swain explained that the Receivers were called in after it had become clear hours earlier that rumours of a split in the boardroom were true: 'A month after David Kohler announced his wish to resign as soon as he could sell off his 60 per cent controlling interest in the club, negotiations between him and the other three directors were still deadlocked.'

The Receivers issued a statement: the club was insolvent, with debts to Mr Kohler and the other directors totalling more than £3 million. They would look into the full financial position in the hope that the future of the club could be safeguarded, but were keen to hear from potential investors who may be interested in funding the club. There might have to be cuts in the Kenilworth Road payroll, but the Receiver had been impressed at the quality and 'lack of dead wood' he had found among the staff.

One of the Receivers' early tasks was to render David Kohler's managing director role redundant. Mr Kelly said this was necessary because he was the biggest wage earner, apart from the players. Meanwhile, an advertisement was placed in the financial press offering for sale the business and assets of Luton Town as a going concern. Before long twenty responses were logged. 'It's been a strange week,' said club secretary Cherry Newbery, with a touch of understatement. 'The attitude has been one of roll up the sleeves and redouble our efforts – most of us who work here are not just employees but committed supporters of the club as well.'

Shortly after the Receivership news broke, among the calls to the club was one from former striker Bontcho Guentchev, who offered to come back and play in Town's time of need. The offer was reportedly 'politely declined' and a month or two later Bulgarian Bontcho joined Hendon of the Ryman Premier Division. Manager Lawrence, who had been in charge at Charlton when they were wound up in the High Court due to tax debts, said he understood the complexities of the situation. The transfer of fullback Graham Alexander to Preston was soon approved, bringing in much-needed cash, and subsequently young midfielder Sean Evers moved to Reading for a gratefully received £500,000.

The football world in general seemed to regard Luton Town's plight sympathetically. The *Sunday Mercury* in Birmingham reported that Luton were only the latest club to teeter on the brink, with Crystal Palace, Oxford United and Portsmouth also in desperate straits. Never before had so much wealth existed at the top end of the game, they said, with the Premiership almost drowning in a sea of cash, yet increasingly reluctant to share it. The paper called for big clubs to turn the strugglers into nursery clubs to safeguard their future while creating a breeding ground for young talent.

Pre-deadline sales meant the future of Luton Town was secured until the end of the season, and the spirit at Kenilworth Road seemed to be on the up. Having made the MD redundant and sold Alexander and Evers, the Receiver even allowed Lennie Lawrence to bring two men in on loan – Sean Dyche and Tony Thorpe – both from sympathetic Bristol City. Lawrence noted: 'The predators gather when they hear receivers are going in. There were many offers and telephone calls about our players, some of them derisory. The receivers backed me in not selling off players cheaply, and their decision to allow the two loans to come in helps us secure Second Division football and go for a strong finish to the season.'

Various supporters groups joined forces to rally public backing for the club. Their umbrella organisation was named FLAG (Fans of Luton Action Group) and declared that AFC Bournemouth's 'community' survival plan should be a model for what could be achieved at Luton. Leading members of Luton Town Supporters Club, Loyal Luton SC and the *Mad as a Hatter* fanzine united to launch the FLAG campaign at a public meeting attended by a turnout of around 1,200. A bucket collection raised £10,000 on the night, plus the inevitable assortment of foreign coins, and pledges to try to buy a controlling interest in the club passed the £140,000 mark. A Luton estate agent offered FLAG free use of a town centre office and MP Margaret Moran came forward to support the idea of a community-owned club. Whether or not the idea would prove workable, the level of response and great spirit being shown was encouraging.

Luton finished the 1998-99 season mid-table in Division Two, which was satisfactory in the circumstances. It was reported that Tottenham chairman and future reality TV star Alan Sugar was sniffing around with a view to buying Luton. But his proposal had strings attached, for he intended to reshape the British game by making the Hatters an official nursery club for Spurs. FA rules, of course, currently forbade one man from owning two clubs. Sugar was said to have opened talks with the FA, having already discussed them with his director of football – David Pleat. The whole idea met with a muted response from Luton fans, and subsequently failed to run with the FA too.

As the Luton players headed off on summer holidays, the Receivers worked to engineer a secure future for the club. Over the summer five approaches were considered. Players Chris Wilmott and Kelvin Davis were sold to Wimbledon for six-figure fees and – taken as an isolated six-month period – meant that under Receivership the club had done pretty well financially. They'd raised some £1.4 million in the transfer market, the wage-bill had been slashed and, thanks to a marvellous response from fans, well over £400,000 had been banked from season-ticket sales. Prices had been frozen while the club remained in Receivership. Given these sorts of figures, most fans were under the impression that the storm had been weathered. Surely there were no more dramas to come?

Behind the scenes there was still frustration. Despite the outside interest, the deal favoured to save the club still involved David Kohler's shares transferring to Cliff Bassett, the director who'd called in the Receiver in the first place. However, agreement could not be reached. As the matter dragged on, the Football League called time and set a deadline of midnight on Friday, 6th August, the eve of the 1999-2000 season. The deal had to be done and the paperwork completed, otherwise the plug would be pulled. If Bassett, Kohler and the Receiver could not agree terms there seemed a very real possibility that Luton Town would be no more.

The deal was apparently struck with seconds to spare. A Nationwide Football League spokesman later said: 'Midnight was the deadline. The message confirming the agreement started to come over on the Football League fax machine at 11.58pm and it actually finished two minutes past midnight. You can't get any closer than that! The agreement that was put in place on the Friday was enough for us to be able to think that the receiver will be able to extricate himself from the club this week and we were happy to let the game [the next day] at Notts County go ahead.' The Receiver, confirmed: 'It had to be done by midnight or Luton would not have played on Saturday. But there was a whole range of quite complicated issues involved in the agreement and we got very near the deadline.'

Secretary Cherry Newbery recalled: 'I will never forget the massive feeling of relief when I received a phone call from Richard Scudamore of the Football League ten minutes after midnight on the day the season started … it was a matter of being happy just because the club was still alive.'

David Kohler reportedly walked away after nine years at Luton with a deal worth around £1 million. Cliff Bassett, long-time supporter and boss of club sponsors Universal Salvage Auctions, was now the new owner but had never been a publicity seeker and seemed reluctant to acknowledge that he was the hero of the hour. Looking exhausted, he joined more than 1,500 fans heading up the M1 for the Notts County game. They turned the day into a party and unfurled a huge banner at the game which made it clear they were glad to see the changes in the boardroom.

Bassett did not talk publicly about the boardroom feud which led to Receivership and the ensuing drama, but the first home programme of the new season made clear that one sticking point had been Kohler's wish to retain rights to the stadium development, with Luton becoming rent-free tenants. That was apparently scrapped by means of payment to Kohler for his services on the development scheme. The new owner was keen to see any new ground owned by the football club and not rented.

Technically, Luton Town was still in Receivership until formalities were concluded some weeks later. Bassett's take-over package included other investors, and he was keen to address the immediate problems of strengthening the squad. He did not want to be chairman but conceded: 'I might, realistically, as majority shareholder, have to become a reluctant chairman for a time, but part of the restructuring of the club will consider that matter. To be honest, I hardly knew where I was at over the weekend after a long and difficult period. It was a relief to get it settled, in time to enjoy the match at Notts County.'

So Luton Town had been saved, temporarily. Many observers saw the Hatters' troubles of 1999 as symptomatic of deeper issues within the game. It was certainly a cause for alarm that summer when it was calculated that around 600 players were on the move as the 'Bosman ruling' began to bite. The 1995 European Court of Justice decision, which had allowed players to walk out at the end of their contracts and offer their services for signing-on cash instead of transfer fees, had made a few very rich, but the vast majority had suffered. Clubs everywhere were slimming down and many young players found themselves unemployed. Money and power was by now concentrated in the hands of England's top twenty clubs, and the rest of the professional game was facing a battle for survival.

Postscript

Later, when the money-spinning Premier League was close to celebrating its tenth anniversary, David Kohler looked back on how he and Luton Town had signed up to the revolution in early 1992, but then narrowly missed out on the gravy train. Had Town held on, life might have been very different for both Kohler and Luton Town. He told the *Evening Standard*: 'You never get over something like that result against Notts County [in May 1992]. You are always thinking, if only we had won that game and stayed up, we would have had all that money to build a team. The history of football is that fans will always turn on the chairman if things don't go well. But what happened with the petrol bombs and protests, that was an ugly, horrible mess. But am I jealous of people like [Arsenal's] David Dein? No. Luton has always been a small club in a small town. If we had stayed up we might have had some good times for a while, but we probably would have found our level. When the twenty clubs were sitting around the table we were always aware that two of us would not be there a few weeks later.'

CRISIS 7 (1999-2003)
A Birthday Present with a Difference

Amidst all the fall-out from recent events, Lennie Lawrence, by now the fourth-longest serving manager in Luton Town history, got his side off to a better start to the 1999-2000 campaign than anyone had a right to expect.

Stripped of his most valuable players over the last couple of seasons, Lawrence's squad had a very inexperienced look, but emerging talents like Matthew Taylor, Liam George and Matthew Spring gave great hope for the future. Taylor, in particular, exploded on the scene as a 17-year-old, and seasoned supporters were soon debating how long it would be before he was sold on to a bigger club.

The club only officially came out of receivership in October 1999, at which point the new majority shareholder Cliff Bassett invited all supporters and the wider local community to join forces to realise his ambitions for the club. But the 63-year-old grandfather and long-time Hatters fan clearly did not intend to be a high-profile figure like his predecessor. He said: 'I don't really want to be seen as the owner of the club. I don't really want to be chairman, and certainly I would never be a hands-on chairman working as a paid full-time chief executive. The original deal to bring the club out of receivership was agreed the night before this season started, and it has taken until now to sort out all the details. There were a lot of legalities and formalities to be taken care of, and it has not been easy. Now I need a little more time to think about where we go from here. But clearly there are two priorities: more funding, and a new stadium.'

One of a three-man board, Bassett was by this time owed more than the £2.8 million reported at the time receivership started. He wanted ownership of the club spread as widely as possible, and not to be in the hands of one individual. He hoped the various names and business groupings who showed an interest during receivership would now come on board, including the fans group FLAG: 'I would be very happy to see FLAG involved, but the reality of the situation is that while I am happy for supporters to be part of the structure running the club, major finance has to be found. I am owed a lot of money, and I hope that eventually I will get it back under a structured scheme, but that is for the future.

'We have to address the short-term first, and I don't think anyone will be surprised to hear that while it is a very welcome boost to come out of receivership, we are still losing money. I expect it to take about three months to work out the situation, and the ways of dealing with the problems. Paramount is the need to get more finance in as quickly as possible.

If someone like a Jack Walker [benefactor at Blackburn Rovers] came along, that would be wonderful. But I don't think that is going to happen, which is why we need a wider spread of owners prepared to put money in. Traditionally this club has sold players to stave off recurring financial problems, but that's the last thing I want to do at present. We have received offers recently, but they were turned down.'

He added that David Kohler's dream was to have an arena near Junction 10 of the M1, and his, without being so adventurous in terms of high technology, was for the same thing. Despite everything that had happened, he believed it was still achievable.

Fans welcomed the fact that Bassett was the first chairman for some time who could claim a long-term history as a true supporter of the club. He first went to matches in the 1970s while running his own small business in Lyndhurst Road, close to the ground. He went on to expand his business into Universal Salvage Auctions, which, as the financial press reported later, would eventually be the subject of a £57 million takeover by its rival Copart. According to the *Daily Mail*, Bassett started in 1968, 'dabbling for years in repairing old Volkswagens' and, when he sold up, his family received a £15-million-plus windfall. Bassett said he had temporarily stopped attending Luton games when the members-only scheme was introduced in the 1980s, but returned later when that era's boardroom changed. He hoped that fans disenchanted during the recent Kohler era would now follow his example and return to the fold.

Luton spent much of the 1999-2000 season hovering round mid-table, never far from mounting a play-off challenge, and certainly never looking likely to plummet downwards. Just after the halfway point Bassett met the Supporters Club and said the long-time dream of a new stadium could become a reality within three years. It was reported that Bassett 'spoke from the heart' at this meeting, and after two hours of answering questions was given the longest ovation anyone could remember in the thirteen years the LTSC had been inviting guest speakers. Rod Fountain, the football club's new director of business development, gave a hint of what was to come when he told the meeting: 'Cliff Bassett does not want to continue with everything on his own shoulders. He wants others to be involved, and running a football club must not just be a one-man ego trip. We have been inundated with people willing to invest, and our task now is to analyse who is best to take the club forward. We have received a number of very interesting applications and proposals, and we are reviewing them … people will have to show they have deep pockets, not just by buying stock in the club, but by introducing working capital, certainly until a new stadium can be built. And we don't want the club to be put into a position where people put in their money, and then take it out by player sales.'

The latter point, in particular, was music to the ears. For a number of years now, Luton fans had been under the impression, rightly or wrongly, that the best players were regularly being sold purely in order to pay back loans by directors. And, encouragingly, Fountain promised safeguards to ensure the situation did not arise again where any one person could have total control of the club without the financial muscle to back it up. When a questioner steered the discussion back to the question of a new stadium, Bassett said Junction 10 of the M1 seemed the only realistic answer: 'It's a great place for a stadium, and if we can build there the development potential will aid funding of the stadium. It would take about eighteen months to build, and from what happened over the previous scheme, we believe that if we went for something with a capacity of between 12,000 and 15,000 it would not be called in for another public enquiry.'

Compared to previous seasons, Luton negotiated 1999-2000 with little drama, although events in the closing weeks were disappointing to the 6,000 faithful. First, versatile local product Gary Doherty was sold to Spurs for an initial fee of £1 million; then a goal conceded by an unnecessary handball in the last minute of the season's final game saw Town finish 13th instead of 10th. The difference of three places was not merely academic, as far as angry Lennie Lawrence was concerned, and the perpetrator, defender Alan White, never played for the club again.

Shortly after the season ended, the boardroom changes Cliff Bassett had hinted at became a reality. And they were not merely minor adjustments either, more like a revolution. Bassett sold his controlling interest to Mike Watson-Challis, a 74-year-old businessman who had earlier done a seven-year stint (1984-91) as a Luton director. Bassett would remain as a director, but colleagues Chris Green and Nigel Terry stood down to become vice-presidents. Watson-Challis, the former owner of Baldock Town FC, was said to be a tax exile who spent much of his time abroad. He brought with him to the board his company secretary and financial expert, Eric Hood, plus the former Fulham player John Mitchell, who had tried to buy into the club in 1993. Rob Stringer, a senior vice-president of Sony Music and long-time Luton fan, was added to the board along with supporters' representative Yvonne Fletcher, former chair of the official Supporters Club and a driving force behind the fans group FLAG. Shortly afterwards, Graham Kelly, the former FA chief executive, joined the board, playing a largely 'ambassadorial' role.

For Watson-Challis, becoming the majority shareholder in his favourite club was said to have been a birthday present from his businesswoman wife Sheila. In a later interview with Tony Francis of the *Telegraph*, Sheila admitted: 'We were enjoying a glass of wine in the garden, thinking how lucky we were to have money in the bank and the children set up for life. I asked

Mike if there was anything he'd always wanted. If I'd known he was going to say Luton Town, I'd have kept quiet.'

Battle-hardened Luton fans are not easily shockable, but there were certainly raised eyebrows when the new regime's first major step in the summer of 2000 was to sack Lennie Lawrence and replace him with former Hatters midfield star Ricky Hill. Although Lawrence was not widely popular among the fans, during his four-and-a-half years in charge he had made a tidy £5 million transfer profit and was a reliable and stabilising influence. However, the inexperienced Hill was an exciting if risky appointment which caught the fans' imagination in a big way. If Watson-Challis chose Hill in order to court popularity, he certainly succeeded.

Watson-Challis promised that he and his new board were true 'football people' who were willing to dig deep to back their new manager. He immediately put his money where his mouth was and splashed out a huge fee by Luton standards, £425,000, on Bournemouth goalkeeper Mark Ovendale. Another Hill swoop saw the return of a second former star, Mark Stein, 34, who had been on the verge of signing for Swansea.

For his part, the amiable Hill was like a child in a sweet shop. He said managing his former club was the 'ultimate' job as far as he was concerned: 'I cannot tell you how proud I am to be manager of Luton Town.' He promised to try and reproduce the attacking excitement of the Pleat era when he'd won full caps for England. Watson-Challis wanted Hill, together with new assistant Chris Ramsey, to revive Luton's image and former glories. Many fans applauded the appointment and agreed that if anyone could do this it was the popular Hill. Were we looking through rose-tinted spectacles again? You bet we were.

As one of the first black players to play for England, Hill had overcome racist abuse and demonstrated deep resolve despite his 'nice guy' image. He had also bounced back from several bad injuries and showed great loyalty in fourteen years at Luton, during which he played more than 500 first-team games and stayed put despite overtures from Bobby Robson's Ipswich, Atletico Madrid and Paris St Germain. A row over a free transfer tainted his 1989 departure, after which he played and coached in the United States with Rodney Marsh's Tampa Bay Rowdies (winning Coach of the Year) and at Cape Canaveral. Late he linked up with mentor David Pleat to coach at Sheffield Wednesday and Tottenham.

'It still feels a little strange to be back and walking up these stairs as manager, but I am getting used to it,' he said. 'Nothing has really changed. It's the same as always. So, it is easy. In a way, yes, it's a bit like coming home but I'm here to do a job and do it properly.' Hill insisted his experience had ensured he wasn't 'soft', despite his apparently easy-going nature, and that he was ready for the battleground that was English football's third tier. In his own career, incidentally, he could recall only two bookings in eighteen years as a player, and one of these was merely for handball.

Off the field, an intriguing innovation was the inclusion of a supporters' representative on the Board of Directors. Yvonne Fletcher had started supporting Luton as a small girl and was now sports desk manager at *The Guardian* in London. She said: 'I grew up in Stanton Road, Luton, a street full of boys who used to play football, and I joined in. I loved football then, and still do. My dad took me to my first match in 1970, standing on the Kenilworth Road terrace to see the Town beat Portsmouth 2-1, and I was hooked. I switched to standing in the enclosure so that I could be near the tunnel and collect autographs, and a little group of us became friends then, and still are. Now we all sit in that area as season-ticket holders.'

Yvonne was a key player in FLAG, whose bid to take over the club failed, but had led to an offer of a place on the board. After consideration FLAG accepted the offer, and a secret ballot nominated Yvonne to occupy the seat. She said her early impression of the board was encouraging as there were no ego-trippers, but a good mix of experience. 'I suppose that I have to prove myself twice over – as a woman in what is traditionally a man's game, and as a supporter in an environment where few fans go.'

At the beginning of the new 2000-01 season all the exciting changes at the club masked one fundamental problem. The reshuffled team wasn't good enough. Ricky Hill probably knew he wouldn't quite achieve the blend he wanted in the early games, but surely didn't envisage the struggle that went into October and beyond. Fans suspected all was not well when his assistant Chris Ramsey parted company with the club, ostensibly by 'mutual consent' but amid gossip about discontent over training methods. An awful run of thirteen league and cup games without a win was halted by victory over Brentford, but then came a calamitous home defeat by Wrexham in which Luton amazingly frittered away a 3-0 lead. Universally popular or not, the writing was on the wall for Hill. He hurriedly thrust a couple of new Scandinavian signings into the side to try and improve things, but after a 0-3 home defeat by Bristol City on 11th November the board reluctantly called time.

A parting of the ways had become inevitable, even though Hill enjoyed, and still does, the sort of 'special' relationship with supporters that meant in many eyes he could do no wrong. His record was two wins, eight draws and eleven defeats (six at home) from 21 league and cup games in charge. Even his most loyal disciple couldn't blame the Luton board for wanting to change things before it was too late. Hill's recently recruited assistant Lil Fuccillo, another popular player from an earlier era, was put in charge and reserve coach John Moore promoted to be his assistant. Was Fuccillo purely a 'caretaker' or in the job for the long haul? The answer remained unclear so far as the fans were concerned, but it was certainly a chance for him to prove his worth while the board weighed their options.

Fuccillo was a Bedfordshire boy of Italian extraction who first came to Kenilworth Road as an apprentice in 1973, overcoming two broken legs to make nearly 200 first-team appearances. More recently he had stints as coach and manager at Peterborough. He admitted he was stunned at the speed of events, having returned to Luton only recently as a scout. He'd been quickly promoted to a coaching role when Ramsey left and had now moved up the ladder again. It was highly reminiscent of what happened to David Pleat back in 1978. Fuccillo declared his first priority was to find a natural leader on the field, someone in the mould of ex-Luton skippers Brian Horton or Steve Foster.

Fuccillo shook things up but couldn't create a winning team overnight, and by January 2001 the board was evidently starting to think about recruiting a manager from outside the club. Watson-Challis confirmed later that the directors had become concerned over the club's prospects and had drawn up a list of 'household names' they might approach to take the reins. Their first choice was Joe Kinnear, the former Wimbledon boss, who was now recovered from a heart attack and working in an advisory role for fellow relegation candidates Oxford United.

Kinnear had joined the Manor Ground club in the autumn as a consultant, and then agreed to become director of football in November. But less than two months later he walked out on Oxford, saying he was taking time out to look after his health and spend more time with his family. Oxford fans were furious when he then pitched up at Luton just days later at the beginning of February. He was announced as Luton's director of football, to work alongside Fuccillo, but before long was occupying the manager's seat himself, Fuccillo shunting back into a coaching role. Viewed from the outside it was like a bizarre game of musical chairs, but Kinnear was an experienced man with a strong personality who wanted thing done his way. He wasn't afraid to step on toes, and, to the fans' delight, results improved instantly.

Kinnear, who had just turned 54, had been away from the dugout for around eighteen months following his heart attack at Hillsborough while managing Wimbledon. He enjoyed great success on limited resources with the Dons, winning more than one third of his 364 games in charge there. His outspoken, fearless style of management quickly won the hearts of Luton fans, who loved the way he acknowledged their songs, even when the lyrics made reference to the portly Kinnear figure. He showed he wouldn't stand for any nonsense early on when bringing on Tresor Kandol as a sub at Notts County, decided he didn't like what he saw and promptly replaced him with another sub just minutes later.

Early on, Kinnear's arrival was like a whirlwind through the Kenilworth Road corridors and Luton's form was transformed, with five wins and a draw from his first seven games. Sadly the magic started to wear off after this, even though he spent £50,000 on Northampton's burly striker Steve Howard on deadline day. The final thirteen games of the campaign resulted in six draws and seven defeats and Luton were relegated to the basement division for the first time in 33 years. They had used 33 different players, operating with probably the weakest squad since the miserable days of the mid-1960s. Clearly the summer of 2001 would be one of change, and one development that gave instant cause for optimism was the news that chairman Watson-Challis had purchased the 55-acres of land near the M1 which the club wanted for its new stadium.

Writing as both newshound and fan, Brian Swain reported this as 'the news some of us have awaited for 50 years or more'. He said the greenfield site near Junction 10 was the same one David Kohler had wanted to acquire, but which the Luton Hoo estate refused to sell, although Luton council was reportedly ready to consider a compulsory purchase order if necessary. Watson-Challis said his negotiations to buy the site had started soon after he took control of the club in 2000. Swain reflected: 'Fifty years ago, we thought the new ground would be at Skimpot, on a sports field which was owned by Laporte's and which was later used as a training facility by the Town. It never happened – a Tesco superstore now takes up most of that area, with Beds FA's offices behind it. The new ground project still has some way to go, but Luton Borough Council, owners of the Kenilworth Road stadium, and keen to regenerate the Bury Park area [around the current ground], is backing the scheme in principle, and a planning application is being prepared by the club's architects.'

Watson-Challis said his purchase of the land was the first step in protecting the long-term future of the club, and he was delighted the club would remain in Luton: 'Along with the club's projects directors, Eric Hood and John Mitchell, I will work exhaustively over the coming months to secure appropriate planning permission. I believe our dream and vision can become a reality, and begin a new era for the town. Coupled with the appointment of Joe Kinnear, it demonstrates our long-term commitment to once again make the club a major force in football.'

Meanwhile, the national sporting media was fascinated that a high-profile heart-attack victim was undertaking the stressful task of trying to revive Luton Town's fortunes in League Three, particularly as he'd turned down an offer to manage better-placed Sheffield Wednesday. Kinnear told the *Independent* Luton was a tough challenge, reminiscent of the one that faced him at Wimbledon in 1992: 'When I arrived here, confidence was a bit low, understandably. They'd only won four [league] matches [out of 26] and had

conceded goals for fun. But I've impressed on them the importance of tac-
tically shutting up shop once we get in front, and improved our scoring
from set plays – something we concentrated on at Wimbledon.'

There was great curiosity about the state of his health, but Kinnear
insisted he was over his coronary crisis. 'When you're laying in hospital,
staring at that heart monitor and listening to that ******* bleep going every
day of your life, you just give prayers for the fact you're alive. Football is
the last thing on your mind. Even when you get up to walk, you're so out
of condition, it's like climbing Mount Everest. Then, after the surgeons
had cleaned out all my pipes they discovered I was committing cholesterol
suicide. Now it's porridge for breakfast every day. I should have the three
bears sitting round the table with me. Then it's apple and banana for lunch,
and in the evening I have the luxury of a piece of fish staring at me.'

Kinnear admitted that relegation (four months after his arrival) was the
most sickening experience of his 37 years in football. The record books
showed that Luton were the first club to have sunk from the top division
to the fourth twice. To reverse the decline Kinnear rang the changes over
the summer and recruited his former Wimbledon assistant Mick Harford
as coach (it was Harford's third stint at Luton) and the former Olympic
gold medallist Daley Thompson as fitness coach. Nine players were
released on free transfers, two others were put on the transfer list, and Paul
McLaren and Petri Helin switched to new clubs. Coming the other way
through the revolving door was a procession that included Kevin Nicholls,
Aaron Skelton, Adrian Forbes, Carl Griffiths, Carl Emberson, Paul
Hughes, Russell Perrett, Ian Hillier, Chris Coyne, Ahmet Brkovic, Dean
Crowe and Jean-Louis Valois.

A good start to 2001-02 was clouded by news that former goalkeeping
legend Les Sealey had collapsed and died at just 43 years old, but the smiles
returned as the Luton promotion bid gathered momentum through the
autumn of 2001. The fun and games included a strange episode that almost
resulted in banishment from the club for centre-forward Steve Howard.
Desperate to get off the mark for the season, Howard insisted on taking a
penalty at York even though he was not the appointed taker of spot-kicks.
After he missed, the referee ordered a re-take and Howard, defying teammates and management orders, insisted on stepping up again. The crowd
couldn't believe their eyes as a fracas developed with Howard resisting all
efforts to wrestle the ball from his clutches. He then missed again with a
poor kick and was immediately subbed by a furious Kinnear. He was
dropped and threatened with the sack, but was given a second chance after
apologising and accepting disciplinary action. Kinnear called the incident
unprofessional, but said dealing with it had been no problem after his years
of supervising Vinnie Jones and John Fashanu at Wimbledon. Howard

returned to the team and quickly became a consistent goalscorer, going on to muster one of the highest goal tallies in the club's history.

After the worst performance of the season, a 1-4 defeat at Macclesfield, Kinnear saw his squad decimated through injury and illness. He decided it was impossible to field a credible team and refused to travel to the scheduled away game at Kidderminster. The League took a dim view and came down heavily despite Kinnear's claims Luton should have been exonerated because 24 players were unavailable, and he had made strenuous efforts to sign replacements at short notice. The League felt Town should have gone to Aggborough with whatever team they could muster, including youth players, and fined them £20,000 for not fulfilling the fixture, plus £10,000 compensation to Kidderminster to cover their costs. Kinnear reckoned fielding a team of youth players would have been a 'dis-service' to the rest of the teams in the division.

By the time Christmas came and went, Luton were established in a two-way fight for the Nationwide Division Three title with Paul Sturrock's Plymouth Argyle. The two clubs opened a gap at the top and were clearly a cut above the rest of the division, much of Town's attacking potency coming from the left flank work of Matthew Taylor and Frenchman Jean-Louis Valois. Skipper Kevin Nicholls and the rejuvenated Howard added the muscle and physical commitment needed at this level.

Success on the field in early 2002 was matched by positive developments off it, and the Watson-Challis regime seemed pleased at how their plans were progressing. The Head of Planning at Luton Council issued a report in February which seemed encouraging as regards the prospect of a new stadium. It gave an illuminating summary of the current state of play and listed certain 'changed circumstances' which had recently boosted the stadium proposal. It said that Luton Airport Parkway Station had now opened and could provide rail access close to the Watson-Challis land at Junction 10. And the proposed local Translink bus project included an extension from the new railway station to the site.

Meanwhile, the Government had agreed in principle to funding £21.3 million for improvements in the 'East Luton Corridor' which should also aid development of the stadium. Another Government project – the London-South Midlands Multi-Modal Study – was in progress, including the M1 corridor and assumptions about a stadium coming to Junction 10. Additionally, the Highways Agency and National Express were understood to be looking to provide an M1 coach stop facility at Junction 10. It seemed as if the people who mattered recognised that a stadium was coming.

The council report stated that the owners of Luton Town had maintained a dialogue with council officers, retaining some of the consultants who worked on the Kohlerdome proposals, and bringing in others. Plans indicated a 'traditional' but modern stadium, such as those built for Bolton and Huddersfield. The primary function would be for football, but there would be facilities for general use, including conferences and functions and supporting developments including a hotel, restaurants and enabling development, as well as a park-and-ride and coach stop facility.

Councillors were told that if Luton Town was relocated, the Borough Council would be able to take possession of the existing ground and the club's parking areas on Maple Road and Hazelbury Crescent. An obvious advantage in removing the 96-year-old stadium would be the improvement to the quality of life of existing residents. Any new use of the Hatters' land that generated additional traffic in the narrow surrounding streets was likely to be unacceptable on highway safety and environmental grounds. There was a lack of open space in the whole of the Bury Park area, and the ground represented a rare opportunity to provide new space.

Meanwhile, March 2002 saw the collapse of ITV Digital which would leave the Football League owed £178 million, a situation that would have serious consequences for hard-up clubs like Luton, most of whom had budgeted to receive a share of the ITV money. However, by now the title race in Division Three was entering the home straight and most Luton fans preferred to keep their eye on the ball at this exciting time.

A 3-0 victory over Bristol Rovers in February launched Luton on a run of twelve consecutive wins, which not only smashed the previous club record, but saw them clinch promotion with four games still to go. The Hatters briefly held top spot after a crushing 4-0 win at Hull, but Plymouth kept winning too and held on to pole position, Town's run ending with a 0-0 draw against Macclesfield. Not lifting the title was a disappointment, having amassed 97 points, but overall it had been a magnificent season and the celebrations were loud and long. A highly significant statistic was the tally of 15 away wins, helped in no small part by the magnificent away support Town received – over the course of the season the club was accompanied on the road by an average of well over 1,000 Luton fans per match, a real rarity at 'fourth division' level.

The new season of 2002-03 started with the directors unable to name a date for submission of their planning application for the new ground, but deputy chairman Eric Hood said much work was going on behind the scenes and it would happen soon. Weeks later they would be frustrated by snail-like progress but still making positive noises. On the field, there was plenty to cheer about, however, particularly a 2-1 Worthington Cup win at local rivals Watford, which featured brilliant goals by Matthew Spring and Steve Howard. Sadly the occasion was soured a little by outbreaks of hooliganism, and later fourteen individuals would be jailed for their part in the trouble.

The Hatters were in the top six by the start of 2003 and spent the latter half of the season on the fringe of the play-off race. The majority of fans were happy with the team, happy with the manager, and even happy with the chairman when he conducted an 'Any Questions?' session in the Eric Morecambe Suite at Kenilworth Road. The standing ovation he was afforded at the end was almost worthy of the man the room was named after. Along with directors Eric Hood and Yvonne Fletcher, the chairman was grilled for two hours about the club's plans, its prospects and the money situation. Watson-Challis was coughing up £4.5million a year to cover current losses, it was stated, because like most Nationwide League clubs, home gate receipts fell well short of running costs.

The push for promotion was still on target, but Hood admitted that the stadium scheme had 'slipped a little' with more paperwork and funding arrangements to be worked out. With reference to a previous owner, Watson-Challis promised he wouldn't name the stadium after himself. The plan was currently for a ground with a capacity of 15,000, capable of being increased to 20,000 or 25,000 seats later. Other uses would enable it to earn revenue day by day, instead of being a once-a-fortnight operation. Building costs would be around £15 million, but there would be other expenditures, including the moving of a huge electricity pylon on the site. The club expected to receive a grant of around £2 million from Sport England. Hood hoped the planning application would be ready for submission but as it would be referred on to the Secretary of State there would be further delays.

At the end of 2002-03, with Kinnear and Harford having steered the Hatters to finishing ninth, the final home programme sent the Town fans on their summer holidays with a message of hope regarding the future. Given the storm that was about to break, the optimism would prove somewhat misplaced. Vice-chairman Hood told the fans: 'Many people have been working extremely hard to turn our long-held dream into reality. I am really encouraged by the amount of goodwill that exists towards the club, and the determination to ensure that it has a bright future. In particular, we continue to benefit from Luton Borough Council's excellent support and guidance on the proposed stadium and its enabling development. We can now pencil a date into our diaries by which time we have a realistic chance of being in our new, purpose-built stadium. That date is the start of the 2005-06 season.

'As much as I would like to say more, there is a limit to what I can add at the moment. Details of the enabling development, so vital to the success of the project, must remain "commercial in confidence" for now. But in the next few months we should be able to announce all our relocation and development plans. I am sure you will find them worth the wait. The club has been trying to relocate for the past 30 years. But never before have we been this close to making it happen. And, arguably, this is the most important issue of all. We own the land and are investing in its development to ensure the long-term future of the club is secure. That is why I believe the future looks good.'

Taken at face value, it was a bullish message which sounded full of hope and good intentions. But among those not fully convinced was non-executive director Graham Kelly. The former FA chief had watched carefully the events going on around him recently and began to wonder whether it was worth continuing in his so-called 'ambassadorial' role on the Luton Town board. Reflecting later that summer, Kelly said: 'It became clear to me that, although the chairman was a man of considerable means, he could not continue to pour money into the club the way he had done. I reluctantly decided to resign after a rollercoaster three years, mainly because I was unable to influence affairs sufficiently. I was very sad to leave, because I was proud of my association with Luton, who were the south's first professional club, founded in the century before last and before some of the current giants of the game.'

Most of the supporters who took the trouble to consider the statement by Eric Hood must have concluded that things were moving, albeit slowly, in the right direction. All the more mystifying then, when a mere week or two after it was published, chairman Watson-Challis suddenly announced he was selling up. The club was to change ownership yet again. It was a bewildering and unexpected development and one that would plunge Luton Town into the club's deepest crisis yet.

Watson-Challis was by now in his late 70s reportedly £20 million lighter than when he bought Luton from Cliff Bassett three years earlier. He had decided the time was right to retire, but reassured supporters the club would still be moving to the 55-acre site near Junction 10. It was not immediately clarified if he would retain ownership of the land. He now wanted to take a back seat as a Life President of the club, and would be letting others do the donkey work, he said. He reportedly sold his majority shareholding for a nominal fee of just £4, a deal which presumably meant the new owners were taking on the debts and commitments that went along with their new acquisition.

An injection of new blood was all very well, but what soon began to worry everybody was the fact that the new owners refused to identify themselves. The local press struggled to confirm who they were and Watson-Challis wasn't saying either. Why was there a wall of silence?

A scoreline to savour from October 1986 (Mike Newell bagged three of them)

Luton's second FA Cup semi-final defeat in three years was by Wimbledon

Popular Mick Harford on the
20th anniversary of the
Littlewoods Cup win

Mark Stein scored goals in two separate stints at Luton, as did elder brother Brian

A glorious 3-0 win at Upton Park helped Luton to Wembley in 1989

Marvin Johnson (left) and John Dreyer, defensive kingpins during the 1990s

Chairman David Kohler rewards loyal travelling fans with free tickets in 1995

Home, sweet home: Kenilworth Road, pictured 50 years after the first plans to scrap it

Fans welcome a new era at the club on the first day of the 1999-2000 season

Record signing Lars Elstrup, who walked out on the club in 1991 in bizarre fashion

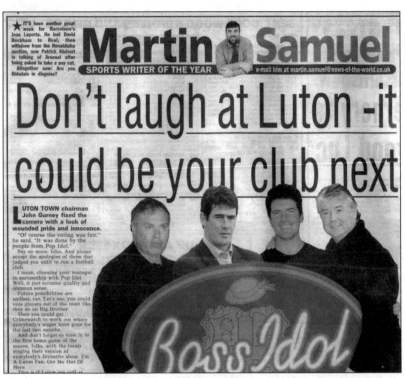

News of the World coverage of the strange events of June 2003

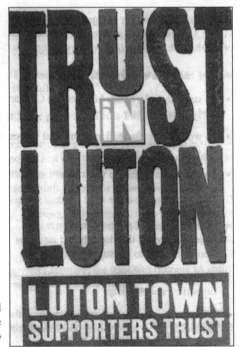

Trust in Luton was formed to represent the fans in the summer of 2003

LUTON TOWN SUPPORTERS TRUST

Share Number
119

Registration Number
29061R

Registered Office: 17 Grove Place
Bedford, MK40 3JJ

Registered with the Registrar of Friendly Societies as an Industrial & Provident Society

This is to certify that
Rob Hadgraft

Is the registered proprietor of a £1 fully paid up share as a member of the Luton Town Supporters Trust, subject to the constitution of the said society.

Given under the Common Seal of the said Society this day the 11ᵗʰ July 2003

Tony Murray
Chairman

Kelvin Dunn
Membership Secretary

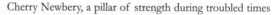

Supporters came forward in numbers in 2003 to buy shares in Trust in Luton

Cherry Newbery, a pillar of strength during troubled times

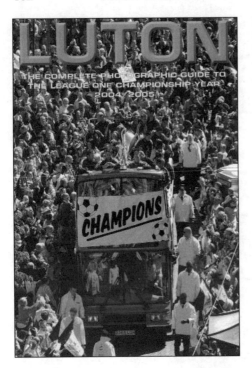

Mike Newell and Kevin
Nicholls led Luton to
League One glory in 2005

Away fans are amazed to
enter Luton's ground via
neighbouring 'backyards'

1980s heroes Steve Foster (left) and Darron McDonough greet Luton fans in 2008

Skipper Kevin Nicholls, back at his 'spiritual home' in the summer of 2008

Cliff Bassett had spells as supporter, director, chairman
and majority shareholder at Luton Town

Before the popularity of
websites, fanzines represented the voice of the fans

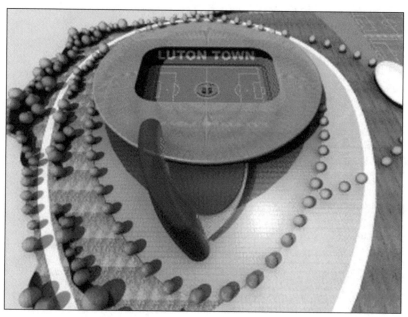

Ambitious plans for Junction 12 of the M1, drawn up in 2006

Mike Watson-Challis sells up in 2003 to spark yet another Luton crisis

The front-men for LTFC2020:
Gary Sweet (left), Nick Owen (centre) and Stephen Browne

Luton legends Mick Harford
(left) and Ricky Hill pull on
the shirt one last time in 2008

Loyal Luton Supporters Club make their presence felt during the 2008 troubles

Old friends meet up at the 20th anniversary of the Littlewoods Cup win

Help our Hatters

To the Football Association,

\>> I believe that the FA punishment against Luton Town over the irregular payments to agents is grossly unfair. A £50,000 fine and a 10-point penalty for next season is totally unreasonable and should be rescinded.

\>> The guilty parties are former directors of the club, so why punish the supporters or LTFC2020, the new consortium looking to take the Hatters out of administration?

\>> It was a Luton Town employee who drew the FA's attention to the financial irregularities. How does punishing the club so heavily encourage a whistleblowing culture to keep football clean?

\>> The fans have suffered enough. Two relegations in two years, a points deduction for entering administration and the consequential sale of our top players last season. Plus a likely further 15-point penalty from the Football League for exiting administration.

\>> Luton Town did not gain an on-field advantage from the rule breaks. Our punishment is not consistent with previous decisions, eg West Ham's unregistered players.

\>> I appeal to the FA to show some compassion for one of the oldest professional football clubs in the south of England and reconsider the club's penalty if it decides to appeal.

Even *The Times* was sympathetic towards Luton's plight in August 2008

Leading articles

Who Would Crush a Hatter on a Wheel?

Luton's almost certain relegation from the Football League is a kick too far

In 1961 the great Denis Law managed to score six goals against Luton Town, and still lose. Torrential rain forced the FA Cup tie to be abandoned when his Manchester City side were winning 6-2, and Luton (the Hatters) won the rearranged match.

Recently, the story of Luton Town's finances has been more dramatic than the club's most extraordinary game. A happy ending, however, looks less likely than it must have done at the moment Mr Law completed his second hat-trick.

The Football League has informed Luton that it will start the season with a deduction of 30 points, meaning that it has to win ten games simply to return to zero (see page 100). Ten of the points were docked by the Football Association because of a breach in the rules regarding agents' fees, the other 20 for failing to meet the league's conditions on arrangements with its creditors.

The administration of the Football League in recent times has been impressive. Its progressive leadership has seen crowds grow. This time, however, it has made a mistake.

Finishing in one of the bottom two spaces in Luton Town's division means being relegated from the Football League. The probability of a side avoiding this fate when it begins at a 30-point disadvantage is vanishingly small. Deducting so many points amounts to expelling the club from the league. Such a punishment is too harsh.

Of course the football authorities must enforce rules. Yet they should also have regard to the emotional and financial investment made by supporters in their team. The league's administrators should take a look today at the faces of Luton's devastated young fans and ask themselves — is this really what I took up this job to do?

CRISIS 8 (SUMMER 2003)
Champagne Ideas, Coca-Cola Pockets

As far as all Luton fans are concerned, the summer of 2003 was an emotional roller-coaster ride that is never likely to be matched again. In the wacky world of the Mad Hatters, that is saying something. Rarely can a single football club have generated as much interest and gossip over an eight-week period without a single ball being kicked in anger.

The 56 days from mid-May to mid-July 2003 saw fans glued to their computer screens as more and more improbable developments unravelled at Kenilworth Road, the websites and message-boards providing 'live' sources of information that the press and broadcast media couldn't match. The story of what was happening to Luton Town FC became so weird and wonderful that fans simply couldn't bear to wait for the evening news, or the next day's papers. They were compelled to seek out the latest gossip immediately and the supporters' websites reported record levels of hits. The saga began around a fortnight after the 2002-03 season ended. This is how it unfolded:

DAY 1: TUESDAY, 20TH MAY 2003

Disturbing rumours circulate in Luton that chairman Mike Watson-Challis is ready to sell his majority shareholding in the club, a big surprise considering the recent success of the team and the fact he had purchased the land for the new stadium. A worried Supporters Club chairman Mark Chapman contacts the *Luton News* today to express his fears and seek more information. Just minutes after Chapman's chat with a reporter, a statement is issued on the football club's official website. It confirms that Watson-Challis is retiring, selling up and swapping his chairman's role for that of Life President.

Watson-Challis says: 'When I took over LTFC, it was on its knees. I gave myself three years to get it back on its feet and to put in place plans that would secure its financial future. With the team looking stronger than ever and well-placed for an excellent season next year, now seemed the right time to secure a deal that will allow the Club to realise its full potential. We are convinced the deal struck today is the best one for the future of the Club.'

DAY 2: WEDNESDAY, 21ST MAY 2003

Phone and e-mail lines are red hot among the curious fans, particularly Supporters Club officials. There has been no clarification over the identity of the new football club owners or their plans and all remains quiet at Kenilworth Road, with no further clues issued about what is going on. It is the lull before the storm.

DAY 3: THURSDAY, 22ND MAY 2003

Unconfirmed rumours are circulating that the front-man for the consortium that has reportedly bought the club is John Gurney, a businessman who was a key figure in a recent episode that saw Bedford Rugby Club nearly go to the wall. Staff at Kenilworth Road are thought to be largely in the dark over what is happening. Unbeknown to them, and to just about everyone else, two official letters have been posted by recorded delivery today which will see the mayhem really kick off.

DAY 4: FRIDAY 23RD MAY 2003

Today we know for sure that disturbing things are happening at our football club. It emerges that manager Joe Kinnear and his assistant Mick Harford, arguably the most popular management team in the club's history, have been sacked. They learned their fate via recorded delivery letters in this morning's post. Harford's postie knocked on his door at 7.40am and after signing for his letter and reading the contents, Harford phones Kinnear to ask why he's been sacked. Kinnear is shocked and assures Harford he knows nothing of this. The little red card on his doormat tells him he also has a letter to collect, so it's off in the Bentley to the local sorting office. Kinnear finds he too has been dismissed. When the bombshell news reaches the fans it has more impact than even the selling of the club – this was truly the moment when the excrement hit the air-cooling device. The rumour mill goes into overdrive and news spreads that ex-Portsmouth and Northampton manager Terry Fenwick is likely to be Luton's new manager. One bright spark even insists ex-England boss Terry Venables was seen at Kenilworth Road yesterday. Rather unsatisfactorily, fans are merely told a meeting at Kenilworth Road next Tuesday will be followed by an official statement.

DAY 5: SATURDAY, 24TH MAY 2003

Mick Harford speaks to reporters and tells how he and Kinnear were escorted off the premises when they drove to the club to collect their possessions and say their goodbyes. He says: 'I think it's a very sad day. I think in fairness it's the worst decision in the club's history. I had no inkling this was going to happen. There was a total lack of compassion from the football club. I woke up and there was a letter on my doorstep. What I did to deserve being dismissed in such a cold, callous manner I don't know. It was disgraceful really. My heart and soul was always at Luton. It was totally out of the blue. We've had players and other managers ringing up saying "We can't believe it." I turned up at the club to clear my desk and take my personal belongings. I said goodbye to the staff. It was a sad day basically. I don't know who the [new] directors are and who the board are down there to be honest. How they can make a decision based on football without even talking to us is beyond me. We were told to leave the building, believe it or not, which is a sad thing. My heart and soul is in Luton, and when that happened I was totally devastated. I personally believe we had a fantastic chance of getting into the First Division next year. And the fans – it's been nothing more than sensational the response we've had from the fans over the last two years. I've always had a tremendous relationship with the fans. I can't thank them enough. They're fantastic. I spoke to Joe half an hour ago and he said, "Please tell them thanks for singing [the] Big Fat Joe [song] and stuff like that".'

Meanwhile, former England defender Terry Fenwick confirms he has been interviewed for the vacant manager's position: 'I will be told on Tuesday if I am being offered the job. That does not mean for certain I will take it as I am also in discussions with another Second Division club further north.' This is mystifying, for Fenwick's recent managerial track record is five defeats from seven games in a brief spell in charge at Northampton.

Day 6: Sunday, 25th May 2003
Fans livid over the sacking of Kinnear and Harford spend today publicising a protest they are planning outside the ground for Tuesday, when the still-unnamed new owners are expected at the ground, along with potential new managerial candidates. Many have decided not to renew season-tickets as they don't wish to hand over cash to owners who have yet to reveal themselves.

Day 7: Monday, 26th May 2003
It is confirmed there will be a board meeting and press briefing tomorrow at Kenilworth Road, and the fans' protest plans gain momentum, with support on the message-boards indicating hundreds are planning to attend. Among the postings and messages, someone has managed to publicise e-mail addresses for Terry Fenwick, and over the past couple of days hundreds of messages urging him to stay away have apparently been sent.

Day 8: Tuesday, 27th May 2003
Fans gather at the ground, some at breakfast time, although many miss the first significant action when a Bentley pulls into the Maple Road car park around 9.15am and Joe Kinnear emerges, accompanied by three smartly dressed associates. Fans crane their necks and cheering breaks out as they

spot their hero. He waves as he makes his way inside. He returns barely ten minutes later stating that the new owners had failed to show. Asked who the new owners were, Kinnear replies, 'It's out of my hands now.'

The protest had been called for 10am, but resourceful members of the group find out the board meeting will now be 3pm, so many disappear and return later. The crowd in the street swells to more than 300 by mid-afternoon and they are joined by journalists, camera crews and police. Cherry Newbery emerges from the club offices and tells the fans the meeting has been delayed until 4pm and she is booed and jeered, which seems a little harsh as she is merely passing on news.

The noise level suddenly soars when a number of vehicles arrive at the top end of the ground, behind the Kenilworth end, containing men in suits. Vehicles are pummelled and spat at, and the occupants look shocked. A Range Rover, thought to be occupied by a representative of the new owners, is seen to turn away after hesitating and then drives round the block before reappearing, thus giving the crowd time to prepare a hail of eggs. No board meeting actually takes place, as there was not a quorum of directors present, but after a while the assembled press is allowed into the building. The police presence increases slightly as people inside the offices make to leave, but there is more car kicking and egg throwing and one fan is led away by police. The demonstrators begin to disperse around 6.30pm, although some stay to speak to Yvonne Fletcher, the fans' representative on the board.

Two of the abused visitors, it transpires, were Roger Terrell and Lee Power, sent in by the mystery consortium to run the football side of things, and expecting to be appointed as Luton's new chairman and vice-chairman. The former is a recently resigned Peterborough director and the latter an ex-player with Norwich, Bradford City, Peterborough, Hibs and Dundee. The pair spoke to reporters to explain they were not investing in the club or being paid by the consortium.

Power said: 'We thought we were coming here today to be appointed but after what happened on the way in we are reconsidering our position. We were approached by someone representing the directors, asking us to run the football side of the football club, which obviously we were delighted to do at that time. We would be looking to appoint a manager in the next seven-to-ten days. We have spoken to three or four people over the weekend but I would like to stress that we were not involved in the decision about what happened to Joe and Mick. We inherited that. It was there long before we came along. We both love football. Me, personally – having played – thought it was a fantastic opportunity to be on the board and to help run a football club. It was an experience I was looking forward to until about 45 minutes ago.'

DAY 9: WEDNESDAY, 28TH MAY 2003

The *Luton News* runs a story naming Mr John Gurney as the man they believe has taken over Luton Town FC. Meanwhile, director Yvonne Fletcher issues a statement promising to do everything she can to help and says she is 100 per cent behind the idea of forming a Supporters' Trust in order to prevent one majority shareholder being able to control the club in future. She confirms that the only people who turned up at the ground yesterday were the 'hired hands', none of whom were part of the 'mystery' consortium. Nobody would tell her who the new owners were, she said, and as she and Cherry Newbery were the only directors present, they were unable to hold a proper board meeting. When a shaken Terrell and Power told them they wanted to reconsider their positions, the meeting was adjourned. 'I am as frustrated as every other supporter,' she adds.

DAY 10: THURSDAY, 29TH MAY 2003

Former owner Mike Watson-Challis calls the club from abroad to issue an angry reaction to a BBC interview in which Supporters Club chairman Chapman claimed nobody knew the club was up for sale and, now it was sold, a 'wall of silence' had been erected. Watson-Challis said he did the deal with the new consortium in the best interests of the club and he remained part of the new set-up. He said the future of the club was guaranteed, the funding of a new stadium at junction 10 of the M1 guaranteed, and changes now made were a responsibility of the new management team. He couldn't continue to fund the club indefinitely and it may have folded if it wasn't for the takeover. He appealed to the fans to give the new consortium a chance to prove themselves and said their identity was far less important than what they were able to do for the club. However, Watson-Challis' assertion that the club 'had been on its knees' when he took over back in 2000 angers the man who sold it to him, Cliff Bassett, who is critical of what has gone on since then.

DAY 11: FRIDAY, 30TH MAY 2003

Another amazing twist to the saga as the new owners post a message on the club's official website inviting supporters to vote for the next team manager. They call this opportunity 'a unique exercise in sport'. The statement reads: 'Beginning next week, we will be taking nominations for people you want us to approach. Following that, we will draw up a shortlist and again supporters will be able to phone in their votes for their favourite from the shortlist. This will give us the final selection. The final vote will then be taken with three groups having a say: Season Ticket-holders, all other supporters, and the Board. Season Ticket-holders will have five votes each, other supporters will have one vote each. To qualify for the additional voting rights, supporters must buy their Season Tickets by close of business next Friday, June 6th. More details will be given next week.'

Far from being happy at being asked for their opinions, the vast majority of fans treat this idea as ludicrous and unworkable. Most of those who take part will clearly vote for Kinnear/Harford and a few comedians might choose big names such as Ferguson or Wenger, and of course the whole thing would be open to abuse from rival fans. 'You just couldn't make this sort of thing up,' says one amazed respondent. There is more bafflement when one news source quotes deputy chairman Eric Hood as saying Kinnear and Harford have not actually been sacked at all. It seems there is a difference of opinion over the authority carried by the letters of dismissal.

DAY 12: SATURDAY, 31ST MAY 2003

It emerges that the person who signed the letters to Kinnear and Harford was Peter Miller, a commercial consultant working for Northampton Town FC. The Football League says it will investigate as their rules state nobody can have an 'interest' in two member clubs simultaneously. Mr. Miller is quoted as saying: 'I very much regret signing those letters. I went to Luton only twice. I was asked to sign the letters because I was the only person at the club that day able to do that [on behalf of the new owners].' Meanwhile, further gossip this weekend surrounds the players and staff allegedly not being paid their wages for the month of May. This is denied by the club.

DAY 13: SUNDAY, 1ST JUNE 2003

Roger Terrell appears on BBC Radio 5 Live's *Sportsweek* and says he knows little about the consortium but believed it involved overseas investors. He said he had nothing to do with the sacking of Kinnear, whom he believed had the best managerial contract outside the Premiership. The BBC's Gary Richardson concludes that it didn't bode well for Luton that the club's [potential] chairman didn't know who he was working for, and didn't know why the manager had been sacked.

Now that John Gurney is widely recognised as being the front-man of the new consortium, local news outlets have been probing his background. He is reported to be 57, hailing originally from Hemel Hempstead and the *Beds on Sunday* newspaper group recalls he took over Bedford Rugby Club in 1999, buying it from boxing promoter Frank Warren for just £1, along with its debts. Popular coach Rudi Straeuli was surprisingly sacked within a few days, and before long various plans were announced involving moving or selling the club to Coventry or Ashford. Local enthusiasts rallied round to raise £750,000 in the space of five days to save the club, and control was seized from Mr Gurney by a local businessman. The current Bedford Blues chairman was quoted today: 'We just keep our fingers crossed that the same awful shenanigans will not repeat itself at our beloved Luton Town.' It is also reported that Mr Gurney had been involved in takeovers at non-league football clubs Farnborough and Southall. It was also reported that he was accused in 1999, but not convicted, of importing with others millions of pounds worth of cocaine.

DAY 14: MONDAY, 2ND JUNE 2003

As many expected, after the rocky ride they were given at Kenilworth Road, Messrs Terrell and Power have now confirmed they won't be joining the Luton board after all. Power has already had a hand in shaping Luton's future, however, for he has used a mutual friend (Tim Sherwood) to approach Mike Newell about becoming the club's next manager. Newell played with Sherwood at Blackburn and welcomed the call, for he is currently out of work, having just parted company with Hartlepool. Newell has fond memories of his playing days at Luton and agrees to be put 'in the frame', presumably blissfully ignorant at this stage about the plan for a phone vote for the Luton job.

Today's other big news is that a newly formed supporters' action group, Trust in Luton (TiL), is up and running and already urging Hatters fans to boycott the phone vote, dismissing it as a PR stunt and a cheap and unworkable imitation of the hit TV show *Pop Idol*. The Trust feels the vote is a tactic to draw attention away from the major debate of who the new owners are and to encourage season-ticket holders to renew. They also believe the voting system could be flawed as there is no indication how many votes the Luton Town board would have and whether the club could veto any specific candidate. 'Should a premium rate telephone line be used for these purposes, it could spell a £5 effective increase in your season-ticket price with no hope of your nominated manager being employed,' said the Trust. 'We know it is imperative to embrace the fans' legitimate opinions in the running of any football club. We therefore ask you to decline to vote in this senseless scheme.'

Trust in Luton also announces it has put together a working party and is inviting fans to attend a public meeting inside the Luton ground next Saturday. It has joined forces with Supporters Direct, a Government-funded body whose aim is 'to offer support, advice and information to groups of supporters who wish to play a responsible part in the life of the clubs they support.' Many fans are pleased to hear something positive and constructive is happening and a big crowd is expected.

Fans also welcome today's article in a national newspaper by former FA executive and Luton director Graham Kelly, who ponders the intentions of

Luton's mysterious new owners. He said he had called the FA for a chat about their inordinate delay in introducing a 'fit and proper persons' criterion for the ownership of football clubs. He writes: 'Needless to say, the fans are now worried sick. They have no idea who owns their club, which is astonishing. Why the big mystery? If I had bought a club with a proud tradition I would be shouting it from the rooftops even if they were a bit rickety.' He added that some fans feared a possible ground-share proposal 'with a certain peripatetic First Division club whose name I vowed never to utter again' [Wimbledon/MK Dons].

DAY 15: TUESDAY, 3RD JUNE 2003

More remarkable developments as the saga enters its third week. The club has apparently written to Mick Harford offering him his job back, and are talking to Joe Kinnear about a possible return. They have also 'regretted the actions' of Peter Miler in sending the letters which sacked them. They say: '[We are] committed to the democratic process, however, and any return would have to subject to selection through the polling system that is currently in place.' But with a 50p-per-minute premium phoneline in place, many fans see this as an attempt to get them to pay through the nose simply to get their favourites back.

Meanwhile, the man lambasted for sacking the Luton heroes, Peter Miller, responds with his side of the story. He denies any business partnership with John Gurney but says he met him fairly recently in connection with providing commercial advice for a planned purchase of Peterborough United. This was followed by a similar meeting regarding Luton Town. As a consultant he visited Kenilworth Road twice and on the first occasion was given the letters and told he was the only person present appointed by the new owners and should therefore sign them. He confirmed he had recommended Messrs Terrell and Power to the new owners, and at all times both Luton and Northampton were aware he was advising both clubs as a consultant. He'd now resigned his Luton duties and had been appointed commercial director at Northampton Town.

DAY 16: WEDNESDAY, 4TH JUNE 2003

Mick Harford says he is not accepting the invitation to return to his beloved Luton: 'For reasons best known to themselves, the club and the faceless new consortium have treated me as if I have done an injustice. Nothing can be further from the truth, and in my opinion it makes the offer of employment in these circumstances totally untenable. I would like to give my heartfelt thanks to the fans who have supported me so tremendously over the years and continue to do so at this difficult time.' Meanwhile, Town's chief scout Trevor Hartley joins Harford among the ranks of the unemployed. He was made redundant, rather than sacked, meaning the club cannot replace him and will therefore be operating without a chief scout. Among the fascinated but horrified onlookers as events continue to unfold is Barry Fry, outspoken boss of Peterborough. He knows many of the people involved and says he finds it all very disturbing: 'The invisible men worry me to death.'

Day 17: Thursday, 5th June 2003
News of another initiative guaranteed to upset the fans leaks out and is covered on local radio. Luton's new owners have apparently had preliminary talks with the local airport about a commercial link-up which could lead to the football club changing its name to mirror that of the airport – i.e. London-Luton FC. Supporters Club chairman Chapman is enraged: 'It's a disgrace. It's like changing Bolton Wanderers' name to Manchester-Bolton. We are nothing to do with London.' The football club reacts to the publicity by faxing the radio station and requesting an apology. On top of all this, the *Daily Mail* reveals today that the Luton players are being asked to take a pay cut, a move that angers their union, the PFA. Trust in Luton announces plans for this Saturday's big meeting, with guest speakers from a variety of backgrounds and publicises messages of support received from ex-FA boss Graham Kelly and the broadcaster and long-standing Luton fan Nick Owen.

Day 18: Friday, 6th June 2003
Fans' representative on the Luton board, Yvonne Fletcher, reports back after a meeting with Gurney, attended by his associate Esther Chan, but is frustrated at having learned little of real substance. She also attempted to get answers from Watson-Challis about why he felt his deal with Mr Gurney had been 'in the best interests of the club' but had got nowhere.

Later this evening a statement is posted on the club's official website stating the new owners have the express desire to build a new ground and keep any supporting revenues within the club. There would be no developer 'creaming off the profits' from a new stadium complex, and the revenue streams from car parking, for example, will go to the club. It pointed out the club had contracted nineteen players for 2003-04 season, whose salaries meant the club's budget is one of the three highest in the division even before any new players were added. The statement complained that the income deficit was being aggravated by the fans' boycott of season-ticket renewals and warned that the 'negative' atmosphere currently around the club was putting off potential commercial sponsors and investors. It also warned that Luton could not go into Administration again as this would lead to liquidation as in the case of Maidstone FC in 1992. Luton

were losing just under £500,000 per month, it was claimed, and any organisation or Trust wanting to be concerned with running the club should bear
in mind that £5-6 million would be required. The statement reads like a real
tale of woe and some interpret it as a signal the new owners are struggling
with what they have taken on.

DAY 19: SATURDAY, 7TH JUNE 2003
More than 2,000 defiant fans turn up and sit in the Main Stand on a sunny
afternoon to hear the Trust in Luton speakers. Dave Boyle of Supporters
Direct, a Wimbledon fan who now follows the new club AFC Wimbledon,
receives a rousing reception as he proclaims: 'This is your club and you're
not going to let anybody mess around with it.' He explains the purpose and
aims of a supporters trust and reckoned all the skills needed to run a football club were sitting in front of him already: 'Harness this and you've got
a club to be reckoned with.'

Ian Pearce, BBC Three Counties Radio presenter and long-time Luton
fan, raises a laugh by saying that after only one speech they were already
more organised than the people allegedly running the football club.
'Pearcey' says before the fans hand the club any more money for season-
tickets and replica kits, they need to know exactly who was running things
at Kenilworth Road: 'The cameras are here today. They will show intelligent, caring and passionate supporters who care for the plight of their
club,' he adds. Borough councilor Peter Chapman, a Hatters fan for 37
years, reminds the crowd that although the Council owned the current
ground, this ownership was on behalf of the people of Luton. The meeting finishes with an overwhelming show of hands to agree to the Trust's
formation, which Dave Boyle describes as a resounding message that the
fans want their club back.

John Gurney, who has still not named any of the purported consortium
members he is supposedly representing, reacts in friendly fashion to the
fans' show of strength and purpose. He posts another statement on the
official website welcoming formation of the Trust and even pledges £1,000
towards getting it started. He also pays tribute to Cherry Newbery ('who is
Mrs Luton Town') and Yvonne Fletcher for their efforts in liaising between
board and fans. The conciliatory mood continues as he admits: 'We have all
started badly, but the last three weeks have shown that Luton Town still has
fierce – perhaps too fierce at times – and passionate support … We apologise for the fact that our silence up to this point has created speculation,
but any comment would have been nearly as ill-informed as the comments
made by those with no authority to comment, or by the media reporting
bus landings on the far side if the moon.' He promises that detailed plans
for Luton's future have been documented and are about to be released.

Another message has filtered through from former owner Watson-Challis, who says he is disappointed to learn that supporters were giving the new management a hard time. 'Whatever the new people are arranging or organising, rest assured it is for the benefit of all concerned.' He says full support was needed from everyone, not criticism. The club was not under attack and the withholding of season-ticket money was 'not an intelligent way to keep the club going up or encourage more supporters'.

DAY 20: SUNDAY, 8TH JUNE 2003

Watson-Challis' request for patience is not welcomed by fans who prefer to echo the sentiments of the sacked Harford in today's *Sunday Mirror*. Harford says: 'I fear for the Hatters. It's like a *Carry On* film. The club has become the laughing-stock of football.' The *Mirror* says the Football League has asked Luton to explain the chaotic takeover. Spokesman John Nagle said: 'The League has written to Luton seeking clarification on a number of issues. But there is little we can do to stop a takeover. And the club would have to apply to the Football League to change its name [to London-Luton].'

DAY 21: MONDAY, 9TH JUNE 2003

The true state of the nation behind the closed doors of Kenilworth Road is finally confirmed today when Cherry Newbery and Yvonne Fletcher resign their positions as directors, saying they are unable to continue in the present circumstances. Cherry, who also quits as company secretary, is in a delicate position as she will be continuing her club secretary duties.

Yvonne is walking out altogether, however, and is therefore able to issue a more detailed explanation: 'I feel my position has become completely untenable. My role over the last three years has been difficult at times but became increasingly so this year when very little information was available from the Chairman or his deputy and there was a complete lack of openness about their future plans for the club. I cannot continue to serve on the board while the [new] owners of the club are unknown, the ownership of, and plans for, the land at Junction 10 are unknown, the proposed make-up of a new board is unknown and the plans for financing the club are unknown. The club's management seems to be in chaos, with no professional leadership emerging from the business consortium which, we are led to believe, has bought the club from Mike Watson-Challis. Business is seemingly being conducted via late night web-site postings rather than through the usual commercial channels. I was delighted to be one of some 3,000 supporters who were at Kenilworth Road on Saturday to give a unanimous mandate to set up a supporters trust. I look forward to giving the embryonic organisation, Trust in Luton, any assistance I can to ensure the supporters have a real say in the running of their football club in the future. It is with great sadness that I have concluded that I can best help to secure the future of Luton Town by working outside of the club rather than with the current owners, whoever they may be.'

The 'prospectus' promised by the club at the weekend appears on the official website and proves to be a document far longer and more radical than anybody expected. The first part was apparently prepared before the takeover, and is to be updated by a second instalment 24 hours later. The contents of both horrify fans but give journalists some meaty stories. At one point Luton is referred to as 'a rotten little football club'. It includes ideas that sound ridiculously far-fetched, but which are apparently being pursued in all seriousness. It explains that ownership of Luton Town is the key to unlocking the development potential of the freehold site near Junction 10. It says the annual profit available to the club could be up to £100 million. It alleges Joe Kinnear earned around £400,000 a year and Luton had probably the largest outgoings of any club in its division with virtually no commercial income. Unlike rival clubs, Luton boasted a huge potential catchment area and, with the M1 and Thameslink, was the most accessible club in the south. It said if the club entered into a strategic partnership with the Airport the club name should be changed to London-Luton, a well-established brand name. Also envisaged was a new stadium built on a concrete raft over the current M1 spur road, with a roof kept in place by air pressure similar to the Pontiac Dome in Detroit.

Then comes the *coup de grace* – an idea so wild even the report's author calls it 'the mad part of the plan'. It involves a scheme whereby the roads on the new stadium site will double as a motor racing track. Planning permission would be sought for a Formula One-standard track and one Grand Prix per year would be staged, which would make Luton (or 'London-Luton') the richest football club in Europe. If not possible to stage a British Grand Prix here, a European, Irish or Atlantic States Grand Prix would be sought. Other opportunities included obtaining a NBA and NFL expansion franchise from the USA, in order to set up 'Team Europe'. It all added up to the most exciting development of any sort in Europe in a decade, claimed the report.

Some of the above is greeted by hilarity, but what particularly upsets and disturbs Luton fans is the following passage: 'At the heart of this [development], completely by accident, is a small football club, which has failed time and again in the past and without a major development will fail time and again in the future. The change will be radical and the small mindedness of the "football club people", who will want to maintain the status quo as they feel they will lose the identity of "the rotten little football club" in a large scheme and the opportunities it provides for power to small egos and hooliganism, will be the biggest single challenge. Having fought small-minded interests before in the neighbouring town [Bedford] over the puffed-up middle class members' interest in rugby, the power of the position of the local club in its market should never be underestimated. The club [Luton Town] is available for a nominal sum but the land has to be bought as part of the deal. The problem is the ongoing liability created by the existing owners in respect of player salaries, which the club is stuck with for a further year.'

The document concluded with reference back to John Gurney's past battles with the *Beds on Sunday* newspaper during his ownership of Bedford RFC: 'If negative media starts it is like an avalanche falling down a mountain. No one will stop it until it reaches the bottom. The risks are worth it because it would be impossible to find this opportunity and potential return again.'

DAY 22: TUESDAY, 10 JUNE 2003

Following release of yesterday's pre-sale document, today we are due to see a brand new report which was evidently compiled over the past two weeks by Gurney and his consultants. In his latest website posting, he says: 'It will be hard reading but it is basically about how we turn the present bankrupt club into the largest football club in the country. Yes I hear everyone laughing and I would have been laughing with them until I understood the facts. He then apologises for 'appearing to go to ground' and for the fact that a mess was made in the early days after the sale.

Gurney admits he would love to have Kinnear and Harford back but is now committed to the voting system: 'The nomination process has now finished and some outstanding names have been put forward. Despite the gloom and doom merchants' forecast that the choice would be between Donald Duck and Alex Ferguson, the process has been very productive. Cherry Newbery received as many nominations for the manager's job as Alex Ferguson did. It has produced very good quality nominations from all around the world. Few would be surprised that Joe and Mick are slightly ahead of all the other candidates … nominations include Mike Newell, Gardner Spiers, Terry Fenwick, Iain Dowie, Bruce Rioch, Nigel Clough, Jan Molby, Steve Coppell, John Hollins, Stuart Pearce, Alan Ball, Gudjon Thordarson, Brian Stein, Paul Parker, Kevin Blackwell, Danny Wilson etc.

'Next week, eight names will go forward for voting … and the three candidates with the most votes [will] form a shortlist. The club will agree terms in advance with all three candidates so that if they are elected, they will be appointed. Our problem will come next week if Joe should be on the shortlist and refuses to agree terms and come back. We cannot then put him on the short list. I would urge 10,000 fans to vote for Joe this week.

'Yes, the calls cost a little bit of money but so do the calls to Sky, the BBC etc. The club is not making a fortune out of this but if Joe receives an overwhelming vote I can then go to him and show him the results and use these votes to solve the one remaining problem – the cost of Joe.'

He also says a small group who want Kinnear and Harford back have agreed to sponsor their wages and he provided a phone number to receive further offers. It is hard to believe the cheek of it all.

The statement says: 'We have come up with a mind-boggling scheme, which will create in excess of £50 million per year for the football club. This requires a key strategic partnership and alignment with the council and the airport. We can achieve what we want to achieve only if the club, the players, the fans and the sponsors work together. Yes we have made a mess of some things but this does not excuse kicking club officials' cars, death threats to people's families, beating up the club solicitor and all the other undesirable matters on the unofficial websites. Is it any wonder that people are reluctant to raise their heads if they are going to be threatened in this way? This is counter-productive and will scare off investors … Seriously, cut out the threats, the message-board crap and the intimidation. All you are doing is scaring off investment in the club. Constructive comment is welcome.

'Other issues will arise. The Milton Keynes Wombles [sic] are in Administration. Should we buy them, merge them with Luton (kill them off) and call the new club Luton Town (or London-Luton), play at Luton and effectively buy a back door promotion to Division One? If we decide that is what we want to do, let's go and raise the money to do it. If it's a bad idea, let's forget it and slog at winning a place in the First Division the hard way.'

Gurney concludes with an almost plaintive appeal for support: 'I would have given up yesterday if it had not been for one or two positive postings on the websites. If there are people out there who are willing to say let's give it a go, then everyone should try to rally together to save the club. Let's have some more positive postings. So you don't like my ideas. Where are the ideas of all the knockers? If it was not for those few positive postings I would be recommending putting the club into liquidation and catching that jet plane. A last light still flickers …'

DAY 23: WEDNESDAY, 11TH JUNE 2003

Following the internet publication of his lengthy documents, Gurney, who is now described as Managing Director (Designate), stages a press conference. He is apparently undaunted by critics calling his statements 'rambling' and full of spelling and grammatical errors. He complains to the man from the *Evening Standard* that he has become a public hate figure in Luton: 'I am being followed and am receiving hourly death threats. I am now banned from the club by the police as I constitute a potential breach of the peace and they cannot guarantee my safety.'

Bedford RFC reacts angrily today to comments about them. The Blues' board said it was surprised by the 'vitriolic and inaccurate comments contained in the rambling, incoherent statements posted on the Hatters website'. The statements, they said, were similar in content and style to those regularly issued on their own website when Gurney had control of their club. They felt sympathy for Luton and said the similarities between their ordeal and today's situation 'brings a shudder to the spine'.

Day 24: Thursday, 12th June 2003

Amid all this mayhem, some people do seem to be taking sensible steps to stop the madness. Widespread coverage in the media is all very well, but most Luton fans want to stop this soap opera, not sit back and be fascinated by it. It is encouraging to hear that Luton South MP Margaret Moran is raising her concerns in the Commons. And there is also news that the League Managers' Association chief executive John Barnwell has contacted Trust in Luton to condemn the plan to vote for a new manager, which he says brings the job into disrepute. 'It is staggering these people are allowed to run football clubs,' says Barnwell. John Gurney appears on local radio (he reportedly had to speak from a studio outside Luton, for security reasons) and Trust in Luton say they heard nothing in this interview to change their appeal to all Luton fans to withhold cash from the football club until further notice. They called talk of Luton's 'liquidation' just another scare tactic.

Day 25: Friday, 13th June 2003

News emerges today of another new row, prompted by a meeting at the football club premises involving John Gurney, Yvonne Fletcher and former chairman David Kohler. Given that Mr Kohler's last involvement at the club saw it sink into Administration, most fans react with horror. Gurney issues a statement that he believes Kohler was acting as a broker of good faith on behalf of Trust in Luton: 'There seems to be a certain amount of conflict of interest with the role of broker of good faith. Frankly, we don't have the time for this. We have a club to run. It is time to put up or shut up. If the supporters [via the Trust] have the funds and the credibility to purchase the Club then come to the table in the proper way and demonstrate it ...'

Inevitably these comments let loose a hornet's nest and Fletcher hits back: 'I am not an officer of the Trust in Luton interim committee. TiL do not intend to purchase the club, i.e. the majority shareholding, and have never stated that they would. The Trust would like to have a shareholding in the club, as many other supporters' trusts have in their clubs. David Kohler is not acting on behalf of TiL in any capacity whatsoever. He contacted me for my personal opinion on supporters' and potential investors' reaction to any possible involvement he might have in trying to help resolve the current situation at Luton Town. David Kohler clearly stated to me, before asking me about the meeting detailed below, that he does not want to own a shareholding in Luton Town … The purpose of the meeting was to try to establish what John Gurney is offering for sale. Is it the majority shareholding in Luton Town? Does it include the land at J10? What level of debt attaches to any deal, and is Mike Watson-Challis a creditor of the club? John Gurney arrived at the meeting but, when David Kohler told him I would be attending, he refused to take the meeting.'

TiL have also stepped forward to distance themselves from this strange case of 'the meeting that never was'.

DAY 26: SATURDAY, 14TH JUNE 2003

Trust in Luton come up with a new idea, launching a pledge scheme whereby fans can record the amount they will be spending at the football club once ownership issues are resolved to the satisfaction of TiL. This should cover all expenditure, not just season tickets, and involves filling out a special form. It's effectively a means of demonstrating intent to 'invest' when the circumstances are right. TiL says it will send a clear message to the current owners that the fans, sponsors and investors are out there, but not prepared to give their money in the current climate.

Belated but heartening news from the hallowed portals of the FA in Soho Square. Investors in football clubs will soon have to prove their credentials to the FA via a new fit-and-proper-person test. It is in response to the growing uncertainty surrounding football finances – eighteen clubs are now in, or have been through Administration. Referring to recent events at Luton and Exeter City, a spokesman said: 'These cases are becoming more frequent. We do not want to get into situations where someone takes over a club and two months later it is in disarray. These people are often not supporters of the club, but in the end it is the real fans who suffer.'

DAY 27: SUNDAY, 15TH JUNE 2003

One of the many horrified onlookers, with Luton close to his heart, has been David Pleat. Tottenham's Director of Football is today rumoured to be thinking about joining a new consortium to take control at Luton: 'I am sure there are honorable people who must be straining at the leash to try and make a contribution and bring some order to the situation.'

TiL today repeat their offer to meet John Gurney at a neutral venue, in the presence of the media, an offer he accepted earlier but has still yet to happen. TiL say this will allow their aims to be clarified for Mr Gurney's benefit, as some of his recent statements indicate he has been labouring under a number of misapprehensions.

Day 28: Monday, 16th June 2003
The shortlist of three candidates are named for the bizarre managerial election contest. They are the sacked Joe Kinnear, former Luton, Everton and Blackburn striker Mike Newell, and the ex-Cheltenham and Stoke boss Steve Cotterill. TiL emphasise today that fans should boycott the vote altogether, which means the outcome is hard to predict. Kinnear is the overwhelming favourite among fans, but most seem to believe it won't be a fair and true election, and that the winner will simply be the candidate who is available, rather than the one with most votes.

Day 29: Tuesday, 17th June 2003
Luton Borough Council, owners of the Kenilworth Road site, today publicly issue a copy of a letter they have sent to John Gurney, calling on him to explain his development plans for Luton Town. Deputy leader Jenny Davies noted that the success of the club was inextricably linked to the reputation and well-being of the town, and the councillors viewed recent developments with considerable alarm, and called for a meeting with him. The Football League and TiL are among the others currently also asking to sit down with him.

Day 30: Wednesday, 18th June 2003
Trust in Luton speak out again today, outlining worries that a 'smash and grab' is under way at Luton: 'Mr. Gurney must show how he intends to implement his ideas … until he does so, it is difficult to see beyond this being merely a smash-and-grab scenario. [He] must name his investors and the other members of his consortium. Whilst he continues to refuse to do this, we will continue to think that none exist.' The statement continues: 'Junction 10 is obviously the main lure for any potential investor in LTFC and the club is the vehicle towards the granting of planning permission. There are investors with the good of the club at heart and we need them to come forward … This whole sorry mess needs to come to a conclusion very soon because this club is too important to too many people, and we will not allow the greed of a few to come before the good of LTFC.'

Day 31: Thursday, 19th June 2003
John Gurney appears on BBC Three Counties Radio's breakfast show and answers questions from the show's presenters and fans who call in. He says discussions are under way with the previous owner's legal people regarding

inherited debts and loans to the club which had been assigned to the current owners and would have to be taken on by any new buyers. He says he met Joe Kinnear in Spain a few days ago and a draft contract was being drawn up for his return as manager. He says it is extremely unlikely the club would go into Administration, and although creditors could force a winding up, this was also unlikely. Consortium pledges currently total £3.5 million after some of them had withdrawn. He had agreed to take part in a TV programme called *Trouble at the Top* and camera crews were being allowed access to meetings.

DAY 32: FRIDAY, 20TH JUNE 2003
Kinnear is currently on holiday in Spain and won't be back when the club's election results are announced next Monday, whether or not he is declared winner. He is currently said to have captured around 86 per cent of the vote, and if he remains ahead will apparently be asked for his final decision before the big announcement at Monday lunchtime. John Gurneys says if Kinnear rejects the job (as many fans are convinced he will), whoever finishes second will be offered it. Steve Cotterill and Mike Newell have both apparently indicated they would like to manage Luton if Kinnear doesn't return.

DAY 33: SATURDAY, 21ST JUNE 2003
Today is the year's longest day, and midsummer madness is all around. Kinnear is reported to be unhappy over the contract he was offered to return, and has not had assurances he sought about his role at Luton. Some fans who renewed their season-tickets early are said to be asking for their money back. A transfer embargo imposed on the club will go on indefinitely, it is reported. And BBC Three Counties Radio have been told the phone vote is proving a lot closer than expected – with Cotterill the closest challenger to Kinnear.

DAY 34: SUNDAY, 22ND JUNE 2003
The chances of the managerial vote running entirely smoothly always seemed slim, and a spanner is thrown in the works today when the so-called second-favourite Steve Cotterill rules himself out of the running. He states Luton was 'the right club, but at the wrong time'. The 38-year-old led Cheltenham into Division Two from non-league football a year ago, and then had short spells in charge at Stoke and as assistant to Howard Wilkinson at Sunderland. He is currently out of work, but clearly something about the Luton job has put him off.

Nothing is certain at Luton these days, but Mike Newell seems set to get the job tomorrow, by virtue of being the only candidate still interested.

The announcement is in danger of looking shambolic – just as many predicted. Newell, also 38, enjoyed a good career as a striker, representing thirteen different clubs and winning England Under-21 and 'B' caps. After 19 goals in 68 games for Luton in the mid-1980s, he won a Champions medal as Alan Shearer's strike partner at Blackburn. After a spell coaching at Tranmere, he landed his first managerial position during last season, replacing Chris Turner at Hartlepool, with the team top of Division Three. Despite a dip in form, Pool gained promotion as runners-up. Newell didn't see eye to eye with the club's board and his contract was cancelled last month. According to Newell: 'I enjoyed the football at Hartlepool, but the owners were oil men. They wanted to run Hartlepool like it was an oil company. I was not prepared to do that.'

Day 35: Monday, 23rd June 2003

For all his perceived faults, Luton's new 'managing director designate' certainly likes to create a bit of a drama to entertain onlookers. Although everyone knew the likely outcome of his managerial election, Gurney seems determined today to crank up the tension a little more. He delays the 1pm press conference called to announce the outcome, saying there has to be a recount as the result was so close. When finally deemed ready, the results, with very little detail revealed, were read out: Mike Newell had won and was the new manager. The players voted for Joe Kinnear, the season-ticket holders for Kinnear, but the board, shareholders and general fans all voted for Newell. The latter would therefore take the reins and sign a two-year deal.

Gurney says the difference between the top two candidates was a mere four votes when the polls closed. However, as the only candidate waiting in the office next door was Newell, the relevance of today's events was looking doubtful. Would Newell really have travelled all this way from his home in the North had he not known the outcome beforehand? Newell's body language suggests he is highly uncomfortable over the circus going on around him, but when speaking to the media was able to demonstrate he wanted the job badly, despite the problems at the club, and this alone was a positive step as far as the fans were concerned. He said he accepted the job regardless of who did or didn't vote for him: 'I first came to Luton Town aged twenty and enjoyed those years immensely. My first job now is to get to know the squad and their skills and experiences, and I can only do that through working with them.'

Gurney says that as the supporters groups urged people not to vote, they could not have cause for complaint about the outcome. TiL welcome the news that a new manager has finally been appointed and wish Newell success, albeit with huge reservations about the way he was hired. They say it is now obvious that not only the fans have problems with the way business is being conducted by the new owners, but the Football League is concerned too.

DAY 36: TUESDAY, 24TH JUNE 2003

The club has announced that a London businessman called Tony Cooper will be its new chairman. He works in the clothing industry and is not widely known among the fans. Meanwhile, five TiL representatives are reflecting this morning on last night's three-hour meeting with Gurney. Filmed by the *Trouble at the Top* TV crew, Mr Gurney told the meeting an announcement about the owners' identity would be made with a fortnight. He also promises to make the data involved in the manager vote available for TiL's perusal, confirms a Football League embargo on the signing of new players until 10th July, agrees a member of the Trust would be democratically elected to the board of directors, and says there was no possibility of a move to Milton Keynes – although a possible ground-share with another sporting club would be considered. He also asked for a measure of decorum from fans using the internet message-boards.

Meanwhile, one of Mike Newell's first steps as manager today was a promise to try and bring Mick Harford back to the club as his assistant. Newell's former Everton colleague Kevin Sheedy is another man rumoured to be on his way as a coach. Some fans are evidently regularly in touch with Harford and pass him a document containing more than 200 goodwill messages which commiserate over his and Kinnear's sacking. Harford says he is delighted and touched and had read it 'more than ten times' and would be passing it to Kinnear on his return from Spain this week.

DAY 37: WEDNESDAY, 25TH JUNE 2003

Trust in Luton today sets out its aim to represent fans' best interests by working alongside the owners of Luton Town, whoever they are or may be in the future. The Trust was not in a position to own the club outright, but from the outset intended to gain a shareholding, which could be increased over time. TiL talk about upholding and preserving the tradition and heritage of the club, and promoting coaching schemes to develop local youngsters.

DAY 38: THURSDAY, 26TH JUNE 2003

The 26th of the month is pay-day at Kenilworth Road – or rather it was. For the second successive month, players and staff are left angry and frustrated as no wages are forthcoming on the due day. Shocked players have already been in touch with the PFA for advice. There is more positive news from Margaret Moran MP, who has met with Sports Minister Richard Caborn to seek his support in the fight for Luton's survival. She says: 'Following my wide ranging discussions with people such as the Football League and the Football Foundation, I have requested the Minister meet with Supporters Direct and fans' representatives to discuss this troubling situation, and am pleased to say that he's agreed.' The MP also invites Luton fans to this evening's All-Party Football Group Inquiry into football finances, which she calls a tonic against the egos, asset strippers and dodgy dealers that are threatening the national game.

DAY 39: FRIDAY, 27TH JUNE 2003

All the talk in the *Beds on Sunday* newspaper offices is of an order issued by John Gurney that its reporters are now banned from the Kenilworth Road press box for the forthcoming season. The paper's coverage of his period at Bedford RFC, and of recent events, continues to upset Mr Gurney, who delegated the job of imposing the ban to secretary Cherry Newbery. Stalwart Cherry is also busy dealing with the problem of the unpaid wages. She is warmly praised for her efforts by team captain Kevin Nicholls, who tells reporters the players have no confidence in the new regime at the club. Nicholls says he is flabbergasted by the owner, who has promised the players he plans to install a one-armed bandit with £25,000 jackpot payouts in the dressing room, yet is unable to pay the wages on time.

DAY 40: SATURDAY, 28TH JUNE 2003

Penning his column for tomorrow's *Independent,* the ex-Luton director Graham Kelly reflects on his recent visit to Westminster to meet the Luton MP and watch the all-party inquiry in action. He is critical of his former employers, the Football Association, for apparently not uttering a word or registering a flicker of interest about the Hatters, who are 'a full-member club that is wallowing in the mire'.

DAY 41: SUNDAY, 29TH JUNE 2003

Luton fans have lived with fear and worry for 40 days and 40 nights now, but slowly the full story is reaching more and more people across the football world. Today sees more extensive coverage of the club's plight in the Sunday papers, including a feature in the Newcastle *Sunday Sun* which reflects on how life at the sharp end of our national game is now attractive only to 'the quixotic, the eccentric, the feckless or the truly reckless businessman'. They noted that an ex-safecracker was in control at Darlington, a UFO-spotter at Carlisle United, and a 'speed freak' at York City.

'Yet that trio have nothing on John Gurney and the other men now in charge of Luton Town. Gurney is no criminal. We know that because a charge against him of conspiracy to import cocaine was dropped in 1999. And non-Luton fans had hitherto looked on more in amusement than with foreboding as the club's new chief executive, backed by the now customary mystery consortium, led the Hatters from crisis to farce.'

The paper marvels at how, just ten minutes after a recount was needed to decide the manager poll, Mike Newell was unveiled as Luton's new boss: 'Good luck to him. Lord knows he will need it. For the Football League appear ill-inclined to step in and call a halt to the madness afflicting the Hatters and all too many other small clubs besides.'

The oxygen of publicity like this keeps Luton supporters' hopes alive of a quick resolution to the current farce. More encouragement comes today from a lengthy article in the *News of the World* by Sports Writer of the Year Martin Samuel. He writes: 'Choosing your manager in partnership with *Pop Idol*. Well, it just screams quality and common sense. Future possibilities are endless, too. Let's see, you could vote players out of the team like they do on Big Brother. Then you could get *Crimewatch* to work out where everybody's wages have gone for the last two months. And don't forget to tune in to the first home game of the season, folks, with the locals staging their version of everybody's favourite show: I'm A Luton Fan, Get Me Out Of Here. That is if Luton are still at Kenilworth Road, of course. If Gurney has his way, who knows? Milton Keynes, Luton Airport, Silverstone, it would not be a surprise if he announced plans to make them the first club in space. Looking back on the events of the last few weeks, he is halfway there already. In the many column inches devoted to David Beckham's transfer to Real Madrid, his Asian odyssey and his pedicurist, the destruction of a 118-year-old football club appears to be going unnoticed.'

DAY 42: MONDAY, 30TH JUNE 2003

On the day a somewhat bemused playing squad report back for pre-season training, John Gurney speaks again on BBC Three Counties Radio, revealing that 'a legal technicality' is holding up payment of wages. Other snippets he offers include the fact that credit and debit card payment facilities have been withdrawn from the club, and that some of his investors have disappeared due to what he describes as threats, pornographic material and other items on the unofficial message-boards. He also questions Yvonne Fletcher's decision to quit the board in order that she can join the Trust and then begin campaigning for representation on the board.

DAY 43: TUESDAY, 1ST JULY 2003

After his first glimpse of the squad he has inherited, new manager Newell makes a public call for the club's transfer embargo to be lifted. He joins up with coach Brian Stein to take training and takes part in the long-distance running himself. He says the players look fit and eager and remained focused despite their concern at some of the behind-the-scenes issues at Kenilworth Road.

DAY 44: WEDNESDAY, 2ND JULY 2003

Joe Kinnear is back at his north London home after sunning himself in Spain and shows he is in fine form by coming up with a quote that features in many of the next day's papers and news bulletins: 'Luton's new owner has Champagne ideas, but Coca-Cola pockets.' Kinnear says he would consider returning to Luton if another takeover happens ('I had two smashing seasons at Luton and loved every minute of it'). He says he's been offered a two-year contract to return now, but needed more time to consider the wording of a thirteen-page document: 'There were 101 different things in the contract. There was gobbledegook like "he does this, you will do this, he will do that" … but I'm not a puppet manager.'

DAY 45: THURSDAY, 3RD JULY 2003

Trust in Luton announce today that their pledge scheme is flourishing, with pledges now totalling almost £200,000 – and more coming in every day. The scheme shows how much money fans would have spent at the club – on tickets, merchandise or sponsorship – but are withholding until the new owners answer fundamental questions about plans for the future. TiL chairman Tony Murray says it's a fine response, but knew there were many other fans who share the concerns over the club but haven't yet filled in the forms. He said it all helped underline the fact that a football club's main source of income was always the cash the loyal fans spent week in, week out.

DAY 46: FRIDAY, 4TH JULY 2003

It seems the players and staff have now been paid their wages for June, but skipper Kevin Nicholls says a PFA official who came to the ground had warned them not to over-spend as the same sort of delays looked likely in a month's time. Nicholls said: 'It's all down to Cherry [Newbery] for the hard work she's put in and really she's worked miracles. She just thinks she's doing her job, but she's done unbelievably well and everyone appreciates it. She's managed to get us all off the hook this month, but I don't know what's going to happen next month because we're going to be back to square one again.' He adds that the players' growing disenchantment with the new owners was stretched further this afternoon when the managing director (designate) failed to turn up for a scheduled meeting between squad members and PFA representative Bobby Barnes.

DAY 47: SATURDAY, 5TH JULY 2003

Despite the unusual scenario surrounding his arrival, Mike Newell has got cracking with the task of preparing the team for pre-season friendlies and the big kick-off on 9th August. Reflecting on his first eventful week back at Kenilworth Road, he says: 'I'm fine. I am enjoying the job. It's my job to be strong and lead the others, so I don't have any problems about the job or the situation at the moment. I won't let it worry the players or me. It's a difficult period for the club and a lot of clubs are going through financial problems at the moment. It's a strong club and I'm sure we'll get through them. It's also tough for the people working inside the club – the staff – they do jobs day in, day out that go unrecognised and keep the club going and it's difficult when they're not collecting their wages [on time]. The fact that a lot of them have been working here a long time is a massive bonus for us and has been a big help to me. Obviously as the manager of a football club you have to put the players at ease, but there is not a lot you can do when their wages haven't gone in.'

DAY 48: SUNDAY, 6TH JULY 2003

Rumours are surfacing that something is about to happen at the football club that could spell the beginning of end of the current unhappy saga. *Beds on Sunday* speculate that the club will go into Administrative Receivership in a short while, while other sources believe that Joe Kinnear might be joining forces with former Leeds chairman Peter Ridsdale to buy Luton. Meanwhile, David Ledsom, the man who led the purchase of Bedford RFC from John Gurney four years earlier, is interviewed on BBC Three Counties Radio and it makes fascinating and rather worrying listening for Luton fans as he gives a lengthy run-down on the state of Bedford during that period.

DAY 49: MONDAY, 7TH JULY 2003

Graham Kelly, bless him, has been rooting for Luton fans once again in his weekly column in the *Independent*. He says that after criticising his former employers (the FA) for not helping Luton, he has been reminded that the FA's financial advisory unit have in fact been heavily involved, alongside the Football League, in seeking to obtain answers from Luton. He reckons the effectiveness of the football authorities' intervention at Kenilworth Road may only become apparent in the fullness of time. This is reassuring for those fans who didn't realise there actually had been any intervention. Kelly said that Ken Bates' recent sale of Chelsea to a Russian billionaire had provided the perfect illustration of why he wanted to raise concerns about the stewardship of football. Kelly also reveals how he has been asked to consider acting as an independent mediator in an effort to secure agreement between Trust in Luton and John Gurney. Having agreed to this, he'd visited the Centre for Dispute Resolution in East London to brush up on his knowledge of arbitration procedures, but on arriving back at his office was 'mortified' to learn that Mr Gurney did not regard him as an acceptable independent broker and he wouldn't be needed.

Day 50: Tuesday, 8th July 2003

Today's news includes the intriguing revelation that Margaret Moran MP is said to have pulled some strings in order to expedite a Trust in Luton plan to become the major creditor at Luton Town. To the ordinary supporter who doesn't understand insolvency issues, the implications of this are not immediately clear, but it is thought to be positive news. When TiL issue a statement today, things become a little clearer as they confirm they are now 'a newly-established Industrial and Provident Society', and had today met with the Sports Minister Richard Caborn. According to TiL: 'Our representatives' main concerns were for the need for football clubs to be owned and run by open, accountable, fit and proper persons, and for clubs to be recognised as important community assets.'

Mr. Caborn said the Department was working with the FA, Football League and Supporters Direct to introduce regulations and discipline with regard to the management of the national sport, and expressed his wish for the problems at Luton to come to a speedy resolution. He was writing to John Gurney to express his concern at the current situation, and to advise him there needs to be better communication between the Club, the fans, and government on a local and national level.

Day 51: Wednesday, 9th July 2003

Joe Kinnear is contacted by the media about his rumoured involvement in a takeover bid at Luton. With typical candour, he says: 'I've been in the game 30 years and the last thing I want to do is ruin my reputation working for Mr. Blobby. I've been speaking to a lot of people about putting something together, but the thing that makes you really sad is how he was allowed to come in and do this to a smashing club like Luton. I think it's shameful really, especially as we were on the verge of doing big things.' He reveals that his former assistant Harford had finally received outstanding wages after meeting John Gurney this week, but Kinnear claims he was still owed two months wages from last season, plus another year's contract and various bonuses.

Day 52: Thursday, 10th July 2003

The football club's owners are today said to have presented the Football League board with what is described as the first instalment of information about their controversial takeover. The League board specifically asked for this information in order to clarify that Luton had actually been taken over. Last month a League letter asking for such clarification had received no reply.

Day 53: Friday, 11th July 2003

A major breakthrough. Central funding from the Football League to Luton Town Football Club is to be cut off forthwith, the League announced today, and compliance officials are to personally visit the club. The League explains:

'Despite [our] request for details of the club's new owners, Mr John Gurney, the Managing Director of Luton Town FC, has failed to provide details of his consortium. This lack of co-operation is further demonstrated by the club's failure to furnish the League with its business plan or any financial projections as requested at a meeting held on June 19. Information on the club's indebtedness, including a full list of creditors, has also not been forthcoming. In view of the fact that the club has so far been unable to show that it can meet its obligations, the Football League has no option but to withhold all central cash distributions due to Luton Town FC until further notice and maintain the player registration embargo already imposed.'

The decision to withhold the TV monies was greeted by TiL as vindication of their appeal to fans to withhold season-ticket and other monies. The FA's Advisory and Compliance Unit will arrive at Luton's offices next week to begin investigations.

Day 54: Saturday, 12th July 2003

Today is the deadline for discounted prices on season-tickets, but TiL have urged fans to resist the temptation to renew now and to continue to withhold their cash. Their appeal seems to be having a big effect and it is thought only around 1,200 season-tickets have so far been sold, which is far less than normal for this stage of the summer. It has been reported that disillusioned members of staff from the football club have been standing outside the ticket office alongside members of TiL to urge supporters not to purchase tickets at the current time.

Day 55: Sunday, 13th July 2003

The lull before the storm. Something significant is about to happen, and those close to events, particularly the TiL interim committee, spend this sunny Sunday on tenterhooks and barely able to contain themselves. For club secretary Cherry Newbery this weekend, as she will reveal later, was when she finally 'saw light at the end of the tunnel'.

Day 56: Monday, 14th July 2003

After a torrid eight weeks, John Gurney has lost control of Luton Town. The club was today put into Administrative Receivership by its major creditor, and Mr Gurney is no longer in charge. The news this afternoon is greeted with glee by fans who swamp the internet message-boards with messages of a 'good riddance' nature. Even the club's official website struggles to maintain a sense of decorum and keep the excitement in check.

A manoeuvre involving complicated legal issues has seen Mike Watson-Challis' Hatters Holdings company (the major creditor) pass into the control of Trust in Luton, who then inherited the power to call in an Administrator as a protective measure. An insolvency practitioner called Barry Ward was said to be heading to Kenilworth Road immediately, with the upshot that Mr Gurney was no longer in control of the football club. The latter was said this morning to be either in Spain or the Canary Islands, and his financial director and company secretary Andrew Zimbler had resigned from the Luton board. To add to the fun and games, the FA's compliance and advisory unit arrive at the ground to begin their investigations.

An emotional club secretary Cherry Newbery says it is all 'great news' and immediately appeals to all supporters and commercial clients to begin renewing season-tickets, sponsorships and commercial packages safe in the knowledge that their money would now definitely benefit the football club. There is a party atmosphere at the club and arrangements are made to extend ticket office opening hours well into the evenings to cope with the sudden return of the anxious fans, albeit with a warning that recent events mean the club can't accept credit or debit cards.

Many observers identify Cherry Newbery as one of the main heroines of the hour and she sounded jubilant as she said: 'I am very emotional at the moment. I just want the club run properly again please! It's been a manic day, but we'll all be having a little drink and celebrating. It's been a tough, tough time and I want to thank all my staff that have worked so hard under extreme circumstances. I am proud to work for Luton Town and I am a supporter and I am just so glad that this day has come.' She said that telephone calls, messages and e-mails had helped the staff get though 'some very dark days', particularly the messages of a humorous nature.

Newbery told the *Guardian*: 'There had been no hint from the chairman that he was selling the club. At our last away game of the season, like a bolt from the blue, he said "I'm retiring". There was no mention of John Gurney. It was cloak-and-dagger stuff. I saw Gurney, without realising who he was, a number of times in our boardroom during that first week. But he said nothing. It was only with the sacking of Joe and Mick that his name was uncovered.'

Most fans appreciate that Trust in Luton's leadership has done a heroic job too, and a TiL spokesperson confirms that today's events have seen control of the football club wrested from its owners into the hands of an independent Administrator. They praised fans for their solidarity and urged them to honour their spending pledges. Although many issues remained unclear and the club was still in deep trouble, the atmosphere had changed entirely and there was an air of celebration around the place.

Broadcaster Nick Owen, president of the Supporters Club, tells the BBC he's been celebrating and admits 'the old neck oil was shooting down last night I can tell you.' He tells the *Daily Mail*: 'This is everything we've dreamed of after a hellish couple of months when we really didn't know where the club was going – except downhill. What we need is a very strong consortium of fans with money who are keen to be investors, hopefully along with a property man with serious money who can move forward on the construction of a new stadium. Supporters have been nearly killed in the rush to buy season-tickets because now they are prepared to do it.'

The Loyal Luton Supporters Club sound a note of caution by pointing out the football club would need to run a far tighter ship in future and that a degree of understanding and patience with the Administrator would be required as he looked to create a foundation for the future. John Gurney's reaction to developments is reported to be one of anger, with the promise of a legal challenge. He called Luton 'narrow-minded and parochial, like a Lancashire mill town in the South' and said the only future for the club was extinction.

Joe Kinnear continued to be open to a possible return to the club, and, with interesting timing, was invited this week to the University of Luton to receive an honorary Master of Science degree for his services to football. He joins a procession of more than 100 graduates from the Town Hall through the town centre to St Mary's Church. Along the way, Luton fans cheer him heartily and he tells reporters: 'It's a sunny day for me at the moment. It's been a wonderful morning and to get this honour and be able to put some letters after my name for my services for football is fantastic. I'm also so proud it's in Luton because my last two years here have been my most enjoyable in football. I've had a magnificent relationship with the Luton people I'm just saddened and angered at what's happened and that I haven't been able to finish what I've started here. The way back is, unfortunately, not in my hands. If it was I'd already be back [at the football club].'

Luton folk were certainly smiling again, but the question remains – as Nick Owen pointed out on BBC radio – how in the first place did this club ever get sold to a man who 'came from nowhere' when other, better known parties had apparently been in the process of preparing a bid? Perhaps the full story will never be known.

For now it was a case of facing the fact that more difficult times lie ahead for the Hatters, unless a billionaire unexpectedly rides over the Chilterns and ties his horse to dilapidated Kenilworth Road. The new man in temporary charge, Administrator Barry Ward, is about to ask the players to take a pay-cut, the transfer embargo is to continue, and before long players will inevitably be sold. Nevertheless, despite everything, our club is still alive.

POSTSCRIPT

The BBC finally broadcast the edition of *Trouble at the Top* featuring Luton Town in October 2004. One national paper suggested the delays were due to complaints and legal threats by certain people close to events. The show proved a highly illuminating glimpse behind the scenes and compelling viewing for Luton fans. The following passages are taken from reviews of the programme:

The *Independent*: 'Luton Town were taken over 18 months ago by a shadowy Asian consortium linked somehow – we were never quite sure – to a property developer called John Gurney. If Gurney was the villain – he looked like Kerry Packer and moved like a mob heavy – the heroine was the club secretary, 20-year veteran Cherry Newbery, in tears for the staff as pay-day came and went without a sniff of a wage packet. As Gurney led out a couple of the consortium after a tour round the club shop, she whispered to camera: "They're going to destroy us. Without a shadow of a doubt."

'Fortunately, she was wrong. Gurney was history, and showed his true colours at the end. "The people in the Trust have made a very big mistake," he warned. "I never walk away from a fight. And if they expect me to walk away from Luton with nothing, I'll make sure there's nothing to walk away from." Those words should be emblazoned on the office wall of every supporters' trust in the land.'

Evening Standard: 'This story of Luton Town FC is an uplifting David v Goliath tale, showing that the big-money guys don't always win, even in the murky world of modern football. The programme drops the cameras into the club immediately after it has been taken over by a consortium led by property developer John Gurney for a rumoured £4. Needless to say, there are deep suspicions about what Gurney plans to do with the 100-year-old club. Is he planning to asset-strip it, for its valuable town-centre ground and its prime piece of land right next to the M1? Or is he really a keen football fan, anxious to pump money into a lowly club? (Answers on a postcard, please.) Even Gurney admits that he is now in a "superstar hate category" with the Luton supporters, but he doesn't seem too bothered.

Another thing he's not too bothered about is paying the club's staff. Gurney and his chums are so hated that over the summer fans boycotted the purchase of new season-tickets – which means there is no cashflow to keep the club going. It's a tactic aimed at squeezing out the new owners. But can it work? The answer is, yes it can. But Gurney won't go quietly.

Independent on Sunday: 'Think David Brent of *The Office*. Think Major Charles Ingram on *Who Wants To Be A Millionaire?* Add Jeffrey Archer and Neil Hamilton and you might have come up with John Gurney. A man with "champagne ideas but Coca-Cola pockets", in the words of Joe Kinnear, the manager he sacked two days after taking over Luton Town in May 2003. The narrator of this documentary is the excellent Tom Baker, though you can hear *Little Britain* in his voice, which makes it difficult to take him seriously. By 14 July, Gurney had left the club, who are placed into administration. He is last seen riding off into the sunset on a horse called Good Riddance. Secretary Cherry Newbery's impassioned plea to fans everywhere is, "Don't ever let this happen to a football club again." But you just know it will.'

Carlisle United Fans Website: 'It was impossible not to watch the BBC2 documentary *Trouble at the Top* without seeing the similarities to our own position a year or so earlier. Unfortunately there are still stories like Luton's around every season. Currently Wrexham are battling against the machinations of property developer Alex Hamilton, who wants them out of their Racecourse Ground by the end of the season and who could ultimately cost them their place in the Football League. There have been similar tales of woe at Swansea, Exeter, York and Darlington in the last few years. All these clubs have come through the crises but there will be many more battles to be fought in the future unless the football authorities wake up to the dangers and act accordingly.'

POST-POSTSCRIPT

In April 2008, five years after he moved in on Luton Town, John Gurney was declared bankrupt in the High Court. A Football League spokesman confirmed this would bar him in future from owning a football club under the 'fit and proper person' test.

CRISIS 9 (2003-07)
'May You Live in Interesting Times'

Relieved that the midsummer madness was all but over, Luton Town began the new season of 2003-04 in buoyant mood, although still shackled by the restraints of Administrative Receivership. The threat of having to sell the most valuable players at short notice remained, and there would be no chance of replacing them due to a strict Football League transfer embargo.

Nevertheless there was a certain feelgood factor around the place when the campaign kicked off with new manager Mike Newell at the helm. Fans could console themselves that Luton were certainly not the only club suffering severe financial problems just now. An investigation by the *Independent* reflected that although the Nationwide League's clubs these days huddled in the shadow of the media monster known as the Premiership, they were watched last season by nearly 15 million, the highest aggregate attendance since 1965.

But despite these encouraging figures, Oldham nearly went out of business altogether, the wreckage of Wimbledon finally plopped into Administration, Notts County were facing possible expulsion in September, Barnsley were barred from playing friendlies by their Administrator, all in addition to Luton and their troubles. Significantly, all five of these troubled clubs had played in the top flight in relatively recent times.

As widely anticipated, popular Mick Harford returned to Luton as director of football and first-team coach on the eve of the season, just two months after being sacked. And Cherry Newbery, enjoying new heights of popularity, was made chief executive by the Administrator/Receiver Barry Ward. One of their first steps was to announce that the club would allow the club offices to remain open until 7pm on the first Monday of each month as a gesture to allow fans to come in and talk to her directly about club affairs. This 'open door' policy was welcomed, but subsequently only one fan appeared at the first Monday night session (he enjoyed a coffee and a chat) although others did send in questions and comments via phone and e-mail.

Through the matchday programme, the club announced that the events of July had left John Gurney with the controlling shareholding in the club 'through his overseas companies', but he had not been seen at the club since it went into Administration. Mr Ward was now very much in charge – and many money-saving measures had already been taken, including withdrawal from the reserves league and talks about wage-cuts for players (reportedly 30 per cent). The club was effectively up for sale again and there had been plenty of interest following advertising in the national press.

In late August 2003, just as the club was getting back to some sort of normality, there was another burst of bad feeling as star striker Tony Thorpe quit the club to join QPR for a cut-price £50,000. This left a sour taste as it came just a short while after the player had pledged his loyalty to the Hatters and called on the fans to pull together to help them. The fans and manager were livid. In a sign of things to come, Mike Newell was critical of how the deal was done, lambasting 'mercenary, faceless agents with one thing on their minds – pound signs'.

Newell pointed out: 'The FA and FL will have you believe there are rules preventing clubs approaching a player who is under contract. But it seems to me that as long as it's done through an agent, they will be prepared to bury their heads in the sand. As a group I don't like agents and have little respect for them. I never had one as a player – I never felt it necessary. Money has been allowed to pour out of the game in the last decade, money it clearly could not afford. That is still being allowed to happen and I wonder why.' Just for good measure, Newell added a dig at his former employees (Hartlepool, who were Luton's opposition that day): 'I normally say [welcome] to [opposition] directors [in these notes], but in my time as manager of Hartlepool they travelled to only one away game, so it's unlikely they'll be here.' Luton fans loved all this. Here was someone who had strong views and was not afraid to express them in an articulate manner. Although they'd loved his predecessor, Kinnear, they were warming to the new man quickly.

Results were mixed as the season picked up steam, and time passed with the transfer to new ownership dragging on through various legal processes. In November the Administrator put forward in court the three consortiums who had bid for control of the club – and he confirmed one headed by former Luton Town employee Bill Tomlins as his favoured candidate. A representative of former owner Gurney was also present, but the case was adjourned so that Mr. Gurney and his legal team could look at all the offers. The final decision would ultimately be down to Judge Norris QC at Birmingham High Court. A week later the BBC reported a 'green light' for Mr Ward to sell the club to the Tomlins group, despite objections and a new bid from Gurney's Melodious Corporation.

More legal manoeuvrings from the football authorities would be needed before the saga could be brought to a close. League spokesman John Nagle said: 'What we're looking to do is make sure that the creditors are satisfied and that the club isn't going to fall back into Administration within two months. We need to ensure that the club has a future.' He said the rolling transfer embargo would continue and that budgetary targets would be set for 'an indefinable period' until the club was in a stable financial position. Monies currently being held back from the Hatters would be made available to the club only after it emerged from Administrative Receivership status.

By the time Christmas 2003 had come and gone, the Hatters had chalked up enough points to be challenging for a play-off place, and Bill Tomlins was able to talk confidently of being given official control of the club in a few weeks. His people were hoping to take the club to a new stadium by as early as August 2006. He said: 'The stadium where it is now, is not commercially viable to take the club forwards but the council is fully behind the football club and has been a very understanding landlord since the ground was sold to them.' A new planning application for a stadium on the land at Junction 10 of the M1 could be submitted by the summer of 2004, he added.

In February 2004, Joe Kinnear, by now installed as boss of Nottingham Forest, tried to lure Mick Harford to the City Ground as his assistant. Harford wavered, and eventually declined, but Newell was angry over what he saw as poaching: 'While I can maybe understand Joe's feeling of owing nobody anything [at Luton] after the events of the summer, I cannot allow Nottingham Forest the same excuse. As I said earlier in the season, when we lost one player and could well have lost more as a result of unscrupulous agents and managers. There are rules to abide by, set out by the governing bodies. I may be in the minority or might just be very naive, but I intend to obey those rules and also show people the common courtesy I would expect in return.' He added that the emotional ovation Harford received from Luton's travelling fans at Wycombe had gone a long way towards convincing Harford to stay.

In March the League's executive board finally gave the power to authorise the sale of the club, eight months on, and Trust in Luton explained the delay to puzzled fans: 'It's been frustrating for all of us. Matters have been moving along at such a slow pace ... the Football League's strict insolvency rules and their painstaking overseeing of this sale are both positive things – they just want to make sure that this club, one of their members, is all set up safely for the future.'

A creditable finishing position of tenth was achieved, seven points short of the play-offs, before the new owners were finally in a position in May 2004 to introduce themselves properly. Front-man Tomlins was already well known, having joined the club as business development director in April 1982 from the club's shirt sponsors Tricentrol. Described as a staunch Luton fan for many years, he was 43 when he took on the role of general secretary of the Hatters in late 1986, and he remained at the club for a further six years in a number of roles, before becoming a victim of a

David Kohler's reorganisation in the early 1990s. As the new chairman, Tomlins was joined on the board by former Fulham player John Mitchell, an associate of previous chairman Watson-Challis, and Derek Peter, a former financial director at Spurs, Richard Bagehot, and the Trust in Luton interim representative Mark Thompson. The new board was said to have stumped up £1.7 million to take the club to the end of the forthcoming 2005-06 season.

Luton soared to a tremendous start in the new campaign, winning ten and drawing two of their first dozen league games to open up a lead at the top of Coca-Cola League One (the old Division Three). Newell and Harford reached new heights of popularity, and the misery of the summer of 2003 was all but forgotten. This euphoria meant the locals could easily brush off the insulting 'findings' of two national surveys, one of which concluded that Luton was 'the worst town in the UK', and the other that Kenilworth Road was the League's 'worst football ground'.

An outraged Bill Tomlins pointed out that the stadium was now 100 years old, and when one considered the numbers that had passed through it during that time, it was ridiculous for the *Observer*'s survey to condemn it on the basis of just one or two people's opinions. And the man who had dubbed Luton the worst town began to sound contrite: Sam Jordison, editor of the PanMacmillan publication *Crap Towns 2*, said: 'I realise that Luton doesn't want that label. Trust in Luton have been doing excellent work with their football club and their community, which is why I've signed up as a member and why I've donated £250 to support them. I can't wait to attend the [forthcoming] 'I Love Luton' evening to see at first hand what Lutonians really think about the town.'

Meanwhile, Mick Harford eventually gave in to the lure of Nottingham Forest and joined Joe Kinnear at the City Ground to help their relegation fight. Sadly Kinnear would shortly be sacked, leaving Harford to suffer the same fate a matter of weeks later, shortly after taking over. Harford then moved on to take the reins at Rotherham, but this proved another ill-fated project, and Luton fans wondered whether he would soon be on his way back to Kenilworth Road. In the meantime, manager Newell seemed to be coping well without his assistant and launched another tirade against agents, expressing fury at the revelation that millions was being paid them by Coca-Cola League clubs alone, let alone the Premiership where the really big money existed.

By the spring of 2005, with Luton racing toward the League One title, Tomlins formally met the fans to reassure them about plans for the future, and to welcome civil servant Kelvin Dunn of the Supporters Club, who took his place on the main club board. The fans these days enjoyed a 10 per cent shareholding in the club with full voting rights. Compared to most recent chairmen, Tomlins appeared to enjoy a good relationship with the supporters, with the *Mad as a Hatter* fanzine describing him as: 'Everybody's favourite uncle – all that was missing was his pipe, cardigan, carpet slippers and his favourite Queen Anne Parker Knoll reclining easy chair ...'

Given the conflict that was just around the corner, it also appeared that Tomlins and his manager were rubbing along together well enough. Newell publicly commended the work behind the scenes at Luton and signed an extension to his contract with the comment that 'this is a proper football club' and he'd enjoyed every moment so far. No wonder he was content, for with four games still to play promotion was sealed. Then four goals were clouted past Brentford, managed by the locally unpopular Martin Allen, which secured the League One title. Celebrations included a memorable parade in the town centre sunshine. It was a record-breaking season with 98 points gathered, 87 of them from 29 victories, of which twelve were away from home. Considering the trauma suffered just two years earlier, the transformation at Luton had been remarkable.

While most of us grabbed this rare chance to celebrate, some longstanding fans were apparently uneasy at what they perceived to be going on behind the scenes at Kenilworth Road. This writer was told that early in the 2004-05 promotion season, two people 'became aware of potential problems' and after what was described to me as 'a little bit of digging around' formed the opinion that the football club was 'rotten to the core'. These vigilantes began planning a campaign that would reach its *denouement* much later in this story.

It was remarkable to think that the manager who guided the club to the 2004-05 League One title had been John Gurney's inexperienced 'Hobson's Choice' candidate. Few fans had celebrated Newell's arrival in 2003, but now he was being spoken of as Premiership standard, much admired as a young pragmatist who didn't suffer fools gladly and knew where he was headed. *The Times* reckoned he mirrored perfectly what he argued the game should be: down to earth, uncomplicated, full of working-class passion and commitment. 'I never wanted to be rich, or to be on the front pages of *Hello!* Magazine,' Newell told them. 'I wanted, I still want, to be the best. and now to manage the best in the game that I love.'

And Newell was, he told another reporter, emphatically a manager, not a coach: 'I don't know if it came from Europe or whatever. But I am a manager not a coach. And you only start being a manager when there are problems. I don't mind putting on training sessions now and again but it's the business of picking your team, going and finding players and dealing with problems that I'm interested in. He also dismissed the story that his old strike partner Alan Shearer had got him his break in management: 'All

Alan did was ask a friend to ask the [Hartlepool] chairman to make sure my CV wasn't overlooked. It was nothing more than that. People liked the story that Alan got me the job but that would be a little bit disrespectful to the chairman.'

Newell was rewarded with the divisional manager of the year trophy in May 2005, while the club's chief executive Cherry Newbery followed in Joe Kinnear's footsteps by accepting an honorary Masters degree from the University of Luton, recognising her work over the years in football and in the community. The *Sunday Times* nominated her as a candidate for the 'Unsung Hero' section of their female sporting awards scheme, stating: 'There might be no football club at Kenilworth Road, no professional team representing the town without Newbery's leadership, without the trust that supporters and staff placed in her, without the instinct of the female to see off somebody who jeopardises her brood.'

Like any good unsung hero, Cherry was keen to deflect all this praise and said the club's current purple patch was down to the strength of her staff, the new board taking on what had seemed 'hopeless', and the team spirit Mike Newell had fostered. And, more than all that: 'Nobody realised the fortitude and the passion in the town for this club.' Cherry's grandfather was Jimmy Yardley, a stalwart player of yesteryear. She had been with the club for 31 years, working as part-time cashier, then programme distributor and ticket office and commercial department worker, before becoming club secretary and then chief executive. Like David Pleat before her, she considered herself 'a true Lutonian', even though she was actually born in Leigh-on-Sea, Essex.

A stunning start to the 2005-06 season, with victories over 'bigger' teams like Crystal Palace and Southampton, was accompanied by news from the chairman that fresh discussions had taken place with Stockwood Park Holdings, owners of the proposed M1 relocation site. A less welcome development was the sale of young centre-back Curtis Davies to West Brom on the last day of the August transfer window for a whopping £3 million. For a home-grown player this was great business, but naturally the fans hated seeing another talent departing. The deal came a few days before Luton joined that select band of clubs to have played at the same ground for 100 years. A special souvenir programme for the visit of Wolves was produced to mark the centenary, and a fascinating illustrated book about the old stadium was published by club historian Roger Wash and Desert Island Books.

Too much nostalgia can be bad for you, but most Luton fans agreed with BBC Three Counties Radio's Ian Pearce when he reflected: 'This old ground oozes nostalgia and history. I'm all in favour of moving on but let's hope that when we do move, something of the spirit of those special games at Kenilworth Road will transfer with the club.' Meanwhile, the chairman was looking ahead: 'A 15,000-seater stadium suits our current situation at the club – we know we can fill it. You don't want to have too big a stadium that you end up rattling around in. But with the progress we've made as a team in such a short time already there's no reason why we shouldn't increase capacity. We've surprised one or two people with the way we've started the season and if we can keep that progress going then we will have to think seriously about increasing the size of the build, in line with the additional costs that will incur.'

The original £19.5 million new stadium plan related to an enclosed-style ground with 15,000 seats on an 18.5-acre site, that could be increased to 26,000 seats later if demand required. But Tomlins admitted the first build could now be of a size between those two figures, probably around the 20,000-seat mark. The club was still hopeful it could have the new stadium up and running by Christmas 2007. Long-standing fans were not so sure. Included within the stadium would be 150,000 square feet of office space and club suites, and 215,000 square feet of commercial retail space. A hotel would be built within the complex, with a second following later. Discussions had already taken place with relevant bodies over gas and water supplies to the site, we were told, while works to widen the M1 would mean the Highways Agency subsidising the cost of removing electricity pylons from the land.

Tomlins added: 'It's nice to be celebrating 100 years at Kenilworth Road [but] I'm totally focused and committed on getting the club to Junction 10. There is a time element, but everything revolves around having the right deal for the club to move forward.' Once the land agreement was secured, a planning application would quickly follow and consent would hopefully be given by April 2006, allowing completion by the end of 2007, he said. Tomlins' optimism and sense of purpose was admirable, but the autumn bad news that followed seemed all too familiar to Hatters supporters.

The big spanner in the works would not be thrown by the council, nor the Highways Agency, nor the landowner, not even any nearby 'NIMBYS' – it would be by the airport. The announcement of the draft master plan for the development of London-Luton Airport included the proposed building of a new runway. It showed the 'public safety zone' being extended from its current position over Stockwood Park to directly over the proposed new stadium site. This was evidently not good news. The airport intended to submit a planning application in 2007, which would be followed by a public inquiry, thus delaying any decision on the relocation site until 2009.

As far as Luton Town were concerned, even a delay this long might not see an end to the safety zone issue. In short, they were going to have to look elsewhere. The club said it was immensely frustrating that this news should come after eighteen months of protracted negotiations with the landowner. They had now begun, they said, to look at a new site north of the town, adjacent to Junction 12 of the M1 near Toddington: 'We have been encouraged by the positive response we have received from our meetings, and despite the current circumstances it should still be possible to have a new stadium in time for 2008-09 season.' Supporters reached for their road atlases and saw that Junction 12 was some considerable distance from the centre of Luton – in the middle of nowhere with nothing nearby except a motorway, railway line and the odd farm building. Many fans were unhappy about this new, alternative site. How could Luton continue to be a community oriented club at such an out-of-town location?

Speaking on local radio, Tomlins said the Junction 10 situation would be 'sterilised' for around four years by recent developments, so they were concentrating on the 200-acre site at Junction 12 which he felt offered a number of benefits, including its proximity to Harlington Station. He reiterated that the funding of any new stadium had to be generated from the commercial profit of its enabling development, and this was a major consideration in selecting the site at Junction 12.

The Loyal Luton Supporters Club voiced the discontent of many fans in a flyer distributed at the Crystal Palace home match in November 2005. It called the news about Junction 10 'a shock and a body blow to all Luton Town supporters' and called for answers to a number of questions. These included justifying a relocation after 120 years in Luton to a site outside the town boundaries, without prior consultation with the fans. The Junction 12 site sits around eight miles to the north-west of the current ground. It is a short drive outside the borough boundary, halfway between the villages of Toddington and Harlington.

Meanwhile, the shady world of 'bungs' and unlicensed agents was highlighted on a BBC *Panorama* investigation, the content of which seemed to vindicate some of Mike Newell's recent rants, in which he revealed that he too had been offered 'bungs'. Paul Hayward of the *Daily Mail* celebrated the findings of the *Panorama* report and called it a 'Champagne night' for football: 'Thanks to *Panorama*, the armies of the cheated and ripped-off can finally round on the head-in-the-sand brigade who told us it was all rumour and innuendo. Told us we were muckrakers and guttersnipes. Told us to stop seeing phantoms giving and taking bungs. Those lies are finally smashed. Several careers have crashed and burned in front of the BBC's hidden cameras.'

In the *Panorama* expose, Luton's Mike Newell is shown studying footage of an agent apparently incriminating himself with talk of corrupt managers, bungs, offshore accounts and cash 'in bags' and he says: 'Those are the people who tried to pay me money.' Hayward added: 'Over now, to the Premier League and the FA to see whether the old complacency will be replaced by a keener sense of what corruption is doing to our favourite sport: how it turns a game into a vehicle for nefarious deal-making. Maybe now a fraction more of supporters' money will stay in the game and not disappear into carrier bags or offshore. Newell emerges from this a public hero and journalism's battered flag flies from football's ramparts. Finally the moral blindfold is off.'

Newell made headlines for different reasons in January 2006 when his team gave Liverpool a hard time in an FA Cup thriller at Kenilworth Road. Town led 3-1 before being beaten by Rafa Benitez's men in a game that enthralled millions via the live BBC coverage. Shortly afterwards Newell was linked with the managerial vacancy at Leicester City, brushing aside criticism by saying he'd met Leicester 'out of courtesy' and had never discussed a contract with them. 'I can honestly say never at any stage did I decide to, or consider, leaving this club.' For older Luton fans this little episode had echoes of the Allan Brown affair in 1968, when another successful young manager spoke to Leicester shortly before ending his stint at Luton. Many fans feared we were seeing the beginning of the end of the Newell era, and lifelong supporter Graham Sharpe wrote in *Mad as a Hatter* fanzine: 'The Chinese have a curse – may you live in interesting times – and the 40-odd years I have supported Luton have been anything other than uninteresting, and I suspect that times at Luton are about to become more interesting than for some considerable while.' Prophetic words.

A mixed response to the plan to now move to Junction 12 of the M1, instead of Junction 10, led the club to try and clear the air with an emphatic statement of intent. Bill Tomlins said: 'I note that comments are still being made in the *Luton News* regarding our proposed relocation. The priority of the board has always been to achieve what is best for the club in the shortest time-scale possible and that means finding a 30-acre freehold site to be given to the club by a landowner, £25 million from an enabling development to build a new stadium with training pitches, hotel, 2,500 parking spaces, community facilities, restaurants and fast food outlets. This is exactly what we have achieved for the club, subject to planning, at the Old Park Farm site at Junction 12 south-bound on the M1, approximately two miles from the borough's boundary at Sundon Park. However, if anyone can find a site within the boundaries of Luton that meets the above criteria, the board will happily take the club there and sign on the dotted line if the time-scale was right. The board have looked at all options very carefully, as have previous owners over the last 40 years, and as the club has said on many occasions if it was that easy why haven't past boards been able to achieve [relocation]?'

In the meantime, Newell's third season at Luton ended with the side finishing a creditable 10th in the Championship (the highest finish for thirteen seasons), with the highlight of the closing weeks a 3-2 win over champions-elect Reading, who had been unbeaten in 34 league games. Then, a few weeks into the summer 2006 recess, the chairman announced that the club was now significantly closer to finalising the 'major land deal' for a new stadium next to Junction 12.

Speaking on BBC Three Counties Radio, Tomlins said former chairman Cliff Bassett owned the land at Old Park Farm and would be handing over 30 acres to the club – with other developments on the site (likely to be distribution depots, etc) – creating the profits to pay for this. Tomlins pointed out: 'We didn't want to go down the road, as many clubs have, of being saddled with millions of pounds worth of debt. We've been very fortunate in getting a 30-acre freehold site, so the club has a secured long-term future.'

Asked about the fact that the site was well outside the built-up area of Luton, and might therefore be unpopular with fans, Tomlins replied: 'Hopefully we'll convince them, because there isn't the option to build inside the boundaries of Luton. We're going to be something like one-and-a-half miles away from the boundary of Luton on the Old Park Farm site. We have looked at all the other options; we've spoken to the Council, our Supporters Groups have had referendums looking at all the alternatives and the options which have been spoken about for probably 30 years now. But at the end of the day, we're left with only the one viable alternative at Junction 12 in the timescales needed to take the club forward.' He was confident the club could move ahead quickly, overcoming the fact that this was green-belt land and that local villagers were likely to protest.

After the promise shown the previous season, Luton fans were hopeful that a genuine promotion challenge could be maintained in the Coca-Cola Championship during 2006-07. But, not for the first time, their dreams were blown out of the water even before a ball was kicked. For the club decided to sell arguably its two most influential players, i.e. the leading scorer, plus the captain and midfield kingpin. Steve Howard, 30, who had exceeded 100 goals in five years at Luton, joined Derby for £1 million, while skipper Kevin Nicholls, 27, signed for Leeds for £700,000, having likewise completed five years' service. New signings, costing far less than the £1.7 million received, would replace them, but there was no denying the gaping holes they left behind. Newell papered over the cracks by saying Luton would always be a selling club, and that it was good money for players of their ages, but he didn't sound convincing.

Newell's firm anti-corruption stance continued to grab headlines, but he scoffed at the sentiments of an unnamed 'high profile chairman' who condemned him for only raising these issues publicly in order to increase his own profile. Newell said he'd been in the game for twenty years not twenty minutes, and was in it because he loved football. He recalled that BBC's *Panorama* investigation into football corruption had been launched before he raised the matter anyway. 'Fame or celebrity status was never on [my] agenda and never will be. I don't do egos or self-promotion.'

Soon afterwards, for good measure, Newell had a pop at the applied management course for aspiring football managers at Warwick University (which he'd quit early himself) and other 'pieces of paper' supposedly required to be a top football manager: 'You can talk about systems and tactics and you can carry clipboards and make incomprehensible signals and gestures with as many fingers and hands as you like, but you will never kid the ordinary man in the street. I know that for a fact because I am one.' Newell's rants were becoming more frequent, but generally made good sense and went down well with the Luton fans, who found his views a refreshing change from the insipid, inarticulate ramblings of most managers.

One of the many issues which frustrated Newell was the seemingly endless bickering behind the scenes at Luton, arising from the new stadium question. This was illustrated during the autumn of 2006 when an open discussion involving the club and local radio was interrupted by what the Luton board called 'a stage-managed entrance by a former owner with a separate agenda'. They were referring to the arrival at the meeting of Mr and Mrs Watson-Challis, who were evidently aggrieved about the way the club had handled the Junction 10 situation.

On the field, October's highlight was a 5-1 romp over managerless Leeds, which took the Hatters up to fifth in the Championship and persuaded fans that perhaps they could cope without Howard and Nicholls after all. With hindsight, this victory marked something of a watershed: it would now be downhill all the way – and not just for the remainder of 2006-07 season. Four goals were shipped in the Carling Cup at Everton and the following weekend another five in a dreadful display at Ipswich. However, there were mitigating circumstances surrounding the Portman Road thrashing, for the players had witnessed full-back Sol Davis suffer a stroke on the team bus travelling to Suffolk. It was an unusual and frightening occurrence for a fit young sportsman and would cast a shadow over the club for some days. Fortunately the gritty defender recovered after a spell in hospital and confounded the experts by reappearing in the first team less than nine weeks later.

Looking back, Davis recalled: 'I was sitting on the coach to Ipswich. We'd departed Luton and after about 20 minutes I started to feel slightly sick. I expected it to pass but then pins and needles set in my hands. I realised something was majorly wrong with me when I couldn't speak properly. I asked David Bell to grab the physio for me and I just slurred my words. Seconds later I couldn't use my arm or my leg and my mouth had gone as well.' It was the third unusual malady to strike down a Luton player recently, for midfielder Paul Hughes was still out of action with a mystery blood complaint and Paul Underwood had suffered a serious infection following surgery.

The Leeds win sparked a run of eight straight defeats (Luton's worst sequence in over 100 years), during which Newell landed himself in hot water for comments made about the performance of referee's assistant Amy Rayner. Newell was left fuming after Luton were denied a penalty during the visit of QPR. Ms Rayner then awarded Rangers a dubious corner from which they equalised. Newell implied she was not up to the job and accused the authorities of only appointing women officials for political correctness, saying they had no place in senior football. He was forced to apologise after a storm of 'sexist' accusations came his way, but he insisted he was merely being 'traditionalist': 'My values involve holding doors open for women, helping a mother off a train if she had a buggy or bags, worrying what time my daughter will be home and whether she is escorted, buying flowers and paying for dinner … if all of these are sexist and prehistoric then, yes I am a sexist,' he said.

Newell's anger spilled over further after the QPR defeat. He also let fly with an astonishing broadside against his own chairman Bill Tomlins. 'I haven't spoken to him for months … everything he gets into he has messed up and I'm just about fed up with it. I keep getting told that when we get planning permission there will be money to spend, or that next week the club will change hands. I've had it for two years. It was easier when we were in Administration because we had nothing and we just had twenty players to work with.' He warned that the uncertainty behind the scenes was affecting his players, particularly those in the latter stages of their contracts.

Whether or not this was a conscious ploy on Newell's part to force a confrontation, the board moved quickly to respond to Newell's statements. A hastily arranged meeting produced the following statement: 'The club disassociates itself totally with the sexist comments made by him, which have no place in this club and are completely unacceptable. Representatives of the board will be meeting with the manager as a matter of urgency to ask him to explain his comments and other criticisms.'

Later in the week it emerged that the manager had been severely reprimanded and warned, but not sacked, as many had predicted. He was also fined a four-figure sum by the FA. Newell had recently signed a lucrative four-year contract with the club and denied allegations that his outburst had been a deliberate attempt to get himself fired.

Newell added: 'I'm not really worried about how secure I am. It's a fickle job and a fickle occupation. It can end at any given moment at all because we're all answerable to somebody at the end of the day, every single one of us. All I ask is people judge me on what I've done so far and what I'm capable of doing in the future. I'd probably take more care and count to ten next time or maybe a bit more, I don't know! We're in such an emotional game, sometimes when microphones and cameras are thrust in front of you it isn't the right time. My apology is unreserved to Amy Rayner and anyone else I may have offended because it was the wrong time and it was out of order, and anyone could have made that mistake.'

Newell might have patched things up with Ms Rayner, but the relationship between manager and board still looked on very rocky ground. Few expected Newell and Tomlins to remain the club's two figureheads for much longer. Something surely had to give.

Meanwhile, work on the Junction 12 plan continued. The Miller Partnership was appointed architects, having earlier designed the new stadiums at Southampton, Sunderland, Leicester and Coventry. Tomlins said: 'The board are pleased with the progress so far, but please understand that until the planning application is submitted we can't divulge all aspects of our negotiations in the public domain until they are completed. This is not a cloak and dagger exercise, it's just normal commercial practice … although we made an announcement regarding Old Park Farm (J12) back in December 2005, we didn't sign a land deal with the landowner until June 29th this year. We can understand that some supporters have been frustrated by the lack of information, but we can assure you that the wheels have never stopped turning.'

Any lingering sympathy for the board from ordinary fans began to fade when the January 2007 transfer window arrived and they were made to stomach an all-too-familiar scenario – the best players making for the exit. This time it was the team's two star attackers, Carlos Edward and Rowan Vine, sold to Sunderland and Birmingham respectively for combined fees totalling £4 million. The 'spine' of the previous season's excellent team had now been sold in a matter of months. Added to the run of poor results, which Newell seemed unable to stem, there were now major rumblings of discontent among the fans.

It was clear to everyone that Newell had been stripped of his best players, either by sales or injuries. Astonishingly, given the situation just six months earlier, Luton were now heading for relegation. A statement in the programme for the visit of Sheffield Wednesday – signed by 'chairman and directors' – tried to deflect the criticism:

'A number of fans questioned our commitment in signing players during the recent window period. The simple facts are the manager, along with our CEO [John Mitchell], continually looked at making signings through-out this period, but simply would not, as Mike Newell consistently states, pay over-the-odds prices for players. Likewise, we had already signed Matthew Spring and Drew Talbot and were keen to add one or two more signings. However, negotiations are often complicated and it is hard for us at times to compete with other clubs who currently have better overall facilities to offer. It is one of the key reasons why we continue to move for-ward in our relocation plans and the opportunity to genuinely compete on a level footing with most other clubs.

'No doubt most of you will now be aware of the recent statement regarding the appointment of Rosemound Developments Limited as the preferred developer for the Junction 12 site, which represents a major step forward in our relocation plans.'

Between Christmas and the beginning of March 2007, Luton only reg-istered two wins in fifteen games and appeared to be hurtling towards the drop. The squad had had the guts ripped out of it by illness, injury and sales, and there were few signs the slide would be halted. One glimmer of hope came when Kevin Nicholls was quoted as being keen to return from Leeds, where he had only played thirteen league games, largely due to injury. The situation was complicated by the fact that these two teams were both facing relegation and would meet at Elland Road in March. An almighty row blew up, with Leeds manager Dennis Wise clearly in no mood to let Nicholls depart to one of Leeds' closest rivals.

Newell bided his time until after that game, a 1-0 win for Leeds, before letting loose another tirade: 'I stayed very quiet last week in the build-up to the match at Elland Road so as not to stoke the fire. It was always going to be a difficult game for us even as it was, but I will now react to the total lack of respect shown to Luton Town by the manager of Leeds, a lack of respect that has since continued. Perhaps he has forgotten that he has not always been employed by a so called "big football club". People need to know the facts regarding Kevin Nicholls. First of all, I was made aware that Nico was unhappy and that he would like to return here. The first phone call I made was to the manager of Leeds United, not an agent, not a chief executive and not the player. The enquiry surprised him but by the time he had spoken to the player and rang me back at 9 o'clock the next morning, he said that if we wanted Nico we could have him for £700,000.

'He [Wise] has since changed that to "no way would he loan a player to a club that are in the same position as them". Never at any stage did I make that enquiry public, or have any intention of making it public. That was done by Leeds United. Their manager has since intimated that I tapped up the player and have been trying to cover my back and the player's back since. He needs to be very careful in what he is suggesting because I can recall the sequence of events very clearly and people can accuse me of many things, but dishonesty they certainly can't.

'The most galling part of the affair is the contempt with which he treated Kevin Nicholls's desire to move back to this club. He said he could understand "if it was a bigger club. or a club in a higher position, but not Luton". He has since referred to us as a small club in Bedfordshire. Never would I disrespect any football club or its supporters, whether it be a massive club like Leeds United or a club on the bottom of the ladder. This club's supporters have every right to be upset and, as they can't respond directly to his comments and contempt, I will do it for them as the manager. We don't have the resources that other clubs have, we don't have the facilities and we don't have the widespread support that certain clubs have. We have, however, earned the right to compete and compete we have done. The club means as much to any Luton Town fan as Leeds United means to any of their fans and nobody or "nobodies" should ever forget that.'

This would prove to be Newell's final outburst as Luton boss, for – less than 24 hours before the 'Ides of March' – the knives came out and he was sacked, reportedly for 'gross misconduct'. His blunt words of recent months were cited as part of the problem. He had reportedly already had two written warnings about frequent profanity and outspoken behaviour. Recent results were also said to be a factor, of course.

Newell's players rallied round him and striker Warren Feeney told the *Daily Mail*: 'The gaffer's come out with comments about the board in the past but he has background for those comments or he wouldn't make them. The players are shocked as you have to look how far Mike Newell's taken the club and the fact he's made the club a fortune. He had to get rid of players that were the backbone of the team but he's only spent £1.5m in four years. Of course you'll end up bottom if you sell those players.'

Newell's one-man crusade, as the national media liked to portray it, to rid football of corruption had been largely responsible for the Premier League's decision to set up Lord Stevens' investigation into the state of the transfer market. His other legacy was an impressive record at Luton in generally difficult times, which was only spoiled by the results of the final few months, when his team plummeted from 5th to 23rd. Of the 200 games under his command, Luton won 83 and lost 68. The outcome had perhaps been inevitable following his thinly veiled accusations about incompetence in the boardroom and his echoing of the fans' chant of 'Where's the money gone?'

Some conspiracy theorists thought Newell might have engineered his own dismissal in order that relegation wouldn't mar his CV, but this seems unlikely given the well-paid contract he had just signed. After all, he had a wife and five children to support. Not all fans felt Newell had been hard done by, though, for some criticised his inability to stop the recent slide and were critical of his 'tinkering', which included the playing of young centre-back Leon Barnett in midfield and then in attack. Newell had also spent a large chunk of his limited transfer budget on striker Adam Boyd, who proved a major flop and rarely featured in the starting eleven. But the bottom line was that Newell's acrimonious departure seemed sad considering how well things had gone for most of his tenure.

The board wasted no time in finding a replacement, and Luton-born Kevin Blackwell, former boss of Leeds, took over at the end of March. Newell had walked into a maelstrom when he started, and for Blackwell it would also be a rocky ride. He had a major task to try and save the Hatters from relegation, but would have to cope with stormy times in the boardroom too. Just a fortnight after Blackwell took his first training session, chairman Tomlins fell on his sword and followed Newell out of the club. Tomlins quit following allegations about illegal payments by the club to player's agents. The FA investigation that this sparked threw the club into chaos once again.

A club statement revealed: 'Earlier this year Mr Tomlins approached the FA requesting a meeting to clarify certain matters relating to the football club. Following this meeting, the FA is currently carrying out an enquiry.' Tomlins said: 'There has been too much disruption surrounding the club in recent months and I feel it is appropriate for me to stand down at this time.' He elaborated further to BBC radio, saying the main issue was payments to agents that were made by the club's holding company Jayten, and not from the main club coffers, which broke football rules. Jayten had been established in late 2003 primarily to finance the club's move to a new stadium. Tomlins signed off by suggesting a major new investor would be arriving at the club within a few days to take his place.

These dramas left an air of bewilderment over the club. Questions were left hanging. Some would be addressed by Bob Graham of the *Daily Mail* in a lengthy 'exclusive', which was published shortly after the news broke. Tomlins was revealed to have confessed to irregular payments in an earlier interview with FA lawyers investigating the club. Up to thirteen separate payments to seven named agents were specified, although the total sum was not huge– around £150,000. This was not necessarily football's so-called 'bung' culture in action, more a case of technicalities being breached and not declared. But the revelations looked certain to land Luton, already hurtling towards relegation, with an FA fine or a points deduction. They would also re-open the general debate over the way money was pouring out of the game via agents, an issue that had angered Mike Newell.

The Mail showed that in addition to Newell's concerns (both at Luton Town and on a wider basis), club secretary Cherry Newbery had presented football's governing body with documentary evidence of irregular payments in mid-2006, thus 'blowing the whistle' on what had been going on. Tomlins accepted that he had contravened football rules but explained to *The Mail*: 'I didn't murder anyone or do anything illegal. I did wrong and it's now up to the FA to decide what will happen.' He said he felt at the time that he had reasonable grounds to bend the FA rules because Newell's attitude to agents had made it difficult for the club to deal with them, and therefore to sign players.

The sacked Newell was said to be taking legal action against the football club for wrongful dismissal. This created a pending tribunal claim for circa £2.8 million, it was reported. Newell was also currently assisting the FA with evidence for their ongoing inquiry into corruption. It was said that one of Newell's last actions at Luton had been to hand in a three-page letter to the club's board, which demanded answers to a number of probing questions regarding financial matters.

The Newell-Tomlins era had seen Luton move onwards and upwards after the horrors of 2003 with some style. But now, less than four years on, it had all come crashing down around the club's ears – and these two protagonists were gone. Behind them was a club in crisis again. Whither now Luton Town?

CRISIS 10 (AUTUMN 2007)
'The Hatters Screwed up my Life'

The Knight on a white charger, riding in to save Luton Town from financial and scandal-ridden meltdown in the spring of 2007, was a 54-year-old racing driver who admitted to a love of speed and risk-taking.

Yorkshire-born David Pinkney first moved to Luton as a boy and was now a successful businessman based in Harpenden, but best known as a driver in the British Touring Car Championship. His prior links with Luton Town included a 30-year friendship with director John Mitchell and a family connection with new manager Kevin Blackwell. Pinkney went to school in Luton and said he had supported the Hatters since boyhood. He took over as chairman immediately, although his acquisition of a controlling interest in the club's holding company, Jayten Stadium Limited, wasn't confirmed until the summer. He announced a five-year plan of getting the club into a new stadium at Junction 12 and into the Premiership.

His targets were quickly rendered harder when Blackwell only inspired one win from the seven games between his arrival and the end of the season – and the inevitable relegation was confirmed by defeat at Derby two weeks before the season ended in a live Sky TV game. Town finished 23rd and slipped miserably back into the lower divisions. An eventful season ended with Roy Keane's Sunderland strolling to a 5-0 win at Kenilworth Road, an embarrassment that was missed by the new chairman, who was racing his Alfa Romeo that day at the Thruxton circuit.

Over the summer the Pinkney investment appeared to be bearing fruit, with revamping of the antiquated Kenilworth Road ground. The boardroom and former Kenilworth Suite was knocked into one large area as the main corporate hospitality facility, while the Century and Millennium Club bar areas were updated. The dressing rooms and press room were redecorated, and Blackwell was given high-tech presentation equipment to aid his team talks. Plans were implemented to improve the club's youth structure and a new public address system installed. This would be followed by a new team bus, changes to the entry area at the Kenilworth Road end – and, significantly, the acquisition of a new purpose-built training ground for the squad at the former Electrolux sports ground in Ely Way.

This was all good news, but not quite so welcome was the summer departure of two locally developed players, Kevin Foley (to Wolves) and Leon Barnett (West Brom) for a combined fee of around £4 million. Less than half this sum would be spent on new players, so evidently the club's general outgoings were proving higher than Pinkney first anticipated.

A clutch of veteran players were signed by Blackwell to boost his inexperienced squad for the 2007-08 season. With many existing players said to be on well-paid, lengthy contracts, it was clear Luton's outgoings for the new season would be high. A promotion challenge, cup runs and big gates – plus the odd player sale – all looked to be essential, unless we had underestimated the depth of Mr Pinkney's pockets. He said the key to success was to expedite the move to a new stadium and, to that end, work was in progress on a planning application for Junction 12. During the early weeks of the campaign Pinkney went on the injury list himself after a multi-car 100mph smash at Brands Hatch which left him 'very lucky to be alive'.

The talk of major ongoing losses at Luton, despite all the player sales of recent times (roughly £9 million in two years), saw the fans' group Trust in Luton make a request to view the club accounts. The Trust was also keen to reclaim its place on the main board of directors, having resigned this privilege earlier in the year in protest at not being consulted over the sacking of Mike Newell. The first request was subsequently granted, but only after some delays, but the latter met with less enthusiasm. Pinkney would state he was not keen to have the board infiltrated by someone who had an 'agenda' that was not known to him, for there were 'sensitivities' over the relocation plan.

As the fans and the new board continued their awkward dance towards getting to know each other, the team had mixed fortunes on the pitch. Home results were generally good before Christmas 2007 (Sunderland and Charlton were beaten in the Carling Cup and Everton kept at bay for 90 minutes), but away results were disappointing. After six months in the job, the jury remained out on Kevin Blackwell, with many fans convinced his approach was too negative. On paper his squad looked strong enough to do well in League One, but the blend was evidently not right.

The new ground issue received another setback in the autumn when it was revealed plans might not be submitted to South Bedfordshire District Council until early 2008 because of 'fine tuning' now needed by the club's developer partners Goodmans (formerly Rosemound). Pinkney explained: 'Junction 12 will be enlarged and improved when the M1 motorway is widened to 10 lanes, circa 2010, the site also has a direct rail link too, and it has become the only realistic option. We now have a set of plans we are enthusiastic about. We think they'll be really exciting for our supporters. I think we will be lucky to get into the stadium for the start of the 2009-10 season, but would expect to take possession of it during that season. It all hangs on how long the planning consent takes to come through. Rest assured the build will start just as soon as we gain planning approval.'

Pinkney called on fans to unite to help move the club forward before this 'last and only available' local site was also lost.

A few months after completing his takeover, Pinkney admitted to being staggered by the complexities and stresses of running a football club, but vowed to get to the bottom of why Luton laboured under such debts and were losing £3 million a year: 'Until certain player contracts expire, which currently we have no control over, we can't get to the balanced position I want to collectively achieve with our manager. They are set in stone and cost us dearly week on week. They have nothing to do with the current management, but are a legacy of the past and something that we have to deal with.' Another inherited difficulty for Pinkney was the FA investigation into financial irregularities, which was continuing, but which the chairman confidently believed would ultimately prove something of a 'storm in a teacup'. He brought in a new managing director, Andrew Dean, as the new board battled to keep a lid on the club's problems.

Growing fan unrest at this time suggested matters were coming to a head. It was hard to believe, but six months after the Pinkney regime took over, the same old problems were bubbling to the surface. Trust in Luton spoke out angrily at not being allowed to reclaim back their seat on the board. Liam Day said: 'Our members are rightly furious. We have a seat on the board because supporters saved this club from imminent extinction four years ago. Since then we have served faithfully on the board and been fully supportive, even during the disciplinary issues with previous management and when the new stadium plans were originally drawn up. We've been told clearly by the board that they no longer want the fans' voice – they see no value in the opinion of lifelong fans and they don't seem to trust the fans either.' A week or two later the gulf between fan groups and directors was clear for all to see. The Trust issued a hard-hitting leaflet at the Nottingham Forest home game in late October, and stung the board into a lengthy response in a subsequent match programme.

The board were critical of what they called an 'external faction that has a different agenda from the board' and whose protest actions had allegedly contributed to the club's predicament. Dealing with the question of where all the incoming transfer cash had gone, the board said it had been used to meet ongoing commitments and overheads, particularly refurbishments – and insisted no monies received had been taken out of the club. The board again emphasised how the Junction 12 plan involved a development opportunity that would see the club gifted a 30-acre freehold site, plus £25 million towards the stadium construction. The Trust denied ever asking fans to 'protest', as the board implied, and again underlined supporters' bewilderment that after around £9 million in player sales in recent years, the club still claimed losses on such a huge scale.

The Trust's annual meeting on Thursday, 15th November 2007 was a lively affair, highlighted by a speech from Trust president John Moore, the former Town player and manager. Moore reflected on current and past troubles at Luton: 'In my view, the best chairman your club had was Denis Mortimer. He didn't do anything spectacular but gradually built the club. Now I worked for David Evans. I couldn't understand why he wanted to sell the ground, the crown jewel of your football club. You know, you marched against the move to Milton Keynes – you were angry and did that. But there was no supporter opposition to the sale of the ground and I couldn't understand it. I wanted it, but I'm not really a political animal.'

Trust official Stephen Browne outlined the tortuous process of obtaining financial information and statutory documents from the new board. He said a complete run-down of money going in and out of the club was still not known. The £9 million from player sales had funded the club's losses since Jayten took over in 2003, and the problem was that few assets remained to pay off future losses. He said it also remained unclear whether the new stadium would be owned by the club or by another company (parent or otherwise). The plight of Coventry City was cited as an example of the dangers of mortgaging a football club's future to get into a new ground.

Coincidentally, on the same day as that Trust meeting, the FA issued a total of 55 charges in connection with their investigation into financial irregularities during the Tomlins-Newell era. Seventeen were made against the club as a whole, and others against ex-chairman Tomlins, and current directors Peter, Bagehot and Mitchell, plus several against player agents. This news was evidently the final straw for Pinkney and the current board, for, as we would find out later, the very next day they consulted a Sheffield-based firm of insolvency specialists, the P&A Partnership, for advice on how to proceed.

It would take several days before the board broke its silence on the charges, issuing a statement which said chief executive John Mitchell and director Richard Bagehot were stepping down from the board 'in the best interests of the football club'. The pair faced FA charges of failing to notify the FA of rule breaches when they became aware of them.

Just as this news was being digested, along came another, even more explosive, bombshell. To the complete shock of supporters, on Thursday, 22nd November 2007 Luton Town FC was put into Administration – for the third time in less than nine years. Brendan Guilfoyle of the P&A Partnership was one of three Administrators appointed by the Hatters' directors. They would run the club with immediate effect, with a view to finding a buyer. Here we go again!

According to the *Herald-Post*, Luton's directors took this decision because the company couldn't continue with decreasing income and escalating liabilities. An immediate consequence of the emergency was that the club would suffer an automatic 10-point penalty from the Football League for taking this step. It dropped them from 17th to bottom of the Coca-Cola League One table. Their new, adjusted tally of a meagre nine points left them three points adrift of the everyone else. Relegation to the fourth tier of English football was now a very serious threat.

Mr Guilfoyle tried to calm the stormy waters: 'Administration will give the club breathing space and an opportunity to restructure its finances,' he said. 'Our aim is to maximise the value of the company's assets and to place the club on a firm footing for the future. We feel for the fans, the manager and the players but hopefully the long term prospects will overcome the short term disadvantage.'

He was looking for prospective buyers to put proposals to the club's creditors before the end of 2007. He said the recent FA charges were a separate matter and would not be affected by the administration status. He added: 'The survival of this historic club will depend on finding a purchaser,' pointing out that in the short term David Pinkney had agreed to fund the trading losses until the conclusion of a sales process, even though he recognised there was no guarantee he would get this money back.

Within days Guilfoyle reported interest from across the Atlantic and from 'former chairmen', among others, and said one of his toughest jobs was sorting out which, if any, of the enquirers were time-wasters. Guilfoyle asked the players to defer their wages and prepared for a creditors' meeting which would have to be held within three months.

Guilfoyle was reportedly surprised at what he found after examining Luton's books. Not so much by the level of debt, which was around £4 million (£2.5 million of this owed to HM Revenue & Customs), and very low compared to that of clubs like Coventry and Leeds, but by the extent of the ongoing losses of between £3 and £4 million every year, and a wage bill of £3.6 million.

Pinkney admitted that calling in the Administrators represented a very sad day, but insisted: 'I have only ever had the long term future of Luton Town FC at heart, but changing circumstances and the potential huge liabilities surrounding the club have presented me with no alternative but to place the club into the hands of the administrator. My sole intention when I first got involved was to take this club forward to where it belongs. I regard myself as one of the 4,000 season-ticket holding supporters of LTFC that come to every game, year on year to support our club, buy merchandise, enjoy the match and go back home to the family. On that basis, loving the club as we all do, I decided to invest in the purchase of our club – and use some solid business acumen to secure its future. I know football is different and that it wasn't going to be a walk in the park, but I had no idea of what was around the corner.'

Pinkney told the *Herald-Post* the crisis had 'screwed up his life' and left him hugely out of pocket. Asked what had driven the club to administration, he pointed the finger at well-paid players who weren't playing regularly, Mike Newell's claim for wrongful dismissal, the continuing FA inquiry, and the recent leaflet drop by Trust in Luton.

The *Daily Mail* confirmed that Newell was suing the club for around £3 million, a large chunk of which was for lost earnings on the remainder of his contract. Ironically, his claim was nearly twenty times the total involved in irregular payments made to agents, but few saw Newell as the villain. After all, it was his revelations that football was rife with corruption which helped trigger some of the investigations now under way. The Administrator said that when everything was sorted out Newell could become just another creditor. *Sportsmail* reported that the FA appeared to have failed to take decisive action when first aware of the irregular payments to agents by Luton. They described how secretary Cherry Newbery had visited the FA for an 'off the record' meeting, armed with her own dossier, knowing the FA's audit earlier in 2006 had already uncovered two irregular payments. She had been uncomfortable with the situation at Luton and wanted to protect herself and the club. Later, chairman Tomlins met FA officials in early 2007 to confess what had taken place, claimed the *Mail*.

United in adversity by the latest turn of events, Luton's three main supporters' groups issued a rallying call in a joint statement. Going into administration was a major blow, they said, especially given the enormous effort historically made by fans in rescuing the club when faced with similar circumstances. They planned a joint meeting with the Administrator to ensure he was aware of fans' concerns and desires going forward: 'We will look to stress the importance of the fans being considered in the future shaping of the club as well as the added value we can bring to the table.'

Gloomy fans accepted that the club was bound to suffer further disruption. The most saleable assets, such as David Bell and David Edwards, would now be eyed up by bargain-hunters, with the January transfer window looming. The last big sales were less than six months earlier when Kevin Foley and Leon Barnett left, and more were now bound to follow. Perhaps even the stalwarts like Chris Coyne and Matthew Spring would think enough was enough and try and find job security elsewhere. And what about the brilliant loan signing Jaroslaw Fojut – presumably he would have to be sent back to Bolton? For manager Blackwell it was equally frustrating and just the sort of uphill battle he didn't need; he had tangled with Mr Guilfoyle before, when similar troubles befell his previous club Leeds United, and was under no illusions about the seriousness of the situation and the restrictions he would now face.

It was clearly going to be a long, hard winter – again.

CRISIS 11 (2007-08)
Forgive us our Indebtedness

Eric Morecambe / Who art in heaven / Hallowed be thy name
*   Let the goals come / They can have one / So long as our boys get seven*
Give us this day a win / And forgive us our indebtedness
*   As we forgive those who have netted against us / Lead us out of administration*
And deliver us from Guilfoyle / For we loved the Eighties
*   The power and the glory / For ever and ever, Luton*

(Reuters correspondent and Luton fan Mark Ledsom)

The persistent questioning of Luton Town's finances during 2007 by supporters group Trust in Luton had been vindicated by the mess revealed when the club went into Administration. But, explained TiL's chairman Liam Day, although they knew the situation was potentially bad, they never imagined the sheer enormity of the crisis.

'With hindsight, it is no wonder that no club director wanted to fulfil their legal duty and give TiL the information that we repeatedly requested. It can also be seen that [their] protests about "hidden agendas and factions of fans" were shallow attempts to talk their way out of the problems ... Even now, the chairman continues to blame players, fans and external factors for the plight of the club. Let's be absolutely clear: there is only one group of people that signed cheques, contracts and land deals; there is only one group of people that owned a holding company, borrowed money and invested little; there is only one group of people that let the club operate beyond its means and racked up debts of £10 million in just the last twelve months; there is only one group of people who had the authority to do this, have control of the club to allow it and the knowledge that it was happening.'

As news of the situation spread, a number of potential new owners expressed possible interest in Luton Town, including a group of supporters determined to create a consortium capable of buying control of the club. Choosing the name Luton Town Football Club 2020 Limited (LTFC-2020), this group's spokesman said that over recent years many fans had questioned whether there was anyone with enough money and vision to take the club forward, and their research indicated the answer was 'a resounding yes'. Led by Gary Sweet, a prominent member of Trust in Luton involved in the 2003 saga, they met the Administrator to indicate their interest and seek advice. He told them all bids were due in by early January, at which point he would choose a 'preferred bidder' who would then enter into a period of exclusivity with him. Now this timetable had been made clear, the race was on to save Luton Town.

LTFC2020 was able to call upon the communication skills of broadcaster Nick Owen as their front-man, although much of the day-to-day work would be carried out by bid manager Sweet, a former senior executive at Siemens, and his fellow Luton fans and business experts Stephen Browne and Antony Brown. Over the coming weeks, the identity of their consortium was revealed, a line-up of considerable expertise and financial muscle. Importantly it involved genuine long-standing Luton supporters, plus two well-remembered players from the past.

LTFC2020 received expert strategic advice through the inclusion of Keith Harris, former chairman of the Football League and chief executive of HSBC Investment Bank. Also in the consortium was Lutonian Mick Pattinson, who had risen to become President and CEO of the USA housebuilders Barratt American, having once been a Luton youth team player. Mike Roberts was another USA businessman, chairman of The Roberts Companies, a group involved in TV broadcasting properties, real estate development entities and a restaurant chain. Mid-Bedfordshire businessman Bob Curson, involved in player development with Luton for many years, was also on board. They were joined by Steve Foster, the hugely popular former Luton skipper and stalwart defender of the 1980s, who was now in business, plus Godfrey Ingram, an England schoolboy international who played for Luton in the 1970s and whose dazzling skills saw him become Cardiff's record signing, although his best footballing days had been for USA clubs such as San Jose Earthquakes and New York Cosmos. Ingram by now had impressive business credentials in the States and was a business partner of Mike Roberts.

The 'public face' of the consortium in these early days was Nick Owen, the man who helped rescue breakfast-time TV, but who now had an even bigger resuscitation job on his hands. Born locally 60 years earlier, Owen was a true lifelong devotee whose first game was back in 1958. His career began in local newspapers before joining Central TV and then *Good Morning Britain* on TV-AM in 1983, co-presenting with Anne Diamond. Then followed stints as an ITV sports front-man and the *Good Morning with Anne and Nick* show on BBC One in the 1990s. Nowadays he was based in the Midlands but remained a regular at Luton games, and even had a bar behind the Main Stand named after him. He was delighted to be involved, but confessed: 'I've always been happy just being a fan. I've been supporting them 50 years now. I remember going to an away game at Hartlepool in the 1970s when I'm convinced I was the only Luton fan there. I'm actually in love with Kenilworth Road. Others might call it ramshackle, tumbledown, a mess, with bad toilets, but so be it. I know we will have to move to secure the club's future, but I love the place. I was saying to my friend at the Liverpool game, this is what we go through the bad times for. It was just alive. Just magic.

'I know I'm sticking my head above the parapet [by joining the consortium], but I sort of had to,' Owen told the *Telegraph*. 'When you've supported a club all your life, it's part of who you are, you can't let it fold. The thought of Saturdays without Luton playing is just intolerable. What is the town of Luton famous for? Vauxhall cars aren't there any more. So it's the airport and Luton Town. It's the town's identity. You know, when I was a little boy, football was all about small-town clubs. Blackpool, Ipswich, Burnley, they won things, they were at the top of the league. Now, the power and the money is increasingly being centralised to the big cities, Manchester, London. You might call me old-fashioned but I think the small-town club is one of this country's great institutions. It is worth fighting to preserve.'

As the weeks went by, the structure of LTFC2020 would be formalised into three groups of key people. Its operational board had Owen as chairman, Sweet as managing director, Browne as director, with support from managers Pat Thomas and Anna Coultas. Its investment board featured Messrs Curson, Ingram, Pattinson and Foster, plus two anonymous investors from the fan base. The advisory board consisted of Messrs Roberts, Harris and Brown, plus Tenon Accountants and representatives of the supporters groups.

Little was known publicly about the other bidders, but the Administrator made it known he would require all bidders to show proof of funds to the tune of £3 million. Fans who doubted whether LTFC2020 could raise this sort of money were encouraged when the Administrator hinted that they might be in pole position: 'There is a consortium backed by fans and they have issued a prospectus. They are looking for Luton fans to come in and help them make a bid. I've seen some evidence that they are having success in that. I was concerned about the attitude of the supporters' groups, so we got together. We met after the Nottingham Forest match and it was positive – very good.'

No wonder everyone felt positive after the Forest game, for this FA Cup second round tie was won, which meant Luton would have another home tie with mighty Liverpool in round three. The income from the Reds' visit, largely via Sky TV money, would keep the club going and mean the players could be paid. If the game ended all square and needed a replay, even more money would be guaranteed and further pressure relieved.

A salutary reminder of the harsh realities of Administration came when wages had to be deferred and players found themselves short of cash in the run-up to Christmas. It was reported that manager Blackwell twice answered knocks on his office door and was greeted by a plea of poverty from two lesser-paid players who were unable to meet monthly mortgage payments. Each time Blackwell was said to have dug deep and handed over his own money, passing it off as a loan so the young players could save face, but admitting: 'I won't see it again. I have already written it off but that's OK. We're all in this together.'

Seemingly inspired by the off-field troubles, the team pulled together and their fighting spirit started producing away points. Bristol Rovers were held to a draw, even though Luton went down to nine men, and then Port Vale were beaten by a late Matthew Spring drive, the first away win of the season. When Yeovil were overcome on New Year's Day 2008 it was beginning to look as if Luton could emulate Leeds and quickly wipe out the points deficit they'd been handed.

However, the arrival of the January transfer window soon put a stop to that sort of optimism. The excellent centre-back pairing of Fojut and Coyne was broken up, the club unable to renew the former's loan deal, and the latter joining Colchester for £350,000. Powerhouse midfielder Edwards then headed for Wolves for £675,000 and Luton at a stroke had lost arguably their three best players.

The FA Cup visit of Liverpool in early January lightened the gloom, and the fairy-tale confrontation between multi-millionaires and paupers delighted the media. Even new England boss Fabio Capello decided to visit humble Kenilworth Road for a crash course in how the other half lives. As his limousine negotiated the narrow, terraced streets around the run-down stadium he must have questioned whether this was the same club remembered as a force in the English game twenty years earlier. Liverpool may have had their own problems, with American owners worrying about funding a new stadium and at odds with manager Rafa Benitez over spending on players, but Luton lived on a different financial planet. All overnight stays for away games had been stopped, manager Blackwell's scouting staff made redundant, and mobile phone use halted. Loanees Anthony Grant and Marc Wilson had even faced problems at their hotel over unpaid bills.

Luton's veteran sub Don Hutchison claimed he told his young teammates that the ideal scenario would be a draw against Liverpool, partly because the replay would help pay everybody's wages, and partly because as an ex-Liverpool player he fancied one more outing in front of the Kop. He would get his wish, for Luton saved the game with an equaliser that John Arne Riise put into his own net. Sky confirmed plans to screen the Anfield replay live, which meant another huge windfall for Luton to keep the Administrator happy. Valuable savings expected to accrue from the departure of Dean Morgan to Leeds failed to materialise, however, when the player failed to agree terms.

Following the first Liverpool game, it emerged that LTFC2020 was edging towards 'preferred bidder' status. Speculation about their main rival bidders centred on two other groups, one said to be headed by a property developer and the other involving ex-England manager Graham Taylor and TV sports presenter Matthew Lorenzo. The group winning preferred bidder status would be announced around the time of the Liverpool replay, but before then a row developed behind the scenes about the transfers of Coyne and Edwards.

Taking advice to act quickly from an agent, Administrator Guilfoyle accepted bids from Colchester and Wolves and did the deals to sell the pair. This angered Kevin Blackwell who evidently understood they would only be sold after key upcoming games with Swansea and Liverpool. Guilfoyle said he had no choice but to immediately secure the funding to ensure the club could continue to the end of the season and any delay could have jeopardised the deals. With episodes such as these taking place beyond their control, Blackwell and coach John Carver called a press conference in which they unexpectedly announced their resignation. To prevent further immediate chaos for the team, they said they would carry on until early February, therefore effectively serving a month's notice. They explained that as they were no longer managing the team, they had no choice but to step down.

The Administrator had not been warned about this development and was 'rather disappointed' to hear of it following their press conference. Unbeknown to the world at large, Guilfoyle acted immediately and recruited old favourite Mick Harford as Blackwell's replacement, but for the time being kept this under wraps. Fielding a weakened side, the Hatters lost at home to divisional leaders Swansea 1-3, but the Administrator said he was not down-hearted for he had a 'constructive' meeting that day with Lord Mawhinney of the Football League.

With the team and fans heading north for the replay at Liverpool, the administrator announced that LTFC2020 had won the preferred bidder status. Shortly before the big kick-off at Anfield, officials from the supporters organisations involved celebrated the news. Whatever the result of the game, this had already turned into a historic day for the football club. It was reported that LTFC2020 would now make a loan to the club which bought them a period of exclusivity while the sale was negotiated. Weeks and maybe months of work now lay ahead and the purchase of the club by LTFC2020 would still be conditional upon approval from the League and FA. In the meantime, the Administrators would continue to run all aspects of the club. Guilfoyle said: 'This is a very positive development and represents the light at the end of the tunnel that players, staff and supporters have been waiting for since our appointment in November 2007.'

So there was an extra spring in the step of many fans as they made their way into Anfield, for by now the LTFC2020 consortium had persuaded many that after all the years of problems it was high time Luton Town was run by the people who mattered – the supporters. Now that prospect had taken a huge step towards becoming a reality. The news, which reached many followers just before kick-off, did the players no harm either. After holding Liverpool at bay for more than 45 minutes, a Luton side playing without recognised centre-backs (against beanpole Peter Crouch, too) and a half-fit goalkeeper, eventually crumbled 0-5 but won friends for putting on a brave performance in the circumstances. The vocal support from the 6,000 travelling Luton fans was phenomenal.

Blackwell and Carver had reason to be proud of their makeshift side, but this was to be their last game in charge. The following morning the Administrator announced they had been dismissed – and their earlier intention to carry on for a month became history. The timing was particularly galling for Carver, who awoke to celebrate his birthday, only for the phone to ring with news of the sack. Given the events of the previous evening at Anfield, it was hard to keep pace with developments, and things continued to rattle on with the Administrator then calling a press conference for later in the day. What was coming next?

All was revealed when into the room strolled big Mick Harford, to be introduced as the new manager. In different circumstances he might have got a drum roll and a round of applause, but insolvency practitioners don't do ticker-tape, so the stage-management lacked pizzazz. However, the fan websites, message-boards and other grapevine feeders were soon humming with excitement. Even though Harford remained unproven as a manager, his arrival at Luton (for his fifth stint at the club) was greeted with widespread delight. Nationally, however, the Harford homecoming got somewhat overshadowed by a simultaneous announcement that another fans hero, Kevin Keegan, had surprisingly returned to manage Newcastle.

Harford's words were music to the ears of the die-hards, the romantics and even the pragmatics: 'I don't care what people say, Kenilworth Road is still a great stadium and I am glad it hasn't changed. There was a shiver down my spine when I walked into the club. I know that you have faced plenty of ups and downs, but be sure of this – this club will never die. It is great to be back and it is a great place to be.' This writer knows of at least one fan who swiftly pasted those words on his 'favourite quote' section on Facebook. Harford's first game in charge of a squad nearly down to the bare bones was at Leyton Orient, where he received a remarkable ovation from a travelling army of more than 1,000. Town lost 1-2 but restored some pride a week later when Sam Parkin headed a late equaliser against Leeds to keep alive hopes of League One survival.

Gary Sweet, managing the bid for LTFC2020, spoke of his delight at gaining preferred bidder status and explained they were now entering a six-week exclusivity period during which they had to progress to a full agreement regarding ownership of the club. He said: 'The majority of people involved in the LTFC2020 bid are lifelong Hatters and we are delighted to be in a position to be the next custodians of the Club – bringing the club home to the fans. After years of mismanagement, the club is in a dire state and was losing over £400,000 a month. Clearly this is not sustainable, so financial stability and living within our means is of the utmost priority. This will mean some hard, and sometimes unpopular, decisions and, when we take those, we ask fans to stand by us as they have over the past few weeks. We want a long-term dream for our club and not a recurring nightmare.' He added that this was probably the 'last chance saloon' for the club – any more mistakes would prove terminal.

The LTFC2020 bid was described as focusing firmly on key principles such as transparency; the engagement of supporters, sensible, achievable plans within a prudent financial structure, an independent feasibility study to select the future location of a new stadium, the inclusion of the Trust and other supporters' groups in the future of the club (the Trust by way of shareholding) and the inclusion of the community to build a stronger supporter base.

The complex issues now being tackled by the Administrator and LTFC2020 were a little tricky for most ordinary fans to understand, but the various websites made sterling efforts at explaining the intricacies by posting regular updates. Among these, Kevin Lennon, chairman of the Loyal Luton Supporters Club, was able to call on professional knowledge as an executive at a city asset management group:

'We should remember that collectively the football authorities (the FA, League, PFA) are effectively a single club. [Luton] has membership, called a golden share, and there are 92 of these shares. Without this we would be unable to compete in professional football. The PFA insists their members (players) are paid in full once they have signed a contract. So, any deferred wages are just that; LTFC, or whoever owns the golden share, owes those players their debt and must pay in full. The consequence of a breach is withdrawal of the membership/golden share. The League insists that clubs entering Administration must exit through a CVA route (Company Voluntary Arrangement). This means other football clubs and players who are creditors must be paid in full, no matter what. Failure to comply would result in reapplication for membership failing.'

Without a CVA, the new owners would need to prove 'exceptional circumstances' in order to win back the golden share. This had happened at Leeds United, but their 15-point penalty was the consequence.

There was widespread sympathy for Luton's plight, with recognition that whatever, or whoever, had caused the current crisis, it was fundamentally wrong that the thousands of ordinary supporters should suffer. The Mid-Bedfordshire MP Nadine Dorries MP met with LTFC2020 and then called on the Minister of State at the Department for Business, Enterprise and Regulatory Reform, Gareth Thomas MP, to exert pressure on HM Revenue & Customs to be flexible in their dealings with Luton. HMRC was the club's major creditor, the debt said to be about £2.5 million, which equated to approximately 75 per cent of the club's total debts.

Speaking in the Commons, Mrs Dorries (great-granddaughter of a founder of Everton FC), called for a framework to be created so that when another club finds itself in the same position, it knows what to do and where to go: 'The situation is impossible,' she said. 'Fans want to save [Luton], and administrators and local people want to do the best for it, but it seems as though everybody else is against the club surviving. The same thing has happened in Leeds. I have also been contacted by Labour members whose local football clubs have been in the same situation. We need a framework within which small clubs can operate. Football is not just about the Championship, or the Premiership. It is not just about the super-clubs with the big money; it is about the small clubs, too. That is where the passion for football starts.'

Fellow MP Margaret Moran (Luton South) was also galvanised by Luton's plight, and lobbied Sports Minister Gerry Sutcliffe MP, urging him to help in the discussions that would be crucial to the new owners of the club regaining the golden share from the Football League.

The cash from the sale of Coyne and Edwards, plus the Liverpool Cup-ties, and an injection of funds from LTFC2020, meant no further player sales were necessary during the January transfer window, which was one crumb of comfort for new manager Harford. He was convinced Luton could still make a decent fist of battling relegation, despite the 10-point deduction and the makeshift defence he was forced to field in every match. The unlikely centre-back pairing of Keith Keane and Don Hutchison did a sterling job, but the side rarely looked like picking up enough points to halt the slump. Certain players were perceived as 'going through the motions' by the fans, and with a couple of four-goal hammerings in early February the writing was on the wall.

It may have been injury-ridden and unbalanced, but the playing staff was now in place for the remainder of the season, and Harford would have to get on with what he'd got. Major changes would be on the way in the summer, though, with the Administrator warning: 'In the longer term, the salary bill at the club is clearly unsustainable so there will have to be changes, but this is for LTFC2020 to decide as part of their plan to ensure financial stability once they take control.' LTFC2020 confirmed that player wages currently accounted for more than 100 per cent of club turnover, 'a suicidal state to be in and one that the previous LTFC custodians got us into.' Interestingly, it was also confirmed that, before the club went into Administration, an unsuccessful offer had been made by LTFC2020 to buy the club from Dave Pinkney. They had hoped that Administration, the consequent 10-point deduction, loss of loan players and transfer embargo that had led to many of the current problems, could have been avoided if their offer had been taken.

Fellow sufferers around this time were AFC Bournemouth, who were hit by a winding-up order from HMRC, a move that triggered the Cherries joining Luton in Administration. Both clubs were near the foot of League One and Bournemouth's loss of 10 points was of some help to Luton's relegation fight, although this 'boost' was somewhat negated by the Hatters' February sequence of five straight losses. Bournemouth's was their second Administration, ten years after their first – but they couldn't match Luton's record of three Administrations in eight years.

When the two clubs met at Kenilworth Road a measure of 'gallows humour' was evident. Nearly 6,000 turned out to watch the battle of the skint clubs. The public address blared out songs like the *Mission Impossible* theme and *Things Can Only Get Better*. Nor did it escape many fans' attention that the game took place in the same week that Premier League officials stood accused of excessive greed when suggesting a 39th match to be played abroad to generate yet more riches. Unlike Luton, Bournemouth were a team in form and scorched to a 4-1 win, exposing Luton's strange-looking back four, which comprised four full-backs all well short of 6ft tall, three of them left-footed players.

While LTFC2020 wrestled with the immediate problems of gaining full ownership, former chairman Cliff Bassett, who owned the land at Junction 12, issued an open letter, addressed to Nick Owen and LTFC2020. He was reacting to LTFC2020's statement that they would carry out an independent survey of possible sites for a new stadium, before accepting that his Junction 12 plan (agreed with the former LTFC owners) was deemed the best or perhaps the only option. Bassett's open letter re-emphasised how the Junction 12 plan would see the club gifted £25 million towards a stadium, use of 30 acres of rent-free land for parking and a new community sports facility, and be entitled to all income generated from the stadium and the land. Bassett acknowledged that planning consent would require various hurdles to be overcome, but felt chances of success would be increased with the support of the fans.

LTFC2020's Gary Sweet answered this via an open letter addressed to the fans, saying he was pleased Mr Bassett had finally placed on public record the details of the opportunity at Junction 12 for a new stadium. He said LTFC2020 were waiting to see an 'alternative site analysis' promised by Mr Bassett, although this did not negate the need for an independent feasibility study, as this was vital to unite supporters behind any new location. He said they had never ruled out Junction 12, but simply did not yet have the evidence or facts about its suitability compared to any other location. The immediate priority was the financial stability of Luton Town and, once this was achieved, decisions about a new ground would follow.

Kevin Lennon of Loyal Luton SC said it should be remembered that the Junction 12 project had been 'sold' to fans by Luton's previous owners, who had not only moved the club to the edge of financial ruin, but whose honesty and transparency was now under question, and as such they could not be trusted by the fans. 'Therefore if [Mr Bassett] wants the full support of the fans then he will need to provide independent documentary evidence that there are no other alternative options.'

The Junction 12 project, on green belt land near Harlington village, had inevitably drawn opposition from local residents. MP Nadine Dorries presented a petition to Parliament against the plans, signed by more than 3,000 residents. This document opposed the idea of a stadium and warehousing development at the site, and was organised by two local protest groups. One of them stated: 'Lutonians are proud of the Hatters and the club and its stadium should be within Luton where the wider community can enjoy the facilities it could offer. It makes no sense to expect fans to travel out to Harlington to support their club.'

On the field, after five straight defeats, Luton picked up a point against Millwall in late February, but that day will go down in club history for very different reasons – agreement was reached by the Administrator to sell the football club and its assets to preferred bidder LTFC2020. A press conference to announce the news was delayed by late hitches and didn't start until shortly before kick-off. When it finally happened, Guilfoyle said: 'I am very pleased, genuinely pleased, to be able to announce that we have reached agreement to sell the football club and its assets to LTFC2020. I should emphasise that technically it's a conditional agreement – conditional upon the Football League share being transferred to the new company – this will either happen through the agreement of a Creditors' Voluntary Agreement or, if we're unable to agree a CVA with creditors, it will happen through the transfer by the Football League of the share. It's rather like a house purchase – today we have exchanged contracts but not reached completion yet – that won't be until the FL transfer the share.'

Guilfoyle said he was pleased to see that LTFC2020 were backed by the fans, and hoped this was the beginning of a period of stability and an escape from the pattern of repetitive insolvencies that had hit the club. He felt it was better to have a group of people to shoulder the losses rather than one autocratic chairman who could make decisions that may be detrimental to the club's long-term interests.

Guilfoyle warned that HMRC were not likely to agree to a CVA, as their policy was not to support any situation or any rescue where one group of creditors is paid a better return than others, and League rules said all football creditors had to be paid in full – so the 'special circumstances' route might be needed. He also spoke up for previous owner Dave Pinkney, who, 'despite his demonisation in the local press,' had provided funding at the outset of Administration. The announcement was followed by Nick Owen addressing the crowd in optimistic mood prior to the Millwall match. It had indeed been an 'earth shattering' day for Luton in more ways than one, for three hours after the game ended in a 1-1 draw the biggest UK earthquake for twenty years rocked parts of Bedfordshire.

LTFC2020 announced they were now in a position to take the club forward. 'Our club is now safe,' they proclaimed, with Gary Sweet pointing out: 'We are totally committed to rebuilding the youth structure for which this club is famous and we will work within the community. We will bring the soul back to our club. Whatever sanctions the authorities take against us for past wrong-doings, and whatever league we are playing in next season, all at LTFC2020 are totally committed to our long-term plan. During the bidding process we have had literally thousands of messages of support and offers of help from fans both in Luton, the UK and across the globe, and this unity amongst all sections of the fan-base bodes very well for the future. Luton Town is nothing without the support of the fans. We believe the future is very bright. It's taken a crisis to unite the fan base, but united it is.'

Regular communication with the ordinary fans was a welcome feature of LTFC2020's *modus operandi*. In March, Nick Owen issued a message: 'I am proud to be a member of the owners-elect of our beloved football club, although we prefer the term custodians, or guardians of a colourful tradition, dating back to the 19th century. Last Tuesday was an emotional and momentous day – my hands were shaking as I read the announcement over the Tannoy! It has been an exciting but phenomenally stressful few weeks. He said he was only the 'front man' for the consortium and those who had really 'sweated blood' were Gary Sweet, Antony Brown and Stephen Browne.

Later, Nick Owen clarified news that an outline planning application involving a stadium near Junction 12 had been lodged with the local council. This, he told fans, had come from developers Goodmans and was not a joint application with the club: 'As you know, we are not with or against any stadium plan until we have completed our independent feasibility study.' He said that study took on even greater importance, now that news had broken that Junction 11a 'infrastructure' may be built before the 2012 Olympics, meaning that area (which was nearer Luton) could be another possibility for a new home. Administrator Guilfoyle expressed unhappiness that the name, logo, brand and crest of LTFC had been used on the above plans without permission and he'd asked for their removal.

By late March it was clear Luton would be relegated to League Two, so savings on the wage-bill were implemented when three players were allowed out on loan – Chris Perry to Southampton, David Bell to Leicester and Dean Morgan to Crewe. Not unexpectedly, news also emerged that yet another club – this time Rotherham United – had succumbed to major financial distress and had gone into Administration.

Thousands of Luton fans got an unexpectedly detailed insight into their club's financial woes in early April when a hefty wad of documents from the Administrator plopped onto their doormats. As season ticket holders, these fans had paid match admission fees in advance, and were therefore technically 'creditors'. This meant they were entitled to an agenda and invitation to the forthcoming creditors' meeting, along with a fully documented breakdown of who was owed what by the football club. It made fascinating reading.

Unsecured creditor claims included £2.1 million owed to HM Customs & Excise at Liverpool, £500,000 owed to a central London legal services company, £313,934 to new stadium architects, £100,000 to Sheffield Wednesday, and five-figure sums to Bolton, Cardiff and Sunderland. The projected creditor claims showed what the players would be owed if they saw out their entire contracts. There were six-figure sums against the names of Alan Goodall, Drew Talbot, Calvin Andrew, Chris Perry, David Bell, Dean Brill, Darren Currie, Dean Morgan, Marlon Beresford, Matthew Spring, Paul McVeigh, Paul Underwood, Richard Jackson, Sol Davis, Sam Parkin and Steve Robinson. Five-figure sums were listed for Keith Keane, Lewis Emanuel, Paul Furlong, Paul Peschisolido, Richard Langley, Stephen O'Leary and Zac Barrett and also for the now-departed Ahmet Brkovic and Chris Coyne.

Among the season-ticket holders entitled to attend the creditors' meeting in central London in March 2008 was Bernard Elwen. He recalled deciding to attend out of interest, even though he was only 'owed' £34.43 by the club. He was one of just twelve who attended in person to witness a vote on the proposal that the club exited Administration by means of a CVA. He recalled: 'The sums owed, and the range of organisations [Luton Town] owed money to was breathtaking. How on earth had our club got into this state? Anyone would think that all the invoices had just been filed in that little round filing cabinet in the corner of the office by the door.

'Working in central London as I do, I was able to take time off work to go along and see what came out of the meeting. I turned up at the New Connaught Rooms and found the conference room that had been booked. There were over 100 chairs laid out so I was quite surprised to find that I was one of only a dozen attendees, all but one of us being season-ticket holders. Brendan Guilfoyle chaired the meeting and announced that several of the interested parties, such as the Inland Revenue, Football League and PFA, had sent representations by proxy.

Questions were taken from the floor, allowing Guilfoyle to explain that the monies listed as owing to other clubs were mostly loan fees for borrowed players, and the substantial HMRC debt was due to income tax on player and staff wages, apparently unpaid for a considerable time. He said the legal action by former manager Newell had been 'stayed', pending the outcome of the Administration proceedings.

As anticipated, the CVA route was rejected by creditors, a decision Nick Owen later said had been fully expected, and they could at least be pleased the HMRC had made its position clear: 'It means we can move everything forward far more quickly than might have been the case. Now we are putting the finishing touches to our bid to reclaim the club's share from the Football League, in other words our full membership and licence to play professional football.' The prospect of having 15 points deducted at the start of season 2008-09, as Leeds had a year earlier, now seemed highly likely. Trust in Luton urged leniency from the authorities, believing the club had already suffered enough through its second successive relegation, both caused by entering Administration. TiL felt taking more points away from the club would represent being punished twice for an 'offence' committed by people no longer at the club.

Relegation was duly confirmed in April by a home defeat by Brighton with three games still remaining. It was the club's fifth demotion in sixteen years and perhaps the most unlikely, given the bright new dawn that had been shouted from the rooftops back in August. Despite the gloom at the Brighton game, there was clear evidence that a new era of transparency had begun at the club, with several supporters group officials invited behind the scenes, into the boardroom and other areas. Kevin Lennon of Loyal Luton SC recalled: 'It was extremely encouraging to spend time with key members of the LTFC2020 consortium, who are all very positive about the future of the club. Nick Owen is a breath of fresh air and sitting with him during the game you can see that as a true lifelong fan he suffers like we all do when Calvin Andrew misses another chance, or Matthew Spring makes another misplaced pass, and he genuinely hurts when we lose. Nick is also a great ambassador for the club and I think we have all been encouraged by hearing someone communicate in the manner he has and not use the spin we have been accustomed to these last few years. It has also been good to see one of the key investors, Godfrey Ingram, at the last couple of home games. Here is a man who is as enthusiastic about the future of the club as anyone I have come across recently, and he is now really looking forward to the challenge that lies ahead. We all know that local boy Godfrey came through the youth ranks [as a player] and he has some great ideas for regeneration of the club both off and on the pitch.

'On the operational side, Gary Sweet, Stephen Browne and Antony Brown are the pillars and drivers behind moving this club back through the gears and they are under no illusion as to the size and magnitude of the task that lies ahead. All have been long-standing season ticket holders, as were two of the other investors we met on Saturday and this helps them all truly understand our concerns. While trips to Accrington Stanley and Morecambe may not be too mouth-watering for many, I firmly believe that what goes around comes around, and following the rollercoaster ride experienced in the last two decades we now have an exciting future ahead of us.'

Early in May, Leeds United heard that their bid to get their 15-point deduction overturned had failed, a decision that suggested Luton might suffer likewise when the time came. Two days later the curtain came down on a traumatic season with a drab home defeat by Huddersfield, Luton's sixth loss in succession. Despite the gloom, the goodwill towards manager Mick Harford remained remarkably strong. Luton fans can be very fickle when things aren't going well on the pitch, but the enduring goodwill towards Harford, come what may, is certainly unequalled in this writer's 34 years of attending matches. I even found myself shaking the big man's hand as he slowly trudged towards the tunnel after the final ball was kicked. Hope springs eternal.

Harford admitted that relegation was possibly his worst moment in football, but added: 'However it's probably the best thing that could have happened to us as a business. I'm going to build a new Luton Town and bring in new footballers who want to play and have passion. I need a clear-out. I've got tremendous belief in the consortium, the club is in good hands. It's the beginning of a new era.' He released two players and offered six of the higher earners a free transfer in a bid to reduce the crippling wage bill, adding that the club would listen to offers for any players over the summer.

The summer of 2008 would prove a hectic time for the prospective new owners, with plenty of tension as everyone awaited news of the 'punishments' likely to come the club's way. The FA's verdicts on the illegal payments offences, plus the 'golden share', would at some point be issued, but, frustratingly, the timing was unknown. Some light relief from all the worry was generated by the staging of an exhibition match to commemorate the

20th anniversary of the Littlewoods Cup victory at Wembley in 1988. The 'legends' of yesteryear turned out and took the fans on an enjoyable trip down Memory Lane. Most were heavier and slower than we remembered them, but the skills still there in abundance. Albeit only briefly, the feel-good factor returned to Kenilworth Road for a few hours, and if this type of event was a sign of things to come from the LTFC2020 regime, it was highly encouraging.

In late May, *Luton on Sunday* reported that former chairman Tomlins failed to attend FA disciplinary hearings concerning the alleged financial irregularities at Luton, involving around 50 charges, thirteen levied against him. Tomlins told the paper he was out of football now, had no intention of involving himself with FA hearings and that the FA had no jurisdiction over him: 'I made a mistake, which I regret. I got nothing out of it myself but should have managed the accounts differently. I did it in the best inter-ests of the club but did it wrongly. That is why I volunteered the informa-tion to the FA and met them voluntarily.'

The outcome of the FA hearings was made known around a week later – and it was news that shocked Luton and its followers to the core. Despite the offences involving people no longer at the club, and the fact that Luton had 'blown the whistle' themselves, the Hatters were hit by a £50,000 fine and docked 10 points, effective from the start of 2008-09 season. This was widely condemned as extreme, given the club had already had 10 docked for going into Administration earlier on and still faced a further deficit of 15 when coming out of it. Urgent talks began immediately concerning an appeal, and subsequently this was formally lodged.

Thirteen charges against Bill Tomlins saw him fined £15,000 and sus-pended from all football and football activities for five years. Of the ex-directors, Derek Peter – for seven charges of misconduct – was fined £3,750 and suspended for one year. Richard Bagehot and John Mitchell faced one charge each of failing to immediately report the relevant wrong-doing to the FA, and were reprimanded and fined £750 and £250, respec-tively. Six agents, on a single charge of failing to have in place a written rep-resentation contract with Luton Town, each received warnings as to their future conduct. The Regulatory Commission was chaired by Peter Griffiths QC, who was keen to clarify that the case had not involved 'bungs': 'There may have been a public misconception following the announcement of the … inquiry that it might have been thought by some that the directors and agents had been involved, using the vernacular, in 'bungs' and/or 'back-handers' or in some other form of corruption. We wish to dispel any such misconception.'

'Having said that,' he added, 'there can be no doubt that Luton Town between July 2004 and February 2007 was run with a flagrant disregard for the regulations laid down to protect the game. At the heart of the allegations laid against both Luton Town and two of its directors, Mr Bill Tomlins and Mr Derek Peter, was the routing of payments to agents not through the FA as ought to have occurred, but through an associated company, namely Jayten Stadium Limited. This was brought to the attention of the FA by an employee of the club itself. The person principally responsible for Luton's serious misconduct was, without doubt, Mr Bill Tomlins, the former chairman of the club. During the relevant period he worked virtually full-time as the principal director, and was effectively its Chief Executive Officer. It was he who disregarded rules that he knew were in place to protect the game, despite being warned informally that it was wrong. Of the former directors of Luton, the next most culpable was Mr Derek Peter, the financial director, a qualified accountant. It was he who, jointly with Mr Tomlins, authorised the irregular payments from Jayten Stadium Limited to the agents and indeed, continued to do so even after his fellow directors, Mr Richard Bagehot and Mr John Mitchell, made it clear to both of them that all such payments should cease.'

Luton's prospective new chairman, Nick Owen, told the BBC he was 'shattered' by the 10-point deduction: 'Why hit little old Luton with a 10-point deduction when the regulation they have transgressed is a mere technicality, with no advantage to any individual or the club? As the prospective new owners of the club, we really didn't expect to be punished for something that clearly is no fault of our own. We and our fellow supporters are the ones who are made to suffer. The cornerstone of our bid to take over the club has been honesty and transparency and I believe we have behaved impeccably throughout this disciplinary process.'

Owen stressed: 'The Administrator pleaded guilty to the charges, with our support, bearing in mind the long-standing club secretary, Cherry Newbery, had had the courage two years ago today to tell the FA of her concerns at what was happening. If she hadn't done so, would the FA be any the wiser now? What message does this send out to any other dedicated employees who are concerned about activities at their clubs? It's like moving into the house of someone who's robbed a bank, being arrested for the crime yourself, being forced to plead guilty and then being sent to prison. Compare this with West Ham. They breached the rule book and appeared to create an advantage on the field of play. Although they received a fine, they were not docked points. We feel we have become a soft target. Kicked when we are down.'

Officials of LTFC2020 declared there would be 'no rest until justice is served'. They were unable to come to terms with the sheer severity of the sanction, they said, for it was a completely inequitable punishment on the people and fans proven to have had nothing to do with the offences. 'To punish the very people who exposed the irregular payments in the first place is detrimental to an honest business framework.'

Trust in Luton registered 'dismay and disgust' at the outcome, calling it 'a massive kick in the face for Luton supporters and hugely disproportionate to the offences that were found to have been committed.' The Loyal Luton SC called on the FA to clarify exactly what offences the club had committed, in view of the fact that the commission chairman's statement seemed to lay all the blame on individuals no longer with Luton.

National paper sportswriters also questioned the severity of the punishment. David Conn of the *Guardian* said the fees involved in the charges amounted to less than £160,000 for seven deals, which made them very modest compared to agents' mind-boggling takings elsewhere. He also reported a growing recognition in football that league tables were becoming too determined by complicated financial events off the field resulting in clubs being docked points. He said 2008-09 was likely to see Luton, Bournemouth and Rotherham all starting with well below zero points. While most League clubs believed in strong sanctions against clubs that over-pay players then collapse into insolvency, there was now some pressure on the authorities to review a policy where points were automatically deducted. Sports minister Gerry Sutcliffe and Hemel Hempstead MP Mike Penning were two political figures who were quick to support the Luton appeal against their penalty.

There was some light relief from the seething anger shortly afterwards when England cricketer, and Luton fan, Monty Panesar told the *Mirror* that if he benefitted from the huge cash rewards on offer in proposed Twenty20 internationals later in 2008, he would use it to buy Luton Town.

A number of other clubs – in addition to Luton, Bournemouth and Rotherham – were widely thought to be close to insolvency over the summer of 2008. Therefore the news was welcomed that Lord Mawhinney was to step down from the FA, apparently to concentrate on pushing through measures aimed at saving smaller clubs from financial extinction. As chairman of the Football League, Mawhinney had been behind a number of radical reforms in the past. He was now said to be ready to draw up a wide-ranging package of measures that would include a review of the increasingly vexed issue of clubs going into Administration. Strangely, all these money troubles came at a time when football in the lower leagues had rarely been more popular. Figures showed 16.2 million spectators attended matches across the three divisions of the Coca-Cola League in 2007-08, making it the fourth-most watched league in Europe, behind the Premier League, Germany's Bundesliga and Spain's La Liga.

CRISIS 12 (JULY 2008)
Minus 30: The Coldest Place in Football

And so, as pre-season training began for the 2008-89 campaign, Luton Town found themselves still in Administration, its best players leaving one by one, and now deducted a further 10 points due to the misdeeds of people long departed from the club. Plus, of course, they were now set to compete in the league's basement, alongside the likes of Accrington, Aldershot and Morecambe. Could things get any worse? Well, yes, they could.

A date in mid-July 2008 was set for an FA panel to consider the club's appeal against the 10-point penalty for irregular payments to agents. It was felt Luton had a good case, not only because the offenders were no longer at the club, but because the offences only came to light because the club itself 'blew the whistle' on the affair. But before this appeal would be heard by the FA, the Football League would announce what sanctions, if any, Luton would also be facing in order to resume League football after coming out of Administration.

It was not widely known exactly when the League would make their verdict known, but yet another points deduction (Luton's third in the last eight months) seemed on the cards. What was in doubt was the extent of the penalty. Leeds had suffered a monumental 15-point deduction in 2007, but their circumstances had been slightly different. Luton would surely be dealt with less harshly than Leeds – after all, this sanction was intended to punish those 'gaining an unfair advantage' by living beyond their means and then going into Administration. Having finished 24th and 23rd in the past two seasons was surely proof enough that Luton had failed to gain much of an advantage over any of their opponents.

When the news emerged from the League's London HQ in Gloucester Place, on the sunny afternoon of Thursday 10th July, everyone associated with Luton was shocked rigid. Those fans peacefully watching England's cricketers build a big score against South Africa couldn't believe the newsflash that popped on to their screens. To get their 'golden share' back and rejoin the Football League, Luton must accept a deduction of 20 points – in addition to the FA's previous 10-point penalty – meaning the Hatters would start the 2008-09 season 30 points adrift of the rest. Even a record-breaking run of ten straight victories at the start would still leave them on zero points. The severity of the penalty was breathtaking for all concerned. In total, the authorities had now docked the club 40 points (seven more than the team amassed in the whole of 2007-08) in a period of less than nine months.

It was an unprecedented punishment and widely thought to constitute a European record in senior football. Its implications shocked just about everyone in the game. Unless the team's form and results showed an almost miraculous about-turn, the club was surely now on its way to demotion from the Football League. They could well be playing in the Blue Square Premier, just three years after finishing in the top ten of the Coca-Cola Championship. The League explained it was cracking down on Luton for repeatedly living beyond their means and then using the Administration process to clear debts and start again. Having not agreed a CVA with creditors, Luton were applying to start again without paying those creditors in full. On top of the 20-point penalty, they were insisting that LTFC2020 paid creditors 16p in the £1 (more than had been anticipated) and, crucially, they must sign away any rights of appeal.

It was a heartbreaking development for the LTFC2020 officials who had spent many hours on their 400-page document setting out their application to receive the League's 'golden share' (i.e. membership of the 92-Club League) with minimal sanctions. Their case had been smashed and the penalties far worse than anyone expected. Inevitably, talk began of how starting on minus-30 points would surely end Luton's status as a League club – after all, they would now need to accumulate a massive 80 points or so to stand a fair chance of finishing no worse than 90th on the ladder. It was a total surely beyond a cash-strapped club in the process of a complete rebuild.

Reaction to the punishment and its implications led to a wave of sympathy throughout the media and from fans and officials at other clubs. Condemnation seemed universal. Stephen Rhodes of BBC radio compared LTFC2020's position to a motorist being forced to pay good money for a derelict car that had no wheels or engine, and which was covered with old parking tickets that needed paying.

Loyal Luton Supporters Club issued a statement, noting 'the time for diplomacy and politeness is now officially over' and lashed out at the League for bullying smaller and more vulnerable clubs: 'Lord Mawhinney should hang his head in shame. He claims it is their board's responsibility to protect the integrity of their competitions and, yes, we all agree with that, but how has that principle been applied in this case? What other industry blackmails you into accepting their decision to regain membership without any fair right of appeal. How is that viewed under EU law?'

LLSC were not alone in pointing out to the media that the authorities handing out the punishment had themselves approved, via a 'fit and proper persons test', the very people responsible for recent mismanagement at Luton Town. The League board said Luton's three periods of Administration since 1999 had sparked the severity of the punishment, but it was pointed out that one of these had been instigated by the fans themselves in order to end the farcical events of the summer of 2003. It was hard to understand the League's view that Luton had 'gained an advantage' on other clubs – unless avoiding extinction fell into this category. What also rankled among Luton fans was that the League board which issued the punishment included the Ipswich chairman, who took his own club into Administration recently, and the Barnet chairman, who surely had a vested interest, being from a fellow League Two club.

Many observers quoted cases where leniency had been shown in the past. For example, West Ham suffered no points deduction at all when two ineligible players helped them avoid relegation in 2007, and Boston United only had four points docked after breaking regulations on the way to their 2001 elevation into the League. Luton felt victimised. Messrs Logic and Fairness seemed to have gone on holiday. As Jonathan Swift once said: 'Laws are like cobwebs, which may catch small flies, but let wasps and hornets break through.'

A shell-shocked Nick Owen told BBC radio: 'I'm just baffled and bewildered that they can be so harsh on us. We lost 10 points immediately on going into administration last season, had to get rid of our loan players and sell a number of others, this started a downward spiral and we got relegated, which was bad enough. We are saving a football club here which is at the centre of a community and yet we get kicked in the teeth yet again. Perhaps 5 points, or 10 points even, but 20? It's just breathtaking and I can't understand how anyone who loves football and wants to preserve the Football League as it is can be so incredibly severe.'

Gary Sweet, managing director of LTFC2020, was adamant the club was being unfairly punished for the mistakes made by previous owners, but insisted they would stay afloat despite the massive deficit. He said: 'Of course we are devastated once again. We know that all the penalties we face next season are a direct result of the atrocious management of the club from 2003 until November of last year. We are directly paying for the sins and actions of the previous directors. However, now is the time to stand united. Our great club needs the support of the fans more than ever. We are at the lowest point in our history but we will get through this.'

Stephen Browne, director of LTFC 2020, said 'the real sting in the tail' had been the clause preventing Luton from appealing the decision. It read: 'Luton Town Football Club 2020 Ltd will be required to sign a contract agreeing not to appeal this decision at any time in the future, through any method.' Therefore, said Browne, they now had to either accept the penalties and sign, or the League would withdraw the offer of returning the golden share, meaning an end to professional football in Bedfordshire after well over 100 years.

'The Football League consider themselves a private members club, and as such they can have whatever rules they like – you either want to be a member and agree to these rules, or you simply don't join. We have tried obviously to discuss the terms with the League, but they have said in no uncertain terms their offer is not a negotiation and that is why we only got half an hour's warning of their statement – once they went public they will not U-turn. In effect we are left with a *fait accompli* – we play on with penalties or don't play. With so little time to the start of the season they know there is no time to challenge. Fundamentally, it is easy for the League to treat smaller clubs this way. And they know it – they have our detailed financial plans! Protecting the integrity of the game? You decide.'

Support for Luton came from various quarters, including former FA acting chief executive David Davies and ex-Aston Villa chairman and FA councillor Doug Ellis, who called for a rethink on the harsh punishments. Ellis said LTFC2020 should not be penalised severely as it inflicted 'suffering as they try to save the lifeblood of the club'. The *Independent* lambasted the authorities in no uncertain fashion and said it would have made more sense for the sentences, at least in part, to have run concurrently, in view of the fact that all Luton's financial problems and misdemeanours could be traced back to the previous administration: 'Instead there has been an attitude of bang-'em-up-and-let-'em-rot, conceivably Luton could go out of business, which pays no heed to the efforts of those desperately trying to remedy matters.'

The *Independent* went on to report that the apparent contempt for natural justice had provoked one Rotherham fan to suggest: 'I'd love to see all 23 clubs in League Two throw their match at Luton to send a message.' Such an outcome seems unlikely, but sympathy for manager Mick Harford from his fellow managers was seen as a possible source of help in terms of loan players over the difficult months ahead.

While the club took stock, with LTFC2020 vowing to press on regardless, the vultures began circling over the club, and midfielder David Bell and striker Calvin Andrew were sold for combined fees of approaching £1 million, to Norwich and Crystal Palace respectively. Their departure reduced the strength of the ravaged squad yet further, with Harford valiantly trying to plug the gaps with players invited in on a trial basis. Messages of goodwill continued to flow in from unlikely sources, including from QPR and Leeds, two deadly Luton rivals over recent years, whose fans commiserated over the draconian penalty. Even supporters of fellow League Two sides Rotherham and Bournemouth – waiting fearfully for news of their own club's futures – expressed sympathy.

The Times even discussed the issue in its leader column, invoking the famous 1960s 'butterfly on a wheel' controversy involving rock star Mick

Jagger's harsh jail sentence. 'Who would crush a Hatter on a Wheel?' the paper asked, adding: 'Of course the football authorities must enforce rules. Yet they should also have regard to the emotional and financial investment made by supporters in their team. The League's administrators should take a look today at the faces of Luton's devastated young fans and ask themselves – is this really what I took up this job to do?'

Just five days after the crushing news of the 20-point deduction by the League, LTFC2020 representatives, plus a bunch of devoted supporters and one Luton MP, headed into central London to attend the FA Appeal Board's hearing into Luton's appeal against the earlier 10-point deduction. The wave of sympathy for the Hatters after recent events led them to believe they had a good chance of success.

Kevin Lennon, chairman of LLSC, recalled the mayhem of that week: 'The date for the appeal at the FA was released and immediately I had a major dilemma for it clashed with my son's sports day. The one I missed last year which led to him getting upset, and the one I promised him I would attend this year. I knew a hard-core of LLSC members wanted to be there and also knew the media would be there expecting reaction. It was a day that would go a big way towards settling the destiny of the club I had supported since I was my son's age and one that I wanted him to follow supporting in my footsteps.

'The 20-point deduction from the Football League had come five days earlier and was causing outrage among the Luton fan base. I was having to juggle speaking to the media, pacify the fans that wanted to send members of the FA and Football League to the gallows, and tackle the emotional dilemma of what to do with my son. I was up until 3.30 on the morning of the big day, dealing with the media and sending e-mails out to MPs and others urging them to attend. At the sports day, as I stood watching kids hurtle round with eggs on spoons, my phone was red hot as people confirmed they were in Soho Square and camped outside the FA offices. Then, in between the 20-metre sprint and the obstacle race, news came through from Jeff, an LLSC committee member, that word had filtered through that the appeal was actually to take place elsewhere. After some frantic calls it wasn't long before we had tracked down the location.

'I then made my big family sacrifice and departed before the start of the sack race. I finally arrived outside Jurys Hotel in Great Russell Street just after midday. It was a lovely sunny day and all the LLSC members were outside handing out leaflets to passers-by and receiving many comforting words of sympathy. Our new 15ft Loyal Luton flag was proudly draped over some fencing and everyone seemed in apprehensive mood. What should we expect? We were confident in the LTFC2020 case, especially having got football luminaries such as Graham Kelly, David Davies and

Doug Ellis to speak in our defence. However, could we ever trust the FA? These were the people that dealt with Eriksson and McLaren, the Wembley debacle, and who stood accused of bullying small clubs while running scared of the big boys.

'As soon as I arrived, the media wanted a reaction and prediction for the outcome of the appeal. All we wanted was to find out our destiny that day and not have to wait on tenterhooks any longer. We were all busy trying to cheer ourselves up, Jane Ledsom was singing new songs and I was going round thanking everyone for coming.

'Just after 1pm as we were debating whether the result would come that day, Pam from *BBC Look East* emerged from the building and confirmed that the LTFC2020 were being summoned for the panel's verdict. The moment of truth was here. Eventually Gary Sweet and Stephen Browne from LTFC2020 came out. Their heads were down, they looked like the world was coming to an end. There was a stony silence and we all knew. The appeal had been rejected.

'How could they do this to our club? How could they let the guilty get away? How could they make the fans and new saviours pay such a price? We wanted them to see the difference between right and wrong, good and bad, the guilty and innocent, assassins and saviours, yet the FA had apparently failed miserably to do this on all counts. Before too long I was being asked to do interviews for BBC, ITV and Sky Sports as well as local radio. I've never had media training and now, when completely shocked and lost for words, I was being asked for views and opinions and not only that but I couldn't even express my true feelings about the FA given slander laws. We had been deserted by football's supposed guardian in the hour of need. It was blatantly obvious that the truth didn't pay and the only winners were the cheats. We collected our flag, folded it up and trudged off to the nearest pub.

'We tried to find justification for what they'd done but simply couldn't get anywhere near. I eventually got into my office in the city at 3.30pm and the sympathy from fellow workers for little Luton was starting to spread. But I didn't want sympathy, I wanted justice and our 30 points back. This injustice impacts the whole of football and not just our beloved Luton. Lord Triesman and Lord Mawhinney may be proud of having sent a strong message out about their ultimate authority and power, but as soon as fans from all over the country started sending Luton messages of support it only confirmed that both authorities had over-stepped the mark of reason and had just scored the biggest own goal. The journey for justice is only just beginning.'

The FA admitted their deduction of the 10 points had been a heavy sanction for the illegal payments during Bill Tomlins era as Luton Town chairman, but said this was deliberate and not excessive as it reflected the seriousness of the breaches and the need to deter such conduct within football clubs: 'It is highly unfortunate for Luton Town and their loyal fans that shortly after the FA regulatory commission reached its decision the Football League quite separately imposed a 20-point deduction for entirely different actions by the club,' added their statement.

According to *The Times*, the FA felt it was right to deny Luton leniency because the whistle-blower on their illegal payments to agents 'was not a club official'. As the whistle-blower was widely reported to have been club secretary Cherry Newbery, this was mystifying to say the least. The FA argued that Newbery, as a secretary, cannot be viewed as a club official. *The Times* said some in the game felt the FA's decision would deter whistle-blowing in the future. It did appear, remarkably, that Luton's appeal was being refused, at least in part, on a technical point about Cherry Newbery's job title.

The Times added: 'Now that the legal battles have been lost, the fate of the club is in the hands of Harford and his players. Without meaningful contracts and on meagre wages, they are working in circumstances that are a far cry from the buzz and bling of the Barclays Premier League. The next time you hear someone complain that all footballers are spoilt and overpaid, spare a thought for the men who wear the white shirts of Luton.'

Former West Ham boss Lou Macari was another well-known figure horrified by the Hatters treatment: 'Professional sport is all about competition – and hopefully fair competition – but what chance does minus 30 points give anyone? Good luck to Mick Harford, because no manager in the country will envy your task. Once again, it is the fans who suffer most, while I have sympathy for the new administration headed by Nick Owen. They were not guilty of going into voluntary administration to clear debts – and it certainly wasn't them making undisclosed payments when they shouldn't have been. But they will suffer and carry the can for several years to come. Luton Town were a soft target, one that's been kicked in the stomach on more than one occasion here.'

Fans bombarded both League and FA headquarters with complaints and queries about how the various punishments were arrived at. Darren Bernstein, the League's customer services manager, replied: 'Ultimately any new company seeking to join The Football League must decide for itself whether it is prepared to accept the entry conditions set by the League. An alternative would be to honour the debts of the previous club in full, in which case the League would not seek to impose such additional conditions. These conditions reflect the need to protect the integrity of the competition by ensuring that no club should be able to gain an advantage over its rivals by not paying its debts. Owners of football clubs will change over

time, but the club remains the same. It is the club which secures a competitive advantage from wiping out debt through insolvency proceedings,
and therefore, it is only right that it is the club, regardless as to the identity of the new owners, that is made subject to any conditions. Luton Town
FC has now been the subject of insolvency proceedings three times in the
last ten years.'

It was a case of take the punishment or go and join a minor league as
Aldershot once did. This metaphorical right hook had LTFC2020 momentarily on the canvas, but officials got back on their feet to declare they
would carry on, for their investors were still solidly behind them, and
would meet this challenge head on. Going into the new season with minus
30 points did not mean certain relegation, but it certainly stacked the odds
against a Luton squad already in disarray through losing its most valuable
players and unable to sign new ones while in Administration. The average
number of points needed to survive in League Two has been 45 in recent
seasons. Therefore Luton must amass at least 75 points to have a fighting
chance of staying in the League. The bookies are rarely wrong and one
quoted Luton as favourites for the drop at odds of 10-1 on. Harford char-
acteristically brushed this aside and announced he was up for the fight. His
stance was echoed by many fans, as evidenced by the astonishing turnout
of around 1,000 for an away friendly at Bedford Town in mid-July.

By the end of July agreement was formally reached between LTFC2020
and the League and the newly structured club was welcomed back into the
fold. The club came out of Administration on the final day of month, nine
days before the start of the new season. Managing director Gary Sweet
said: 'We are delighted that we can now move on and look to rebuilding the
Club and ensuring survival in the professional leagues. The entire 2020
team have been working tirelessly since last autumn to save this great club
and have shown to the football world that our blueprint to stabilise our
club has the official rubber stamp of all the footballing authorities. No
matter what hurdles we have had to overcome, our backers have never
wavered in their support. Mick Harford, too, has been a rock to us and we
are merely in the shadow of his love for our club. This is just the start. We
now have a huge job on our hands, both on and off the pitch, to finally
exorcise the ghosts of the past. For our part, getting through these dark
days has only given us more energy and determination to move forward
and rebuild. It's a long-term plan as we have always said, but we are on target, we are strong, and there is a unity about the club that I haven't witnessed for many years.'

Season-ticket sales held up well towards the end of July, despite news
of the deductions, and it appeared the world-weary fans were rallying once
again and responding to LTFC2020's call for everyone to 'keep the faith'.

The size of Luton's task was reduced considerably when sanctions against fellow League Two clubs Rotherham and Bournemouth were announced. Both would start season 2008-09 on minus 17 points.

Gary Sweet and fellow director Stephen Browne agreed the 2008-09 season would be the most important in Luton's entire history: 'It's a mountain to climb, but look how far we have come in the past eight months – from no hope, to the brink of exorcising all the ghosts, having our club back, and most importantly, being united. It is obvious no one else is going to save our club, so it is down to us – all Hatters throughout the land and globe. It is now that we must stand up and defend 123 years of history. Our history. A proud history. Our club will never die while we stand together.'

EPILOGUE
The Black and Leaden Porridge

'The pride, the love, the passion
We rise and fall as one,
No matter how you hurt us
We're here for years to come.'
(Songwriter and Luton fan Jane Ledsom)

Why, a Luton fan asked in 2008, does happiness visit so seldom and stay so fleetingly, like an April butterfly alighting momentarily upon your finger, whereas tragedy lurks heavy in your guts like black and leaden porridge?

He had stolen these fine words from an unusually eloquent West Ham supporter, as it happens, but the sentiment certainly applies to the Hatters as well as the Hammers. In fact, Luton fans believe they've suffered the slings and arrows of outrageous fortune more than most clubs, and recent events have only intensified that perception. For 50 years their club has survived crippling body-blows, but somehow lives on, despite its wounds constantly being patched up hastily and unhygienically.

Mid-July 2008 saw what was generally agreed to be 'the lowest point' in the club's 123-year history, with the vultures amassing overhead. Reeling from a huge points deduction that seriously threatens their very League status, the loyalty and patience of Luton's army of fans was tested as never before. But when 2008-09 stuttered to an uncertain start with a makeshift Hatters team emerging for a meaningless friendly at non-league Bedford Town on 19th July, around 1,000 Luton fans showed up in a remarkable show of solidarity.

On that hot afternoon, Bedford's tiny New Eyrie ground reverberated to chants of 'Luton Town will never die', a song reflecting the fact that the club is just about the oldest surviving institution in Bedfordshire's largest town. Only a much-trimmed-down hat industry survives from the days in 1885 when Luton Town FC was formed, soon to become the south of England's first professional football club. The club was established long before the airport came along, long before Vauxhall Motors, and certainly long before the M1 motorway and much-maligned Arndale shopping centre. And although Luton as a place has never been sympathetic to its historical heritage, there is a passion and pride among Hatters fans that suggests the football club will never be allowed to wither on the vine.

The mistakes of the past are all too evident in the town of Luton itself. Beautiful and historic Edwardian buildings such as the Carnegie Library,

Corn Exchange with its magnificent spire, Plait Halls and Grand Theatre were all demolished in the 1950s and 1960s to make way for the dreadful Arndale centre – history swept away in a disgraceful episode that led to Luton gaining its reputation as a grim and ugly place. Luton's developers would surely win a first prize for desecration; in more sensible times the Prince of Wales would have had them flung into Harlech's dungeons.

The borough of Luton was also affected by post-war immigration, drastically changing the nature of the town with huge numbers of incomers settling locally to take advantage of work opportunities. Perhaps a spin-off of the new cosmopolitan mix has been the evident lack of civic pride. The football club's 50 years of repeated crises has been accompanied by the decline in the image of the town itself. At the start of the 1960s the Hatters were in the top division and the town was seen as affluent and thriving, but as the club slipped down the divisions and the horrendous revamping of the town centre took place, the smiles were wiped off local people's faces. By now, the hat industry which gave the football club its nickname was much reduced from its heyday – and no longer were the hatters particularly 'mad' either, for the days of using mercurous nitrate in hat-making were long gone, along with the muscular twitching and hallucinations it could cause in workers.

The only twitching these days is by nervous supporters driven mad by events on and off the field at Kenilworth Road. Supporting Luton can be a painful experience in more ways than one. Celebrity supporter and new chairman Nick Owen recalls once waking during the night with stomach pains and, as he was rushed off in an ambulance, blamed them on a chicken pie he'd consumed in a bar at Kenilworth Road. The club's earlier 'celebrity fan' Eric Morecambe famously suffered from heart trouble, of course, but used to tell his wife watching the Hatters was a release from stress and good for him. The manner in which he fiercely chewed his pipe up there in the Main Stand told a different story, however.

Morecambe joined the Hatters' cause quite late in life, but the likes of Nick Owen are, like many of us, real Luton 'lifers'. That is to say, someone who caught the bug very early on and could no more give up supporting Luton than quit breathing. Don't laugh – there are more of us dotted around the planet than you might think. Nick Owen recalls his first game as being in the autumn of 1958, which was precisely the same season this writer was first exposed to the delights of Kenilworth Road. Although barely three years old, I clearly remember scampering around in the scruffy, tunnel-like concourse under the Main Stand while my dad stood a few yards away on the enclosure terracing. The first footballer I ever heard about was Billy Bingham, who sounded interesting even though the finer points of wing play would have been wasted on a three-year-old.

Morecambe and Owen have over the years gained enjoyment and attention from the fact that they support an underdog club like Luton. These
days the performance poet John Hegley and England cricketer Monty
Panesar, not forgetting comedy actress Nicky Wardley, are also doing their
bit to raise the Hatters' profile. Increasingly, in these days of mega-wealthy
Premiership clubs, supporting a team that is not part of the mainstream is
like belonging to some sort of alternative cult. An addiction to nostalgia
must also be an ingredient in all this, for those of us who have seen better
times cling desperately to the expectation they will return.

Nick Owen was certainly not afraid to trumpet his devotion to Luton
even before he gained nationwide fame. As a young lad he was a devotee
of *Charles Buchan's Football Monthly* and had a letter published in the magazine more than 40 years ago (his one guinea fee perhaps started a taste for
freelance journalism?), telling of his teenage angst caused by a love of
Luton: 'On Saturdays when I have not been able to watch, the condition of
tension and anxiety I attain has to be seen to be believed.'

Perhaps Luton fans are inveterate letter-writers at heart, for poet John
Hegley, a regular on national radio these days and who has a considerable
national following, also had a letter about his beloved Hatters published in
the same magazine during boyhood. He calls publication of that letter 'my
first brush with glamour'. In his missive, Hegley announced his hope that
Luton's cause would be helped by 'more Oak Road shouters' attending
away games so that their away record could soon match that at home.
When student life and work took him away from the town for a few years,
Hegley went without his weekly Hatters 'fix', but on returning to the fold
in the early 1990s he saw a fabulous solo goal by Scott Oakes against Derby
that reignited his passion.

Most of the Luton 'lifers' don't enjoy such celebrity status, of course,
apart from the occasional brief brush with fame that can occur when a *Sky
Sports News* reporter thrusts a microphone in their face and asks for their
views on the latest Hatters crisis. One of this happy band is Jane Ledsom,
a talented Bedford-based singer, who exercises her vocal chords during
Luton matches and hones her songwriting skills by penning lines about her
favourite club. She said: 'I have been a Luton fan since the age of ten, so I
grew up dreaming of a team of Ricky Hills and visiting Wembley twice in
the first few years of supporting the club. I now sit in the Kenny End next
to a little old man called Ron who's like my granddad. The atmosphere and
the pies are much better there but Ron doesn't like all the swearing so I
have to keep it clean. I have no envy for people who support teams that
have always been in the Premiership. It's a totally different sort of support.'

Like Jane, many Luton loyalists speak of being unable to contemplate
ever following a more glamorous club and wouldn't dream of letting their

love for Luton fade, whatever hurdles are put in the way. The English love an underdog and Luton's points deduction in 2008 ensured that a club already in dire straits suddenly became the League's biggest-ever underdog. Perhaps 2008-09 will therefore witness a surge in popularity across Britain for the previously little-loved Hatters?

Just like Nick Owen and your author, Mrs Caz Meers first watched the Hatters when they were one of 1958's leading clubs and could never have imagined the situation facing her favourite team 50 years later. But she admits that her devotion simply intensifies the harder life gets for Luton: 'We have the special spirit of a small club – linked to each other by care and love. The long-term fans will never let go, but I hope that better times are on the way for all involved and that justice will be done.'

Kevin Barrett, chairman of the official Supporters Club agrees: 'Having come through three periods of administration in a short period of time, I think the fans have shown a great spirit to help the club through. It seems the fans galvanise in a special way when adversity comes to challenge us and some club owners of the past have come to underestimate the true power of the fan base.' Kevin Lennon, chairman of the Loyal Luton Supporters Club, concurs: 'It's the old English bulldog spirit and never-say-die attitude. If anything the tough times have pulled us together more. What is really apparent at Luton is the high amount of fans that we get that now live out of the town, but are still very loyal and travel longer distances to watch performances, however good or bad, and still have an attachment to the town.'

After 50-plus years of failing to secure a new stadium, some supporters are beginning to believe the club may never move and that Kenilworth Road, for all its many faults, will always be home sweet home. For even though this lopsided and woefully inadequate stadium may be the subject of abuse and amusement from the opposition, many Lutonians seem to love it like a tramp loves his fleabag dog. Most regular fans would put 'matchday atmosphere' high on their list when describing the appeal of football, and that created at Luton for certain games can be something special. Noise levels can be remarkably high at Luton when the crowd is up for it, even though gates have rarely exceeded 10,000 since the 1980s.

Long-standing fans like Caz Meers talk misty-eyed of the old ground's unique character and the memories it holds, and Kevin Lennon confirms: 'Kenilworth Road definitely has a unique feel to it, with its closeness to the pitch, the restricted views and the atmosphere all part of the essential ingredients of a proper English football ground. It would not be unusual to hear a full house of 10,000 here making more noise than 30,000 in some of the new soulless grounds now popping up all over the country. In my opinion Kenilworth Road is all what is good about English football –

except perhaps the greenhouses [corporate boxes] which should have been knocked down to allow a redevelopment of the Bobbers Stand.'

Kevin Barrett admitted he will be sad when (if?) the club finally moves to a new home: 'I can only put forward an analogy of moving out of your family home for the first time. You know it is something you must do, but you are still sad. Familiarity is the main thing, for all its faults Kenilworth Road is home, it is where we go on a Saturday afternoon and we love it. Coupled with that are the memories, as a fan you remember where you stood for your first match, you can recall the first goal you ever saw, and that can never be replaced in a new ground. I have visited so many stadia over my time following LTFC around the country and it is always the older and smaller grounds which seem to have an atmosphere all of their own.'

'Being a Luton fan is not glamorous,' added Barrett. 'Friends who either do not follow football or are armchair supporters wonder why I persist in going both home and away in all weathers to watch a team like Luton. It seems to me that fans of the top clubs are the ones who are really losing out. Yes it is tough in the lower leagues. Relegation is always a threat and financially you are sitting on a knife edge, but give me that any day over the over-priced, over-paid televised games of the Premiership. They are soul-less affairs and sometimes you really need to experience the tough times to appreciate the good.'

Over the years there have been a handful of club employees who have won special places in the hearts of Luton fans by identifying closely with the support in a way over and above the norm. Two near the very top of the list were key figures at the club in the summer of 2008 – manager Mick Harford, now in his fifth stint at Kenilworth Road – and club secretary Cherry Newbery, who was profiled earlier in this book. Kevin Barrett, spoke for many when he said that Cherry's contribution over the years has been surely unequalled. 'Hers is one name that will always come to the forefront. She has been a rock and a constant at Luton throughout the troubled times. Cherry is not only a loyal club servant but also a fan and will fight as passionately for her club as any other supporter.'

Luton's support may not involve huge numbers, but there is a hard core who are in it for the long haul. These are the stoics who cheer themselves up by recalling the good times of yesteryear, and occasions when they did strange and embarrassing things in the name of supporting Luton. As a responsible married woman, Caz Meers now looks back with horror at some of her behaviour: 'I recall a woman among the travelling Luton fans at Halifax one time, who wouldn't stop moaning, so I went up and knocked her hat off and then ran away and hid. I also remember leaping over a British Rail barrier at Newcastle as I had no ticket and then having to jump on a moving train as it pulled out of the station.'

Kevin Lennon fondly recalls sneaking into a bank vault to kiss the Littlewoods Cup: 'At 18 I had embarked on a career in the financial world by taking up a job offer with NatWest. My first placement was at the Bury Park branch of Luton. Being a mad Luton fan and season-ticket holder since I was seven it was quite surreal that many of the top players such as Ricky Hill, Mal Donaghy, Ashley Grimes and Mark Stein all regularly banked there and I was cashing the wages for my idols. In April 1988 the trophy cabinet at the club was not big enough to store the Littlewoods Cup so while a new one was being built they stored the cup in our bank vaults at night. One morning that week I sneaked in wearing my Luton boater – with its rim having fallen off during the celebrations – headed down into the vault with a camera and a colleague and got the trophy out of its case to pose for pictures of me lifting and kissing it.'

Veteran fan Scotty, a qualified referee and editor of the website *Vital Luton*, recalled a stressful clash of fixtures back in 1971: 'The date was set for my wedding well in advance but when the fixtures came out it was found to be on a match day. I tried to get my fiancee to change the date and she wouldn't speak to me for a week. I was obviously forbidden to go to the match, but half our family guests mysteriously sneaked away to the game after the lunchtime ceremony and didn't return until midway through the reception. About 50 of them came running in at 5.15 pm with red faces and stories of a great win over Middlesbrough I was gutted to have missed it. I also missed the 1983 classic at Manchester City and when the result was confirmed I completely lost it and ran around the garden whooping, before diving fully clothed into the kids' swimming pool. This dislodged the frame and sent gallons of water all over the lawn to earn yet another bollocking from the wife. She said: "For God's sake it's only a football match." They just don't get it, do they?'

What was encouraging during the trials and tribulations of the summer of 2008 was the sympathy and backing Luton fans received from fans of other clubs. To have 40 points deducted over eight months was widely seen as hugely unjust and it seemed true football fans didn't want to see such penalties imposed, even on clubs they traditionally disliked. One writer who understood what Hatters devotees were going through was Millwall fan and broadcaster Danny Baker, who said: 'Needless to say, among we happy band of life-sentence lunatics, this [crisis] situation with all its atten-dant nostalgic intimacy, gallows humour and siege mentality is being daily savoured like an exotic opiate that will always elude the humdrum lives of Premiership supporters. These are the conditions that we understand. Crisis, chaos and desperation replenish our barren, too-long-in-mid-table veins like an eschewed narcotic from which we have been too long in denial. League Two is beckoning and it feels like we're coming home.'

Fifty years of crises but Luton fans are not cowed yet. Far from it. The latest setbacks merely set the scene for new challenges and new dramas to keep the adrenalin pumping. In many ways the challenge before Luton for 2008-09 is the biggest faced by any club, ever. Committed regulars at Kenilworth Road are quite used to spending their Saturdays in an emotional mess, and the rest of the week fretting over the latest developments at the club. We wouldn't have it any other way. There is always something happening, good or bad, and life for a Luton fan has never, ever been dull.

Forty Million in Forty Years

For most of the past half century, circumstances have dictated that Luton Town must be a 'selling club' simply to survive. This has been an eternal source of frustration for fans and managers alike. An exasperated David Pleat once described Kenilworth Road as resembling a 'footballing warehouse'. Between 1989 and 2008 some dozen players were sold for fees of between £1 and £3 million, eight of whom were developed through the junior ranks at Luton.

Listed here are the main sales that have taken place over the past 40 years. It is not a comprehensive list, but does include all the major moves. The total income from transfers on this list alone comes to around £40 million, meaning, on average, Luton have sold at least £1 million worth of talent every single calendar year since 1968.

In a few cases fees have been estimated due to clubs refusing to disclose the exact figure, or due to different values quoted in the media. Those marked (*) were fees settled by tribunals.

MAJOR LUTON TOWN SALES 1968-2008

1969 Rioch (to Aston Villa)	(Division 3 record)	£100,000
1971 Malcolm Macdonald (Newcastle)	(Division 2 record)	£180,000
1972 Chris Nicholl (Aston Villa)		£90,000
1973 Alan Slough and Viv Busby (Fulham)		£75,000
1974 Barry Butlin (Nott'm Forest)		£120,000
Tom Finney (Sunderland)		£70,000
1975 Peter Anderson (Antwerp)		£55,000
1976 Andy King (Everton)		£40,000
John Ryan (Norwich)		£46,000
1978 Steve Buckley (Derby)		£160,000
Paul and Ron Futcher (Man C)		£430,000
Milija Aleksic (Tottenham)		£100,000
1979 Steve Taylor (Mansfield)		£75,000
1980 Bob Hatton (Sheffield U)		£50,000
1981 Paul Price (Tottenham)		£250,000
Alan West (Millwall)		£45,000
1982 Godfrey Ingram (San Jose E'quakes)		£100,000
Mark Aizlewood (Charlton)		£50,000
1984 Paul Walsh (Liverpool)		£750,000
Clive Goodyear (Plymouth)		£100,000
Vince Hilaire (Portsmouth)		£100,000
1985 Frankie Bunn (Hull)		£40,000
Paul Elliott (Aston Villa)		£400,000
1986 Garry Parker (Hull)		£72,000
Mitchell Thomas (Tottenham)		(*)£233,000
1987 Mike Newell (Leicester)		£350,000
Peter Nicholas (Aberdeen)		£350,000
1988 Mark Stein (QPR)		£300,000
Andy Dibble (Manchester City)		£240,000
Mal Donaghy (Manchester Utd)		£650,000
1989 Steve Foster (Oxford)		£175,000
David Oldfield (Manchester City)		£600,000
Roy Wegerle (QPR)		£1 million
1990 Danny Wilson (Sheffield Wed)		£200,000
Mick Harford (Derby)		£480,000
Mick Kennedy (Stoke)		£180,000

1991	Lars Elstrup (Odense)	£250,000
	Kingsley Black (Nott'm Forest)	£1.5 million
	Matt Jackson (Everton)	£600,000
	Dave Beaumont (Hibs)	£110,000
	Sean Farrell (Fulham)	£100,000
	Tim Breacker (West Ham)	£600,000
	Iain Dowie (West Ham)	£480,000
1992	Darron McDonough (Newcastle)	£90,000
	Graham Rodger (Grimsby)	£135,000
	Mick Harford (Chelsea)	£300,000
	Steve Claridge (Cambridge U)	£195,000
	Mark Pembridge (Derby)	£1.25 million
1993	Philip Gray (Sunderland)	£800,000
1995	Juergen Sommer (QPR)	£600,000
	Paul Telfer (Coventry)	(*)£1.15 million
	John Hartson (Arsenal) (Record for teenager)	£2.5 million
1996	Scott Oakes (Sheffield W)	£425,000
	Vidar Riseth (Linz)	£90,000
	Johnny Vilstrup (Aarhus)	£100,000
1997	Ceri Hughes (Wimbledon)	£400,000
	Kim Grant (Millwall)	£200,000
	Matthew Upson (Arsenal)	£1 million
1998	Tony Thorpe (Fulham)	£800,000
1999	Kelvin Davis (Wimbledon)	£600,000
	Steve Davis (Burnley)	£750,000
	Graham Alexander (Preston)	£50,000
	Sean Evers (Reading)	£500,000
	Chris Wilmott (Wimbledon)	£650,000
2000	Gary Doherty (Spurs)	£1 million
2002	Matthew Taylor (Portsmouth)	£750,000
2003	Tony Thorpe (QPR)	£50,000
2005	Curtis Davies (WBA)	£3 million
2006	Steve Howard (Derby)	£1 million
	Kevin Nicholls (Leeds)	£700,000
2007	Rowan Vine (Birmingham)	£2.5 million
	Carlos Edwards (Sunderland)	£1.5 million
	Kevin Foley (Wolves)	£750,000
	Leon Barnett (WBA)	£2.5 million
	Warren Feeney (Cardiff)	£75,000
2008	Chris Coyne (Colchester)	£350,000
	Dave Edwards (Wolves)	£675,000
	David Bell (Norwich)	£500,000
	Calvin Andrew (C Palace)	£200,000

RICHES TO RAGS

Formed in 1885, Luton Town became the first club in Southern England to turn professional, when in 1890 they started to pay three players the grand fee of five shillings (25p) per week. By the following year, the entire team was on the payroll.

Luton were the first club to achieve the 'riches-to-rags' feat of sliding from the First Division to the Fourth Division (it happened between 1960 and 1965), and although they climbed all the way back again (between 1967 and 1974), incredibly they managed to repeat the slump a second time, albeit slower this time around (between 1975 and 2001). Due to the points deductions inflicted over the summer of 2008, Luton began the 2008-09 season facing the rare ignominy of being relegated three seasons in a row.